Authorship and Audience

Authorship and Audience

LITERARY PERFORMANCE IN THE
AMERICAN RENAISSANCE

Stephen Railton

PRINCETON UNIVERSITY PRESS

PRINCETON, NEW JERSEY

Copyright © 1991 by Princeton University Press
Published by Princeton University Press, 41 William Street,
Princeton, New Jersey 08540
In the United Kingdom: Princeton University Press, Oxford

All Rights Reserved

Library of Congress Cataloging-in-Publication Data

Railton, Stephen, 1948–
Authorship and audience : literary performance
in the American Renaissance / Stephen Railton.
p.   cm.
Includes index.
1. American prose literature—19th century—History
and criticism.   2. Authors and readers—United States—
History—19th century.   3. Authorship—History—19th
century.   4. Reader-response criticism.   I. Title.
PS368.R35   1991   810.9′003—dc20   91-607   CIP

ISBN 0-691-06925-5 (cloth)
0-691-01516-3 (pbk.)

This book has been composed in Adobe Galliard

Princeton University Press books are
printed on acid-free paper and meet the guidelines
for permanence and durability of the Committee
on Production Guidelines for Book Longevity
of the Council on Library Resources

Printed in the United States of America by
Princeton University Press, Princeton, New Jersey

1   3   5   7   9   10   8   6   4   2
1   3   5   7   9   10   8   6   4   2
(pbk.)

But when it was midnight Shahrazad awoke and signalled to her sister Dunyazad who sat up and said, "Allah upon thee, o my sister, recite to us some new story, delightsome and delectable, wherewith to while away the waking hours of our latter night." "With joy and goodly gree," answered Shahrazad, "if this pious and auspicious king permit me."

—Richard F. Burton,
The Book of the Thousand Nights and a Night

CONTENTS

ACKNOWLEDGMENTS

MUCH OF the argument of chapter 2 has already appeared in "'Assume an Identity of Sentiment': Rhetoric and Audience in Emerson's 'Divinity School Address'" (*Prospects* 9 [1984]), and in "Seeing & Saying: The Dialectic of Emerson's Eloquence" (in *Emerson and His Legacy: Essays in Honor of Quentin Anderson*, ed. Stephen Donadio, Stephen Railton, and Ormond Seavey; copyright (c) 1986 by the Board of Trustees, Southern Illinois University, used by permission of Southern Illinois University Press). An earlier version of chapter 4 appeared as "Mothers, Husbands and *Uncle Tom*" (*The Georgia Review* 38 [Spring 1984]). I thank Jack Salzman of *Prospects*, the editorial board of *The Georgia Review*, and the Southern Illinois Press for permission to republish.

Quentin Anderson, Alan Howard, William Kerrigan, and Raymond Nelson read various parts of my study at various stages in the writing of it; I remain very grateful for their suggestions and encouragement. The University of Virginia provided leave time in which much of the writing was done, but I also wish to acknowledge the students here, both graduate and undergraduate, who have always helped to sustain and enrich my engagement with the American Renaissance.

Robert Richardson, who read the manuscript for Princeton, gave me very useful advice, which I followed as best as I could. Robert E. Brown, who has been this book's editor, has been a model of efficient support.

And then there's love. Ilene, Ben, and Annie have put up with this book for eight years. I want to dedicate it, with a love and thankfulness that are beyond the reach of both words and time, to my mother and father.

Authorship and Audience

Chapter I

THE ANXIETY OF PERFORMANCE

[In America] the general reader, or the common reader (he who stands somewhere between the avant garde and the consumers of mass diversion), has had a greater and more direct influence on the writer than his counterpart in Europe has had. This statement can be documented conclusively from internal evidence in the work of our greatest writers.
—William Charvat, *Literary Publishing in America*

The child is sincere, and the man when he is alone, if he be not a writer.
—Ralph Waldo Emerson, *The Journals*

MY MAIN concern in this study is with the major prose works of the American Renaissance. My list of major texts is a traditional one—Emerson's "Divinity School Address," Thoreau's *Walden*, Hawthorne's *Scarlet Letter*, Poe's tales, and Melville's *Moby-Dick*—but I try to reread them from a new point of view: as performances. The context I am trying to define can be called a dramatic one, although the drama is peculiarly subjective. The paradox of writing is that it is at once an intensely solitary and an utterly public act. Although I am alone at my desk, you are with me as I write this paragraph. I can shut the door to keep other people out of the room, but I can hardly exclude you from my consciousness. What I think about the major prose texts of the American Renaissance is one thing; what I say about them, however, and how I say it—those things, these words, depend upon the complex and dramatic fact that I am saying them to you. Fully to appreciate the innumerable choices I have to make as I push this sentence across the page means taking into an account of it my ambitions as a person and my sense of an audience as a late-twentieth-century critic. Similarly, my account of Emerson's, Thoreau's, Hawthorne's, Poe's, and Melville's works attempts to relocate them in the space in which they were originally written: the space between the individual author, beset by his own hopes and fears, and the contemporary American reading public for whom he was writing. So while my main concern is with the texts themselves, I must also take into this account what lay behind them—the emotional lives of these American authors—

and what lay before them—the values, appetites, and expectations of their mid-nineteenth-century American audience. Theoretically, this means subordinating the texts to the status of effect. The causes that governed them are to be found, at least for the purposes of this study, in the anxieties of their authors and in the assumptions of their audience.

The premise on which my account is based is that writing should be conceptualized as a public gesture, not as a private act.[1] Experientially, I believe, everyone is already aware of this because everyone has been a performing writer, if only as a school child trying to produce a composition for a teacher and a grade. It is possible that some may be so solipsistic as to remain unaffected by the thought that what they are writing will be seen by other eyes—re-viewed—but surely even most student essayists can recognize their own self-consciousness as writers in Washington Irving's description, in the last paragraph of *The Sketch Book*, of his "peculiar situation":

> The author is conscious of the numerous faults and imperfections of his work, and well aware how little he is disciplined and accomplished in the arts of authorship. His deficiencies are also increased by a diffidence arising from his peculiar situation. He finds himself writing in a strange land, and appearing before a public which he has been accustomed, from childhood, to regard with the highest feelings of awe and reverence. He is full of solicitude to deserve their approbation, yet finds that very solicitude continually embarrassing his powers, and depriving him of that ease and confidence which are necessary to successful exertion.[2]

Although Irving's modesty is certainly exceptional, the situation he is describing is less peculiar than he thinks. The page on which anyone writes for publication is inevitably a "strange land." This page, for instance. Whose is it? Mine? On it I seem to have a godlike creative power and a freedom I could never find in the real world beyond the margins. I could spend two years at Walden Pond or meet Fayaway for a canoe ride. Apparently anything can happen here. Yet when I am finished with it, this page is yours. To the extent that my sense of myself is invested in a concern about your response, my apparent freedom shrinks dramatically. What Irving acknowledges, with a candor that few writers have chosen to imitate, is that the public before which he "appears" stands between him and the page, between his imaginative vision and the words in which he seeks to realize it. Certainly in the case of *The Sketch Book*, the painstaking casualness of Irving's prose, the tortured gracefulness of his style, the provincial cosmopolitanism of his allusions all reflect the anxiety about performing that, as he admits, he "continually" felt as a writer.

It was Cooper's career that first prompted me to think about the role that an audience plays in the work of literature. When, at age thirty, Cooper committed himself to the attempt to become a professional American novelist, he had to begin with his potential readers. If the prospects for American fiction were still an unexplored, largely empty territory (much like the continent), the realm in which his imagination could play rather resembled a baseball or football field; it had already been marked off and defined by a set of rules and conventions, the specific patterns that imported British novels had conditioned American readers to expect. As James D. Wallace has shown in his study of Cooper's first three novels,[3] Cooper's stunning success at the start of his career resulted from his creative acceptance of the conditions that his audience's assumptions imposed on his imagination. In the way he appropriated and reshaped the elements of popular British fictions, he found the means to recondition Americans to read American tales and, as he put it, to please himself as well.[4] Despite his success, however, Cooper was always extremely uneasy with the demands of literary performance. By the end of his first decade as an author, he was anxious to get his "neck out of the halter" of authorship.[5] Disgusted, as he put it in a letter to a friend, with himself; mortified, as he put it in *A Letter to His Countrymen*, with his audience, he announced his retirement.[6] Within a few more years he went back to writing novels, but in most of the fictions he wrote in this second half of his career, his mixed feelings about his audience became an explicit part of the performance. The ground on which his imagination had previously played was now conceived as a battleground for which his imagination had to fight. His quarrel with his country was actually a quarrel with his readers, and what started it was his quarrel with the dynamics of literary performance itself.

As I try to show in my study of Cooper,[7] his various reactions to his American audience's reactions have to be labeled overreactions. Out of the slightest real causes he created another kind of fiction: "The Career of James Fenimore Cooper, Betrayed Novelist," which was then followed by a sequel, "The Revenge of the Writer." In my book I explain his overreactions in the Oedipal terms of his quest for identity as a son. But since the melodramatic shape of Cooper's career also resembles that of a number of others in the American nineteenth century—Brockden Brown's, Melville's, Mark Twain's, even Irving's—I came to realize that it also reveals a good deal about the quest for identity of the American writer: about American writers' peculiarly dependent relationship to the responses of their audience, and the amount of performance anxiety that vulnerability produced. One of Cooper's late novels, *The Crater*, yielded a paradigm, not just for Cooper's career but for thinking about the paradox of writing as both intensely private and utterly public.

Cooper's twenty-eighth novel, *The Crater* tells the story of Mark Woolston, an American seaman who, like Robinson Crusoe, is shipwrecked on an island he first cultivates and then colonizes. Its subject is ostensibly American society in the 1840s. By removing the setting to a Pacific island, Cooper tries to give his polemic exposé of the dangers of rabid egalitarianism the clarity of a political parable. But in its distribution of narrative emphases, the novel is more evocatively a parable about imaginative creation and publication. Effectively alone on the island for much of the story, Woolston delights in his uncontested possession of a realm over which his own will is sovereign. The crater is like the novelist's blank pages, ready to take the impress of his own designs: a new world for him to bring into expression. Indeed, Woolston's efforts "to create, and to adorn, and to perfect"[8] are followed, thanks to a volcanic process that Cooper leaves rather vague, by an enormous enlargement of his kingdom. But he is not allowed to remain alone and undisturbed. Once his realm is exposed to other eyes, the idyll of creating a world in solitude gives way to the violence of having to share it with the public. Initially the violence is moral and emotional, but by the end it has been literalized. Rather than watch his beloved playground be desecrated by the mob of Americans who claim it for themselves, Woolston sails away; when he returns, he finds that another volcanic eruption has carried off the whole island—sunk it like the *Pequod* and its crew. Cooper wants us to accept this destruction as a judgment of God. Most readers view it instead as his own anger at the evils of American society. But we can also see in this apocalypse the rage of a novelist against the inevitable constraints of his art. In Genesis the creator is also the reviewer: "and God saw that it was good." Mortal artists, though, have to live with the fact that others will pass judgment on their creation. Under our eyes Cooper brings a world into being, but because he cannot find his own wishes reflected in those eyes, he destroys the whole world he has made. The pleasures of solitary creation are consumed by the trauma of public-ation.

Writing about Cooper taught me about writing as a performance in a more visceral way as well. I had read what writers themselves have said about reading reviews of their work. On the record they mostly affect indifference to the process of publication. Yet after my book on Cooper was published and I waited for some echo to come back from the emptiness into which it had gone, I came to realize how much I had at stake in what other people, whose faces I might never see, would say about my work. When at last there were reviews to read, I had to give up any lingering pretense to a disinterested sense of achievement. Reading what others said—or failed to say—I learned that it was not just my book, but somehow my self that was vulnerable to their judgments. I doubt my experience was at all unusual. In October 1838, in the midst of the controversy aroused by "The Divinity School Address," Emerson confided to the pages of his journal: "I am sensitive as a leaf to impressions from abroad.

And under this night's beautiful heaven I have forgotten that ever I was *reviewed*."⁹ The italics are Emerson's, and of course, as the passage itself reveals, he had not forgotten.

Probably the most important, at any rate the most inescapable, thing that a critic brings to the study of literature is his or her own obsessions. It can hardly be a coincidence that I soon noticed how preoccupied with their audience are the nineteenth-century American works I teach. Because typically Emerson's audience was in the room with him when he first "published" his essays as lectures, it is perhaps obvious why he devoted so much attention in his journals to the topic of performing, to the anxieties and rewards of addressing a public. It is less obvious, however, why he would erase almost all traces of this concern when he revised his journal entries into lectures and essays. On the other hand, *Walden* and *Moby-Dick* are written works, yet in each a narrative mode is displaced by a rhetorical one; as texts, they are essentially organized around a direct encounter with their reader, who is not merely repeatedly addressed, but even given lines to speak. *The Scarlet Letter* too inscribes an audience right into its text: before the "story" begins, the throng of Puritan men and women is put in place as its immediate audience. Poe's well-known aesthetic doctrine, the theory of a "unity of effect" that he develops in his critical pieces, puts the reader's mind at the very center of his imaginative project; by claiming that the work of literature is to produce an effect, Poe implicitly makes each of his tales and poems as much a performance as any of Emerson's lectures. Writers, as Emerson noted, are never alone. But as a group, the major writers of the American Renaissance were particularly preoccupied with the drama of literary performance. To appreciate the achievement of their works, and the conflict out of which it came, we need to set their texts back in this dramatic context and to look at the role the contemporary American public played, in this drama and in these texts.

It might help clarify my theoretical concerns if I locate them in our contemporary context. As Susan R. Suleiman has pointed out, "in the field of literary theory and criticism . . . [t]he words *reader* and *audience*, once relegated to the status of the unproblematic and obvious, have acceded to a starring role."¹⁰ Within the last twenty years, critics working from such disparate methodological traditions as linguistics, philosophy, psychoanalysis and sociology have arrived at the problem of "the reader in the text." The large and growing body of work on this issue is summarily referred to as "reader-response criticism"; included under this rubric are many kinds of "reader" and many categories of "response."¹¹ My concern with "readers," however, responds to an essentially different set of questions from those asked by reader-response criticism. To put it simply, I

am less interested in the experience of *reading* the major prose texts of
the American Renaissance than in the experience of *writing* them. To put
it positively, I am more interested in the writer's consciousness than in
the reader's, in the dynamics of literary creation than in the dynamics of
interpretive or affective response.

I have no desire to be polemical about this difference. Yet I think criticism should preserve a distinction that is often blurred—as Suleiman
blurs it in the passage above: the distinction between "reader" and "audience." Once I commit my words to print, "you" may be anyone; this
potential and ahistorical "you" we can call the *reader* that most reader-
response criticism identifies as its object of study. But while I write this,
my sense of "you" is more determinant; as a late twentieth-century critic
of American literature, I have in mind a particular *audience* for my prose.
While I have a measure of freedom in deciding what kind of audience I
want to try to address, and while, in any case, as Walter J. Ong points out,
my sense of audience is essentially a fiction—a conceptual category rather
than, say, a real group of men and women, an abstraction rather than a set
of faces,[12] the way I define an *audience* cannot be detached from the circumstances of a particular time and place. As the reader-response critics
say, a *reader* comes into existence every time someone, some place opens
a book and begins to process a text. An *audience*, however, is something
that is there before a writer begins to write—it is "there" in the real world
he or she inhabits, as the set of potential readers for the text; more significantly, it is "there" in the author's mind as his or her sense of the people
to whom the text is addressed.

It could be shown that nineteenth-century writers helped to create this
idea of the *reader*. This is the end, for instance, toward which Wordsworth works in the various prose statements that served as prefaces and
supplements to his poetry. Out of his frustrations with the actual responses of real readers to his poems, he evolved the programmatic belief
that writers had to create the taste by which they were to be enjoyed and
understood, which led him in 1815 to distinguish the contemptible
"Public" from "the People, philosophically characterised."[13] He claims to
make a political or moral distinction, but he seems really to have in mind
an aesthetic one: "philosophically characterised," the People are the readers who can respond directly to his poems, who in fact are largely created
by the way they respond to his poems. This impatient tension between
actual and potential readers runs through a lot of nineteenth-century literature. In effect, Melville makes the discrimination I'm suggesting between audience and reader when, in chapter 89 of *Moby-Dick*, he asserts
that his reader is both a "fast-fish" and a "loose-fish, too." As a "fast-
fish," the reader is bound by the preconceptions of his cultural moment,
the *idées récus* of his society; as a "loose-fish," on the other hand, the

reader is an open mind that can dive into new depths, a consciousness that can be changed by experience—especially by the experience of reading *Moby-Dick*. Writers like Blake or Emily Dickinson, by refusing to address themselves at all to the contemporary public, might be said to have written exclusively for the kind of reader which most reader-response criticism presumes. But as a group, nineteenth-century writers, whether English or American, were stuck with an audience they did not create. They may have longed for the kind of "implied readers" that Coleridge anticipated when he declared that the "willing suspension of disbelief for the moment" is the covenant "which constitutes poetic faith":[14] readers who would open themselves up to the full experience of the text. But they knew, often only too well, that they had to write for a specific audience: men and women who would bring to the text many deeply held, but often unconscious, "beliefs"—values, tastes, expectations they were not willing to suspend, even for the moment, and to which they would hold the text accountable. And while theoretically Ong is right to point out that any writer's "audience"—the conception of his readers that governs his own performative stance—is a "fiction," psychologically, for these writers, that preexistent audience was a very real fact.

Because an audience exists before a work has been written and a reader comes along only afterward, they play very different roles "in the text." The choices you make about meaning and value as you read this sentence—your responses—are prompted by the text itself. As the enormous body of work on the reading process has demonstrated, how readers respond is a complex matter, but they are responding *to the text*. On the other hand, the choices I make as I write this sentence (my pre-sponses?) are shaped by "you." I have to put "you" in quotation marks because it does not refer to any particular person but to my internalized sense of an audience. That "you" is a construct of my assumptions, however, does not prevent "you" from playing a very dramatic role in the writing process. Since I have a good deal of myself invested in "your" reaction, as I write my prose responds *to the audience*. "You" pervade every level of my text. At the most local level of diction, whether I say "interpretation" or "hermeneutics," "work" or "text," "written into" or "inscripted" are choices that I make, in part at least, with "you" and "your" values in mind. This holds at every other level as well. What kind of first chapter I begin with, what critical authorities I cite, what objections I anticipate, and so on, can all be referred to the particular performance I am engaged in. When Emerson noted in his journal that "in composition the *What* is of no importance compared with the *How*,"[15] he was thinking precisely of the active part that the preexistent audience plays in the creative process.

The "how" of Emerson's work was demonstrably responsive to his mid-nineteenth-century audience, just as how I write is a reflection of who is with me in this empty room. If the *reader* can be approached theoretically as a timeless or ahistorical locus of responses that are summoned into existence by texts, the *audience*—in the way I am trying to define it—cannot be abstracted from history, from the cultural circumstances of time and place. Historicizing the dynamic of reader-response has been the most useful contribution of the Konstanz group of theorists. Of these the best known is Hans Robert Jauss, who argues that what literary theory must conceptualize, what literary history should try to concretize, is the "horizon of expectations" that contemporary readers at any given moment brought with them to the reading of a particular text.[16] Such expectations reflect readers' previous experiences with works of literature, but also the preconceptions about "reality" that have been shaped by the norms of their culture. Jauss's version of literary history sees individual works as engaged through time in a dialectic (he calls it a pattern of questions and answers) with the way earlier works responded to and changed readers' "horizons of expectations."

To attempt to establish the horizon of expectations of the American audience to which Emerson, Thoreau, Hawthorne, Poe, and Melville addressed themselves, I spend two chapters on two different modes of popular literature. Stowe's *Uncle Tom's Cabin* was one of the three best-selling novels from the period that F. O. Matthiessen taught us to call the American Renaissance. Along with *The Wide, Wide World* and *The Lamplighter*, it created a kind of separate, unprecedented category of popular success. The books, tales, and sketches that can be grouped under the category of Southwestern Humor were popular in a less spectacular way, but throughout the years between 1836, when Emerson published *Nature*, and the beginning of the Civil War—the twenty-five years that constitute the period of the American Renaissance—the various works of Longstreet, Hooper, Baldwin, and the other humorists enjoyed a steady success with readers. Both *Uncle Tom's Cabin* and Southwestern Humor make a number of claims on the attention of modern criticism. By any kind of reckoning, Stowe's novel is a great book. Historians of American literature have found illuminating connections between Southwestern Humor's repertoire of event and especially its experiments with the resources of vernacular speech and later, canonical authors like Mark Twain, Hemingway, and Faulkner. I include them in this study, though, for the way they can help us gain access to the tastes and assumptions of the contemporary reading public.

I have to be modest about this enterprise. "The contemporary reading public" is a hopelessly vast abstraction. Unless one is simply talking about literacy rates, it has no real historical referent. As Jacques Leenhardt empirically demonstrated at the conclusion of a sociological survey of five hundred readers in France and Hungary, "*The* public . . . can no longer be considered as a valid notion where the process of reading is concerned." "When speaking of *the* public," he wrote, "one frequently sees it as a whole; in actual fact, we only met *readers*, who form *publics* according to their sociodemographical characteristics."[17] From the viewpoint of the sociologist of literature, there is a dizzying number of ways in which the literate persons at any historical moment can be divided into different potential "reading publics": on the basis of class, or ideology, or age, or education, or region, and so on. The distinction that decided my choice of representative popular works was gender.

Because of the circumstances of its publication, one can say with as much certainty as historical research into popular culture ever permits that Southwestern Humor was written by men, for men. "Everybody" read *Uncle Tom's Cabin* in the 1850s, but despite its political subject matter it retains the characteristic assumptions of the "domestic" or "genteel" fiction that was written—regardless of who eventually read it—by women, for women. My decision to give gender such a decisive role in categorizing significant reading publics follows the line that analysts of Victorian American culture have long taken, from Santayana to Fred Patee to Ann Douglas:[18] that Americans at mid-century tended to make increasingly sharp distinctions between male and female realms of experience, that for those Americans gender tended to be a category that took precedence over such other accidentals as age or region or class. But I don't offer it as a definitive way to make sense of the vast, and vastly different, number of actual people who made up "the reading public" at the time. It is simply *a* way to try to gain *some* access to the minds—the literary expectations, the cultural assumptions, the concerns and values—of the audience that was available to writers like Hawthorne and Melville.

There are other means of gaining access to the world of real readers. William Charvat has made a permanent contribution to our understanding of American literature through his research into the empirical history of book production. How and where books were published, how and where they were distributed, how much they cost, how much they made—Charvat's work demonstrates conclusively that all of this had a measurable influence on the authors who were writing the books.[19] In her fine study *Novels, Readers, and Reviewers*, Nina Baym turns to the contemporary reviews that mediated between the individual author and the reading public in Victorian America and that preserve the responses of one group of readers on the brittle pages of old periodicals. By reviewing their reviews, Baym brings to light many of the patterns of assumption that governed the public relationship between novels and the culture.[20]

There is still more progress to be made in each of the directions that Charvat and Baym have blazed. My decision to read two kinds of popular literature to discover what they reveal about the habitus of the general reader is certainly less empirical than either of their approaches. But I wanted to maintain my emphasis on literary enactments. By looking at

specific works in the context of contemporary expectations, I can focus
on the way individual writers negotiate the terms of their relationship
with their audience. One of the things popular literature can reveal is the
operation of the spoken and unspoken bonds that link a writer to his or
her contemporary readers. Although there are (from a sociological point
of view) huge differences to be noted between Stowe's novel and a typical
southwestern sketch, as popular performances they have in common a
presumed and discernible sense of identity with the respective audiences
to which they are addressed. Considered this way, they both can be distinguished from the works of Emerson, Thoreau, Hawthorne, Poe, and
Melville, who all, for various reasons and in various ways, felt estranged
from or at odds with the audience they wrote for. The more we know
about the general reader (and we can never know enough) the better we
can appreciate the drama of their performance. It is that drama, however,
to which I want to attend.

I won't have to use the first-person pronoun much longer, but I
should admit that Jauss's dialectical schema can help only up to a point in
my efforts to understand the drama of literary creation. The audience's
horizon of expectations is one aspect of any literary performance. The
other, though, involves the aspirations, the designs, the anxieties of the
writer. Jauss is concerned with reception, not production, and the figure
of the writer remains at the periphery of his field of forces. This is still
more generally the case with other forms of reader-response criticism,
which often bracket out "the author" entirely. To New Criticism's acts of
attention to the text these theories add the presence of the reader whose
activity recreates the text, but they are uninterested in the nature of the
activity that created the text in the first place. Author—text—audience.
The text somehow occasions the reader's response, but what kind of occasion was the text itself? How was it conditioned by the writer's awareness of the reader? How, then, is a text the record of its own performance? To answer those questions I cannot bracket out the audience, but
I have to put authors, and their human needs, at the center of my analysis.

In our time the most seminal author-centered critical theory is Harold
Bloom's diagnosis of "the anxiety of influence." Bloom takes New Criticism to task on grounds that are more congenial to my own perspective: "We need to stop thinking of any poet as an autonomous ego." He
too locates the writer in a specifically dramatic context: "For the poet
is condemned to learn his profoundest yearnings through an awareness
of *other selves*." Yet he implicitly takes as a given of the "Modern" writer's
situation (and for Bloom "modern" means post-Miltonic) the culturally
impoverished condition of twentieth-century poetry. In his account the
poet neither plays nor can aspire to any social role; sealed off in the separate realm of "poetry," the writer struggles to create himself by encountering and defeating his literary precursors: "Every poet is a being

caught up in a dialectical relationship (transference, repetition, error, communication) with another poet or poets."[21] These are the only other selves that matter. The writer's quest is for originality, priority, authority, all of which he strives to achieve within texts that are ultimately self-referential.[22]

Any future account of intertextuality or the history of influence will find it hard to ignore the explanatory power of Bloom's model.[23] However, I think we should put Bloom's self-conscious poets back into the larger human context from which his analysis abstracts them. The enormous weight that Bloom puts on "originality" is a modernist (by which I mean post-1912) phenomenon. The Romantics who provide the basis for his model were anxious about a very different kind of "influence" than Bloom is prepared to consider: from Wordsworth's definition of the poet as "a man speaking to men" to Shelley's claim that poets were "the unacknowledged legislators of the world," they sought the meaning of their achievement as writers in the difference they could make to history. Once we bring back to the front of our minds their concern with what Emerson called "the conversion of the world," many of the gestures that Bloom italicizes take on a different meaning. Quoting or alluding to Milton, as Wordsworth and Coleridge so often do, may function one way in their private drama as "strong imaginations" contending with "the great Inhibitor,"[24] but in their public drama as prophets with an original vision speaking to a conventional audience, it can be seen as serving a profoundly different end. To the readers whom Wordsworth and Coleridge addressed, Milton was not just a "strong poet"; he was also a consummately *orthodox* one, whose works occupied the same privileged place on bookshelves as the Bible or *Pilgrim's Progress*. Citing Milton could help span or even disguise the gap between the writer's radical newer testament and his audience's horizon of moral expectations.[25] By co-opting Milton's voice, in other words, Wordsworth could use him strategically in the same way that Emerson could impersonate the voice of the King James Bible in his most unorthodox pronouncements.

Because Bloom abstracts writing from any social dimension, he overlooks the way writers, nineteenth-century writers in particular, could feel as burdened *by* originality as they were by the quest *for* it. When we posit a writer looking forward to his audience instead of backward to his predecessors, and forward to that audience's response to his ideas or words, the difficulty of creating himself becomes inseparable from the problem of getting a receptive hearing for his version of the truth.[26] And almost all nineteenth-century writers, especially the Romantics and their American descendants in the next generation, defined their project as a public one. Whether they sought "to arouse the sensual from their sleep / Of Death" (Wordsworth) or "to wake my neighbors up" (Thoreau), to sound "through my lips to unawakened earth / The trumpet of a prophecy" (Shelley) or to "gospelize the world anew" (Melville's *Pierre*), they saw their texts as a means. The end at which they aimed depended on the reaction of their audience.

For this reason they actually were tempted to deny their own originality, as Emerson does at the end of *Nature*, where he blandly refers to his radical and apocalyptic announcement of the divinity of man as "some traditions" that "have always been in the world, and perhaps reappear to every bard." In a long journal entry from 1839, Emerson identifies the most urgent of his anxieties. The passage is addressed to his precursors but winds up confronting much more dramatically his audience. It suggests how, like the other writers I'm concerned with, he was less apprehensive about the past than about the future—the future as defined by his audience's response. The passage can serve to conclude my contention with Bloom and to introduce the next subject I have to take up: the presence of the reading public in mid-century America, the presence that looms so large at the beginning and, even more palpably, at the end of Emerson's journal entry. "Him who said it before" turns out to be a benign, even a nurturing presence; "you" who should hear it are the adversary:

> *To him who said it before.* I see my thought standing, growing, walking, working, out there in nature. Look where I will, I see it. Yet when I seek to say it, all men say "NO: It is not. These are whimsies & dreams!" Then I think they look at one thing & I at others. My thoughts, though not false, are far, as yet, from simple truth, & I am rebuked by their disapprobation nor think of questioning it. Society is yet too great for me. But I go back to my library & open my books & lo I read this word spoken out of immemorial time, "God is the unity of men." Behold, I say, my very thought! This is what I am rebuked for saying; & here it is & has been for centuries in this book which circulates among men without reproof, nay, with honor. But behold, again here in another book "Man is good, but men are bad." Why, I have said no more. And here again, read these words, "Ne te quaesiveris extra." What, then! I have not been talking nonsense. These lines of Greek & Latin which pass now current in all literatures as proverbs of old wise men are expressions of the very facts which the sky, the sea, the plant, the ox, the man, the picture, said daily unto me, & which I repeated to you. I see that I was right; that not only I was right, which I could not doubt, but my language was right; that the soul has always said these things; & that you ought to hear it & say the same.[27]

By "you" Emerson means his contemporaries, the audience he spoke to and wrote for. Yet the fact that he is actually alone here, writing in his own journal, points to a distinction that must be kept in mind throughout this study. At any given time "the reading public" would be the aggregate of all the literate members of a society. That broadest category could be broken down into the various "publics" that define themselves by their appetite for different kinds of texts, as Henry Nash Smith has suggested dividing American novel readers of the 1850s into "high," "middle," and "low" "brow levels."[28] One could strive for greater sociological exactness by breaking down even these divisions into the particular "publics" that read specific works—the fifteen hundred people, say, who bought the first edition of *Nature*, and the interested friends to whom they loaned it.[29] But my focus on the writing process requires me to define the "public" for any given writer as a psychological as well as a sociological fact: "Emerson's audience" as a set of assumptions and attitudes in his mind. Because this internalized audience is different for each author, the "American public" I am concerned with has to change from chapter to chapter, and even within a chapter the concept is not more stable than a writer's own set of attitudes. When considering *Moby-Dick*, for instance, I discuss the way Melville cast his audience into at least three incompatible roles in the course of writing the book.

There is always a gap between a writer's internalized audience and the real men and women who will read a particular work. Often there is an abyss. The conception of "you" revealed in Emerson's journal entry is patently out of touch with reality. Although he sees himself as surrounded by an unappreciative audience—"all men say: 'NO'"—his numerous oratorical performances up to 1839 had generally been met not just with approval, but with great enthusiasm. Like Cooper, he is overreacting to *some* criticism: he construes a few members of his audience as *the* public. Why Emerson was so vulnerable to the responses of his audience is a subject for my next chapter. But before I conclude this chapter, I want to try to suggest why as a group nineteenth-century American writers felt so much anxiety about the American public.

As Ong notes, the basic nature of the relationship between authors and audiences changes over time.[30] Literary performance—how writers conceive of and address themselves to an audience—is at the mercy of cultural-historical circumstances. In imperial Rome, according to Erich Auerbach, authors like Horace or Pliny the Younger first "published" their manuscripts in private readings attended by "their friends, that is, a group of the social and intellectual elite."[31] Since "it was public readings that decided the fate of a work," undoubtedly even this kind of performance aroused anxiety, yet it would hardly have been comparable to what Mark Twain felt about the terms of publication in Gilded Age America. He too often read his works in public, but by the 1880s they were "published," and their immediate fate decided, by an army of subscription salesmen who went from house to house across America carrying a sample chapter from the forthcoming book, complete with specimen illustrations and a choice of bindings and endpapers.

As Ian Watt has demonstrated, the development of a new literary genre reflects changes in the readership patterns of a society.[32] In his essay "The Romantic Artist," Raymond Williams succinctly summarizes the interplay between historical forces and imaginative activity, including the way writers conceive of themselves and the process of publication.[33] Sociological changes in the nineteenth-century British reading public and their impact on literary history have been studied by Amy Cruse, Arthur Simmons Collins, Q. D. Leavis, R. K. Webb, Richard D. Altick, Louis James, and Jon P. Klancher.[34] I mention all these studies to acknowledge the complexity of the ground I have to venture on. For American literature, it is still largely unsurveyed.[35] But I cannot very well proceed to examine specific literary performances without trying to set the stage on which American writers at mid-century had to perform.

Their audience was at the center of the stage. The central circumstance on which my study is predicated involves the unprecedented size and power of the public in the process of public-ation. With all the aggrieved exasperation of a performing writer, Coleridge in 1817 puts in a sociohistorical context the new dynamic that governed the relationship between writers and their audience:

> Poets and philosophers, rendered diffident by their very number, addressed themselves to 'learned readers'; then, aimed to conciliate the graces of 'the candid reader'; till, the critic still rising as the author sunk, the amateurs of literature collectively were erected into a municipality of judges, and addressed as the Town! And now, finally, all men being supposed able to read, and all readers able to judge, the multitudinous public, shaped into personal unity by the magic of abstraction, sits nominal despot on the throne of criticism.[36]

"All men" is, of course, exaggerated; at the time Coleridge wrote the book-reading public was still only a small part of the population.[37] But from the middle of the eighteenth century onward, the rapid spread of literacy was widely extending the franchise by which readers were admitted to the "republic of letters," and dramatically widening the distances that separated writers from their audience.[38] The sociology of literature must resist as best it can the "magic of abstraction" that would turn any modern period's multitude of readers into *an* audience. Writers, however, are not sociologists of literature, and many of them shared Coleridge's apparent alarm at the thought of having to address themselves to this other nineteenth-century Great Unknown: the growing mass audience. Tom Moore, who unlike Coleridge enjoyed extraordinary popularity, nonetheless worried about "the ruinous effects to literature likely to arise from the boasted diffusion of education; . . . from extending the circle of judges; from letting the mob in to vote."[39]

"To vote": the idea of the republic of letters itself was another legacy the eighteenth century bequeathed the nineteenth-century writer.[40] Concommitant with the democratization of literacy was the rise of democratic principles, which gave theoretical sanction to the significance of public opinion while their increasing numbers gave the mass audience more substantive power as consumers in the marketplace of letters.[41] Coleridge refers to this republican assumption when he complains that now "all readers [are supposed to be] able to judge." Nineteenth-century critics often quoted Dr. Johnson's remark about Gray: "In the character of his *Elegy* I rejoice to concur with the common reader; for by the common sense of readers uncorrupted with literary prejudices, after all the refinements of subtilty and the dogmatism of learning, must be finally decided all claim to poetical honours."[42] Although Johnson, writing in the Enlightenment, meant something much less democratic by "common reader" than what the nineteenth century meant by "common man," his asseveration was cited to give authority to the belief that the people could be counted on to determine literary achievement. Literally *counted* on, as numbers came to play an increasing role in assigning status and rank in the republic of letters.[43] As Sir Egerton Brydges summarily put it in the 1820s: "Merit is now universally estimated by the multitude of readers that an author can attract."[44] To Brydges this state of aesthetic affairs was a "vile evil." To others, though, it represented the triumph of egalitarian progress over the elitisms of traditional literature. "The people are always right," Emerson noted in his journal; "the man of letters is to say, these are the new conditions to which I must conform."[45] In the last sentence of the Preface to the first edition of *Leaves of Grass* (1855), Whitman enthusiastically embraced the notion that merit or poetical honor was determined solely by the multitude of readers an author could attract: "The proof of a poet is that his country absorbs him as affectionately as he has absorbed it."[46]

As with so many other aspects of European culture, the development of what can be called a mass audience came later and more precipitiously to America. Its presence was just beginning to be felt in the late 1830s.[47] Although as Smith admits, "It is impossible now to determine just what did happen to the [literary] market in the early 1850's,"[48] by that time, as Smith notes, the reading public as mass audience was a palpable fact that American publishers, reviewers, and writers had to contend with, even though they could treat it as either an opportunity or an intimidation. Publishers, of course, treated it as an opportunity, one that they quickly learned to exploit. Writers, as I hope the following chapters make clear, felt many different ways, often at the same time. But the point for literary criticism to keep in mind is that, if we want to set the works of this period back in an historicist context, the most immediate way in which contemporary society impinged upon a writer—as the audience being addressed—was also one of the most decisive.

The empowerment of the reading public was by no means an exclusively American circumstance. The concern with or anxiety about performing for this mass audience surfaces in many different texts. The kind of narrator Fielding developed, and the avuncular role he plays as the interlocutor between the events of his fictions and the responses of his reader, reflect Fielding's patrician uneasiness about the enormous audience revealed by Richardson's success; such readers do not need their appetites satisfied, Fielding felt, but rather their taste and judgment instructed. An equally self-conscious, though much less self-satisfied awareness of the distance between the writer and the public can be felt in the nervous clutch of the Ancient Mariner's hand as he detains his unwilling listener. The frame of Coleridge's poem, like the narrative strategy of Fielding's novels, is another instance of how a text records the drama of its own performance, and the kind of study that I have undertaken here could certainly find much to attend to in most British works from the second half of the eighteenth century to the end of the nineteenth.[49]

There were, however, factors that made the American writer at mid-century feel particularly exposed to and dependent on the reactions of his or her audience. For instance, in that passage from the *Biographia*, Coleridge calls the public the "*nominal* despot on the throne of criticism." He goes on to say that the real "invisible ministers" behind that throne are the quarterly reviewers who, according to him, control public opinion.[50] In America the reverse was true. In the essay on Hawthorne that Melville wrote in 1850, he protested that "there are hardly five critics in America; and several of them are asleep."[51] It would be hard to vouch for Melville's figures, but reading through the reviews printed in papers and magazines during this period supports his basic contention. In his day Cooper complained that American reviewers deferred too meekly to British judgments; traces of this neocolonial mentality persisted, but as a group American reviewers in Melville's day deferred more profoundly to the "suffrage of readers."[52] In a very representative passage, *Putnam's Monthly Magazine* in 1856 offered this tribute to the sovereignty of public opinion—or, as Tocqueville called it, "the tyranny of the majority":

[The critic's] function, in these days, is not to give a final but an accessory judgment—to speed the good to a readier appreciation, and to dismiss the bad to a quicker oblivion. For the world has come to judge for itself; no man is any more a supreme arbiter; the monopoly of literary opinion, such as was held of old by Scotch reviewers, has passed—and it is before the public that writers must tremble.[53]

Popularity, or the denial of it, seemed an irrefutable aesthetic judgment; reviewers were generally as reluctant to criticize a popular writer as they were to praise an unpopular one.[54] Both Poe and Margaret Fuller worked hard to create an American criticism, but their exhortations notwithstanding, the American faith in the theology of majority rule meant that writers could not look to the structures of a literary establishment to mediate between their work and the larger reading public. In essence, each writer was alone on the stage of literary performance. Writers did not necessarily have to tremble, but it was directly before the public that they had to perform. For almost any validation of his or her identity *as* an American artist, the writer was directly dependent on their response.

And of course, as the world's great experiment in republican government, America had by far the most invested in the idea of popular sovereignty. To the extent that they thought of themselves as *American* writers at all, the writers of the American Renaissance had to concede more to their audience, at least in principle, than their counterparts in the Old World. "Vox populi vox Dei": that the voice of the people was the same as the voice of God was a favorite slogan in Jacksonian America, and not just in the mouths of politicians. Hawthorne offered his variant on it in *The Scarlet Letter* when he avowed that the "judgment" of the "uninstructed multitude," at least when based on "the intuitions of its great and warm heart," can "possess the character of truths supernaturally revealed."[55]

Even more flattering is the tribute paid to "the people" by the author of "Readers By the Million," which appeared in *Harper's Magazine* in 1859, and which (hyperbole and all) can serve to sum up the status of the public as audience in the larger culture of the American Renaissance. "Without doubt," he writes, "literature is now the most democratic thing in existence." "Our firm conviction," he adds, is that "in this matter, as in politics, . . . the people are the soundest judges." With a bit of obviously assumed naivete, he throws a plank across the uneven, conflicted ground where democracy meets literature: "One would think it quite a natural thing that writers should address themselves to the vast body of the people." In his conclusion, however, apparently without quite realizing it, he reminds us of how conflicted that ground really was. The opening of his peroration seems very encouraging to the ambitions of individual writers, but to men and women who sought to express themselves in art, the note he ends on would have sounded ominously: "Authors were never so sure of sympathy, appreciation, and substantial recompense as now. The real state of the case is, that the people consider literature as

their property . . . and they intend to enjoy their sovereignty over it without 'let or hindrance.'"[56] This confusion of the real state of publication
with real estate recalls the paradigm of *The Crater*, where "the people"
decide to treat Cooper's hero's discovery and creation as "their property." The assumption here, that the audience presides over the space in
which literature happens, helps us understand a characteristic of the texts
of the American Renaissance that we will come back to often: the enormous amount of energy given off by the textual surface.[57] One of the
most pervasive and charged conflicts in the works of this period is not
developed inside the text (as narrative or argument, through development of characters and so on), but expressed by the text as a whole (as
style, or rhetorical stance and strategy): the conflict, that is, between the
imperatives of self-expression and the demands of performing for this
American public.

In the studies that follow, my focus is mainly on individual authors—
writers one by one rather than readers by the million. Let me conclude
this chapter by resuming that perspective, with Margaret Fuller's firsthand evidence about the state of mind of the American author in the face
of the contemporary circumstances I have tried to outline. In 1846, having lived in New England near Emerson, Hawthorne, and Thoreau, having moved to New York, where Poe was nearing the end of his career and
Melville beginning his, she wrote an essay entitled "American Literature:
Its Position in the Present Time, and Prospects for the Future." She ac-
cepts, although with misgivings, the democratization of art: in Europe
"there were princes and nobles to patronize literature and the arts. Here
is only the public." The essay's most emphatic passage, however, makes
"only the public" a profound understatement:

> if [literature] bows to the will of the multitude, it will find the ostracism of
> democracy far more dangerous than the worst censure of a tyranny could be.
> It is not half so dangerous to a man to be immured in a dungeon alone with
> God and his own clear conscience as to walk the streets fearing the scrutiny
> of a thousand eyes, ready to veil with anxious care whatever may not suit the
> many-headed monster in its momentary mood. . . . Writers have nothing to
> do but to love truth fervently, seek justice according to their ability, and
> then express what is in the mind; they have nothing to do with conse-
> quences, God will take care of those. The want of such noble courage, such
> faith in the power of truth and good desire, paralyzes the mind greatly in
> this country. Publishers are afraid; authors are afraid.[58]

There is hyperbole here too. "Anxious" describes more accurately than
"afraid" the self-consciousness of the American writer—if not while walking the streets, at least whenever he or she sat down to write. It is also
perfectly specious, as Fuller knew well from her own experience, to assert

that writers could simply express what was in their minds. For writers really to be unconcerned with consequences, they would need more than the faith she recommends; they would need a godlike sense of self-sufficiency. As human beings, however, writers bring their own inescapable needs to the ultimately public process of literary expression. As their texts show, they are very concerned with consequences.

There is one other "author" of the American Renaissance whose testimony is worth recalling here. Huck Finn supposedly writes his book between the end of his voyage downriver and his decision to "light out for the Territory" alone. This would have been just about the time that Thoreau decided to move out to Walden Pond. That Huck decides to escape from "sivilization" is what everyone remembers about his novel's last paragraph. What no one notices, however, is what Huck names as the most immediate problem he wants to escape: "if I'd a knowed what a trouble it was to make a book I wouldn't a tackled it and ain't agoing to no more. But I reckon I got to light out for the Territory. . . ." Of course, Huck did not write the book in the mid-1840s; Mark Twain did, in intervals of inspiration and blockage, between the mid-1870s and 1880s. Huck's exasperated confession here is one of the few places where Twain clearly steps in front of his persona.[59] American literature has often been identified with protagonists like Huck and Thoreau, with the flight from society that Cooper's Natty Bumppo pioneered. But we can only confuse these asocial gestures with the books that contain them because we've overlooked the drama of literary performance. No doubt this neglect has been encouraged by the way the terms of American authorship had changed by Twain's death in 1910. In the style of his late novels, Henry James was the first American writer to put high art beyond the reach of the middle-class audience. Although we should remember that James abandoned the general reader only in reaction to the disaster of his attempt to court wider popularity as a dramatist, his choice helped shape the modernist's assumption that one writes not for the public but for what Wallace Stevens called "a gallery of one's own."[60] Because we have inherited the dissociation of serious art and popular audience from the modernists, we have to make a leap to realize how public reception and aesthetic achievement were bound together in the last century. Moreover, we have missed the hopeless paradox in which nineteenth-century American literature, according to our generalizations about it, is trapped. It celebrates the possibility of escaping society in books addressed to society—that is, Huck heads for "the Territory," but Twain's manuscript goes to the printer, then to that army of subscription salesmen, then into the hands of the mass audience. Protagonists can flee society, but authors cannot. There is a great difference between Thoreau's decision to move out to Walden and his decision to write and publish *Walden*. Perhaps literary creation should mean finding and freely enjoying a territory of one's own imagination, but in fact it means moving in just the opposite direction: toward others. It was such a trouble to make Huck's book because literature was a performance, the demands of which Mark Twain could not escape.

Chapter II

"THE HIGH PRIZE OF ELOQUENCE":
EMERSON AS ORATOR

... if the single man plant himself indomitably on his
instincts, and there abide, the huge world will come
round to him.
—"The American Scholar"

WHERE we begin does not matter, Emerson claimed to believe; "the ultimate fact we reach on every topic is the resolution of all into the blessed
ONE."[1] His concept of unity has complex referents. There is the spiritual
project to reunite people with their best selves, to plant the individual
indomitably on his or her instincts. There is the philosophical project to
reorganize the world of thought—science and religion, history and providence, psychology and ethics—around the fixed point of consciousness,
to make the huge world round again. I am interested, however, in what
can be called his rhetorical project: his need as a visionary performer to
bring the world of his audience round *to him*. Moved as he was by the
spectacle of individuals in society betraying their divine powers, concerned as he was about the rush of the modern mind toward intellectual
chaos, it was nonetheless this private need, I think, that engaged his deepest anxieties and that determined the shape of his career. "The high prize
of eloquence may be mine," he confided to his journal in 1834; "the joy
of uttering what no other can utter & what all must receive."[2] What all
must receive—thus he consecrated himself to his mission as a prophet to
Jacksonian America and identified in a phrase his highest ambition and
his greatest obstacle. For he knew that on the topics most central to his
aim, he and his audience began with profoundly different convictions.
"How hard it is to write the truth," he admitted to himself in 1836; "so
soon as I have seen the truth I clap my hands & rejoice & go back to see
it & forward to tell men" (*JMN*, 5:181). Here Emerson locates the most
stubborn of the antitheses he had to try to reconcile: the conflict between
seeing and saying. If, as a seer, he was "an endless seeker with no Past as
[his] back" (2:188), as a sayer he was always acutely conscious of the
audience in front of him.[3]

While all Emerson's works reveal the anxieties of this performance,
they seldom address the conflict directly, and indeed typically go to great
lengths to disguise the opposition between himself and his audience. Yet

in "The American Scholar," his first major public statement after launching his career with *Nature*, he avows the rhetorical project I am trying to describe, and even indicates the personal urgencies that lay behind it. As Henry Nash Smith pointed out, in announcing the scholar's "duties," Emerson is defining the problem of his own vocation.[4] Those duties, he proclaims, "are such as become Man Thinking" (73)—but he is really thinking about himself, lecturing. "They may all be comprised in self-trust"—but finally he means trust in the possibility of communion with his audience. Speaking in the third person, Emerson obliquely acknowledges the worry and self-doubt, we could call it the stage fright, that often dominated his journal entries during the 1830s:

> For the ease and pleasure of treading the old road, accepting the fashions, the education, the religion of society, he takes the cross of making his own, and, of course, the self-accusation, the faint heart, the frequent uncertainty and loss of time, which are the nettles and tangling vines in the way of the self-relying and self-directed; and the state of virtual hostility in which he seems to stand to society. (73)

It was from this state of alienation that Emerson began his quest for a new identity as a peripatetic spokesman and philosopher. The familiar tropes here recall the proverbial fate of such a prophet, yet Emerson could be characterized as the one prophet with no desire for martyrdom. On this topic too, the way leads back to unity. The scholar's solitary pilgrim's progress ends with a triumphant homecoming:

> Success treads on every right step. For the instinct is sure, that prompts him to tell his brother what he thinks. He then learns that in going down into the secrets of his own mind he has descended into the secrets of all minds. He learns that he who has mastered any law in his private thoughts, is master to that extent of all men whose language he speaks, and of all into whose language his own can be translated. The poet, in utter solitude remembering his spontaneous thoughts and recording them, is found to have recorded that which men in crowded cities find true for them also. The orator distrusts at first the fitness of his frank confessions, his want of knowledge of the persons he addresses, until he finds that he is the complement of his hearers; —that they drink his words because he fulfils for them their own nature; the deeper he dives into his privatest, secretest presentiment, to his wonder he finds this is the most acceptable, most public, and universally true. The people delight in it; the better part of every man feels, This is my music; this is myself. (74)

In Emerson's metaphysics, mind becomes one with and sovereign over matter. Here, though, he announces the kind of narcissistic reunion that was the goal of his rhetorical program. Through the mediation of language—what in "The Divinity School Address" he calls "the speech of man to men" (92)—the scholar's "own mind" discovers its identity with and mastery of "all minds."[5]

The poet Emerson refers to is obviously Wordsworth, from whom he borrows the phrases—"spontaneous thoughts," "speech of man to men"—with which to articulate the orator's function. That Emerson gestures so directly to Wordsworth in both "The American Scholar" and "The Divinity School Address," his two most earnest, autobiographical attempts to define the public role he aspired to, suggests how intently he had read the prefaces in which Wordsworth tried to make his prophetic aims explicit. Coleridge felt that Wordsworth had made a strategic mistake in stating his purpose so straightforwardly;[6] Emerson may have profited by this hint, although the fact that he never sought to explain or justify the aesthetic of his lectures is also entirely consistent with his general determination never to draw a line between himself and his audience. In any case, while Coleridge's prose helped Emerson to understand the range of his themes, Wordsworth's prefaces are the best guide I know of to Emerson's aesthetic, to how and why he expressed those themes.

Wordsworth situated poetry where Emerson situated eloquence: against the background of institutional Christianity's impotence as a means "to cheer, to raise, and to guide men" (73). The poem or the lecture inherited the purpose that had been served by the ecclesiastical ritual of service and sermon. As pastor of the Second Church, Emerson had broken with his congregation over the issue of administering the Lord's Supper, but the transaction between speaker and audience he describes in "The American Scholar" is a secularized communion. Where the Unitarians drank the wine that stood for the blood of Christ, the orator's listeners "drink his words," which embody the divine truth of their humanity. The "pleasure" that Wordsworth said was the aim of every poem was an essentially religious transport: the glow of faith and power felt by a recovered self restored to its own resources, which is what Emerson is thinking of when he says that "the better part of every man" dances to the orator's eloquence.

Wordsworth calls himself "a poet charged with a new mission to extend [the] kingdom" of "the sources of sublimity in the soul of man."[7] It was on the same mission that Emerson traveled and lectured so widely in America. To "arouse the sensual from their sleep / Of Death,"[8] to restore mankind to "our natural and unalienable inheritance," "to send the soul into herself": these are Wordsworth's formulations, but they describe well what Emerson meant by the "wonder" and "delight" that preside over the encounter between speaker and listeners. Whatever the topic pointed to by the titles of his lectures, this conversion of a disparate audience into an awakened soul was the end each lecture worked toward:

In the pulpit at Waltham, I felt that the composition of his audience was not of importance to him who possessed true eloquence. Smooth or rugged, good natured or ill natured, religious or scoffers, he takes them all as they come, he proceeds in the faith that all differences are superficial, that they all have one fundamental nature which he knows how to address. This is to be eloquent. And having this skill to speak to their pervading soul he can make them smooth or rugged, good-natured or ill natured, saints or scoffers at his will. (*JMN*, 5:219)

Behind both these rhetorical projects lay the examples of the great awakenings, the revivalist excitements of the seventeenth and eighteenth centuries. Their mission was national and political as well as personal and religious. "The Poet," writes Wordsworth, "binds together by passion and knowledge the vast empire of human society"; as Emerson put it in his lecture "Society," "an example of a perfect society is in the effect of Eloquence."[9] Under the idiom of a truly inspired speaker, who has carried each listener into himself, to that realm of the Reason where all is unity, where the divided and sundered become one, the audience in a lecture hall is transformed into the archetype of a regenerate society. This may seem a lot to expect of a poem or a lecture, but because both Wordsworth and Emerson made their genres the main heir to the whole Christian tradition, they were forced to put equally great burdens on their powers as performers. In some respects, their design was no different from the one that the Puritans brought with them to Massachusetts Bay: to make the congregation of converted saints the model for a state. Except, of course, that the Puritans had God, the Bible, and the institutions of their faith to rely on, while these secular messiahs had only the soul, and their own words.

Yet to appreciate the burden that Emerson placed on eloquence, Wordsworth can help us only up to a point. The English Romantic movement and the self that emerged with it to shoulder the task of its own and society's salvation rose from the ashes of the French Revolution. Thus Romantic affirmations evolved dialectically out of ruin. In Wordsworth's careful balance of power with form one can detect the grim influence of the Reign of Terror: although he celebrated "powerful feelings" and sought to extend their domain, he did so within the limits fixed by metrical arrangement: "there is some danger that the excitement may be carried beyond its proper bounds. Now the co-presence of something regular [i.e., metre], something to which the mind has been accustomed in various moods and in a less excited state, cannot but have great efficacy in tempering and restraining the passion." Although Emerson's journals admit an occasional apprehension about overturning all traditional forms of authority, his early public work makes no concession to this restraint.

"Wherever a man comes, there comes revolution. The old is for slaves" (89); "feel your call in throbs of desire and hope" (84): Emerson's aphorisms cultivate excess.[10] Rhetorically he hoped to "set the hearts of . . . youth on flame" (58). Buoyed by America's benign associations with "revolution" and his own desire for an imminent apocalypse, he was not afraid of carrying his audience too far. Instead, his greatest anxiety was that he might leave them behind.

On the question of defining an audience, Wordsworth was the most egalitarian of the English Romantics. While the faculty of Reason was equally the property of all minds, Coleridge felt moved to protest "that it is neither possible or necessary for all men, or for many, to be PHILOSOPHERS."[11] Shelley's ardent contempt for all aristocratic privilege was complicated, to say the least, by his decision to address his poetry to "the highly refined imagination of the more select classes of poetical readers."[12] Wordsworth was more consistent in granting even "the most inexperienced Reader" the right "to judge for himself," to "decide" the value of his poetry "by his own feelings." But before letting his readers pass from the preface to the poems in *Lyrical Ballads*, Wordsworth warns them, in a passage that stands on its head his attack on traditional authorities, that "an *accurate* taste in poetry . . . is an *acquired* talent, which can only be produced by thought and a long-continued intercourse with the best models of composition." Wordsworth, in other words, puts his poems, and the effect that through them he seeks to produce on the public of his time, in the midst of a dialectic between feeling and taste, reading and study, the "simple produce of the common day" and the sophisticated achievements of culture.

Emerson, on the other hand, dismisses long-continued intercourse with the best literature as "listen[ing] too long to the courtly muses of Europe" (79). As an American, he refuses to "set bounds to the possibilities of man" (50). "All men," "each man," "every man"—these are his invariable locutions. Even *Nature*, the most Coleridgean of his texts, written to be read in print, often formidable in its use of technical terms, nonetheless gestures in its conclusion to the broadest possible audience: to the "cobbler" and small farmer as well as to the "scholar" (56). Since all humans were divine, Emerson could have replied to Coleridge, it would be an apostasy to presume they could not all be philosophers: "Every ear is yours to gain. Every heart will be glad & proud & thankful for a master. . . . be to them [men and women] a Plato be to them a Christ & they shall all be Platos & all be Christs" (*JMN*, 5:37). In another journal entry he indicates with still more recognizably Jacksonian explicitness that Emersonian man speaks to the largest possible congregation: "I said to Alcott that I thought the great Man should occupy the whole space between God and the mob. He must draw from the infinite source on the one side & he must penetrate into the heart & mind of the rabble on the other. From one he must draw his strength; to the other he must owe his Aim" (*JMN*, 5:249). This dramatically charged space is exactly where Emerson set up his podium: between the eternal truth and the mass audience. And if this passage seems to claim a vast amount for the self, the aim it announces lays down a program that mortgages Emerson to the verdicts of time and place. The true theory may be its own evidence, but true eloquence, as he defined it, depends upon the reaction it provokes. Even the great man's greatness is more like a politician's than a statesman's, for it depends upon its appeal to this broadly conceived public.

One can find the same tension in the means Emerson chose to redeem his age. Wordsworth's decision to "speak" to others as a poet meant working in private on the solitary consciousness of a reader. Emerson was a poet too, of course, and an essayist, but above all he believed in the power of speech. The public lecture or address was the occasion he preferred for "the communication of principles" and "the conversion of the world" (80). Most of his essays, derived as they are from lectures, are organized by the aesthetics of speaking. Not even his journals were written entirely in private, for much of the time we find him there rehearsing an idea for a lecture, soundlessly tuning his voice. Behind this choice to meet his audience face to face lay a long tradition of men literally speaking to others, not just the generations of ministers in his own ancestry but also the prophets of the Old Testament, and especially Jesus, Luther, and Fox, who were the predecessors with whom Emerson identified most strongly. There is something tragically genteel about the lyceum hall— where Jacksonians gathered to be instructed in such subjects as phrenology, classical sculpture, or (segregated by sexes) human anatomy—as the mount Emerson chose for playing Plato and Christ.[13] Yet he celebrated the lyceum lecture as the most modern, most democratic, least encumbered of genres. Unlike the church sermon or the political rally, the ad hoc nature of the lyceum assembly freed the speaker from any obligation to an institutional cause; he was no "retained attorney" (2:32) pledged to the Unitarians or Whigs. "In the lyceum," he wrote to Carlyle, advising him to come lecture in America, "the orator is only responsible for what his lips articulate."[14] In the lyceum all Americans, whatever their creed or class, could take "their place as Men in places of manly culture and entertainment" (*JMN*, 5:104).

Yet this occasion, while it liberated speakers from a priori commitments, bound them more tightly to the demands of a live performance, to the judgments of the listeners seated directly in front of them. "The audience is a constant meter of the orator":[15] Emerson gave his audience an authority over him that he granted to nothing else. This was partly a matter of metaphysical principle; since soul, or instinct, was the only absolute authority, what any man "announces, I must find true in me, or reject; . . . on his word . . . I can accept nothing" (104). More immediately, this authority was inherent in the dynamics of performing itself, a fact that Emerson construed as a matter of republican principle: "At the lyceum, the stout Illinoian, after a short trial, walks out of the hall. . . . Well, I think with Gov. Reynolds, the people are always right, (in a sense,) & that the man of letters is to say, These are the new conditions to which I must conform" (*JMN*, 14:28). The ad hoc nature of an Emersonian lecture made it a truly existential encounter. Exchanging a Unitarian pulpit for the lyceum platform was a brave act of faith. It meant that henceforth he would meet his potential congregation as Ralph Waldo Emerson, not as a minister. Without a commissioned role, with no institutional authority to speak from, with neither Bible nor liturgy to refer to, he took it upon himself—his presence and his language—to work out the terms of a public identity. The people who filled the hall met only on the common ground that Emerson could supply in his text for the evening. As a prophet, he finally had no other sanction for his words than his audience's consent to them. At the lyceum he had "to put on eloquence as a robe" (*JMN*, 2:242). He had no other badge or costume of office.

What did it mean to believe that his audience was his constant meter as an orator? According to Wordsworth, acquiring an accurate taste for poetry requires time, long-continued intercourse. But another distinction between Emerson's creed and that of the English Romantics is precisely his rejection of the operations of time and history to announce an imminent apocalypse. At least in his early work, his most characteristically Emersonian pronouncements, the emphasis is on how quickly the huge world can be brought round. The "Prospects" pointed to at the end of *Nature* are immediately available: "*As fast as* you conform your life to the pure idea in your mind, that will unfold its great proportions. A correspondent revolution in things will attend the influx of spirit. *So fast* will disagreeable appearances . . . vanish" (56; my italics). Similarly, when Emerson measured his own prospects as a speaker, he put the same emphasis on immediacy, instantaneousness:

> We shun to say that which shocks the religious ear of the people & to take away titles even of false honor from Jesus. But this fear is an impotency to commend the moral sentiment. For if I can so imbibe that wisdom as to utter it well, *instantly* love & awe take place. The reverence for Jesus is only reverence for this, & if you can carry this home to any man's heart, *instantly* he feels that all is made good & that God sits once more on the throne. . . . I refer to the discourse now growing under my eye to the Divinity School. (*JMN*, 7:41–42; my italics)

This is a rich passage, identifying Emerson's most crucial message as a prophet and situating him amidst all his hopes and fears as an orator. I will discuss in detail the discourse he refers to. At this point we need only note how much he expected of his utterance, from the moment of live performance itself.

An instant was all it took for one of those mystical raptures he describes in *Nature*'s "transparent eyeball" passage to arrive, and one such instant could transform someone's whole life. Emerson's experience of such influxes of spirit could be considered the basis of his belief in instantaneousness. Or it might be more accurate to turn this around and say that his faith in such immediacy had its roots in what he longed for: in his desire, whenever he spoke, to recapture the feeling of communion by converting the audience in front of him even as he spoke. For that was the goal he set himself as a speaker: to create his own transcendent unity through speech. Mystical experiences are ordinarily found, not made; they happen with apparent randomness as one is crossing a bare common or traveling the road to Damascus. In his lectures, however, Emerson hoped to make them happen, to will them into being. "The length of the discourse," he conceded to his journal, "indicates the distance of thought between the speaker & the hearer" (*JMN*, 7:50). His operative mode of discourse—the Emersonian style—was evolved precisely to try to bridge that distance, erase all human differences, allow each listener and the speaker to lose their separate selves, to be nothing and to *hear* all: "In perfect eloquence, the hearer would lose the sense of dualism, of hearing from another" (*JMN*, 7:52).

Emerson makes this goal a matter of principle as well. As there is one truth, and as it abides in each person's instincts, so the best way to restore people to it is to talk past their disparate social selves to their common soul. "Do not put yourself in a false position in regard to your contemporaries," he reminded himself in another calculation of his rhetorical prospects:

> If your views are in straight antagonism to theirs, nevertheless assume an identity of sentiment, —that you are saying precisely that they all think, & in the flow of wit & love roll out your ultra paradoxes in solid column with not the infirmity of a doubt, knowing that really & underneath all their external denials & diversities, they are of one heart & mind. (*JMN*, 5:504–5)

This is a sweeping repudiation of the prophet's traditional stance and of protest and righteous anger as prophetic resources, but it does sum up the ingratiating way Emerson sought to work on his American congregation. Although at times in his journal he exhorts himself to "deal plainly with society," even to shock his listeners (*JMN*, 7:105), the strategies of his public expression remained captive to the design to "assume an identity of sentiment" with his contemporaries.

And there were moments, at least in his journal, when he could acknowledge his own need, the psychological stake he had in using eloquence to erase the boundary between himself and his audience. There is, for example, this passage, in which Emerson himself sees his platform eloquence as a kind of compensation, in the Freudian rather than the Emersonian sense:

> [Margaret Fuller] writes me that she waits for the Lectures seeing well after much intercourse that the best of me is there. She says very truly; & I thought it a good remark which somebody repeated here from S.S. that I "always seemed to be on stilts." It is even so. Most of the persons whom I see in my own house I see across a gulf. I cannot go to them nor they come to me. Nothing can exceed the frigidity & labor of my speech with such. (*JMN*, 7:301)

This is only one of the many journal entries in which Emerson, with unchanging wonder and dismay, records his crippling diffidence in the presence of other people. His shyness has often been remarked, although no one seems to have made the connection that he suggests here, between the personality he could not escape as one man among others, even in his own home, and the role with which he could clothe this nakedness as the man speaking to others from the platform. I quote only one more such passage, but the extreme of alienation that it describes, the gulf between his private self and other people into which it bleakly stares, marks the fixed psychological point from which Emerson moved again and again to the front of the lyceum:[16]

> The old experiences still return. Society when I rarely enter the company of my well dressed & well bred fellow creatures, seems for the time to bereave me of organs or perhaps only to acquaint me with my want of them. The soul swells with new life and seeks expression with painful desire, but finds no outlets. Its life is all incommunicable. (*JMN*, 7:516)

On the platform frigid and laborious speech could give way to eloquence, estrangement to reunion, frustration to fulfillment. In gaining every ear, in speaking as "the mere tongue of us all" (*JMN*, 5:102), Emerson sought not only to communicate his life but to *live* it: "If I could persuade men to listen to their interior convictions, if I could express, embody their interior convictions, that were indeed life" (*JMN*, 4:346).

Even Emerson grants that this fact of his temperament has a legitimate relevance to the preoccupations of his work. "We love to paint those qualities which we do not possess," he admitted; "I who suffer from excess of sympathy, proclaim always the merits of selfreliance" (*JMN*, 7:371–72). With "self-reliance," of course, we come to the central Emersonian term. Like "unity," it has many referents. Yet if we trace his development of the term through his journals, "self-reliance" turns out to refer mainly to his rhetorical project. That is to say, he uses it less often to evoke the soul's relationship to spirit than to refer to the orator's dramatic relationship with his audience. This, as we have seen, is the context in which "The American Scholar" treats "self-trust." It is even the emphasis of the essay "Self-Reliance," in which topics like conformity and consistency are elaborated mainly with examples that Emerson draws from his career as a public speaker: "He would utter opinions on all passing affairs," "what you have stated in this or that public place," "speak what you think now in hard words," and so on (2:29, 33). On the one hand, that he associated this central term so directly with his rhetorical program reminds us that the conflict between seeing and saying was the heaviest burden of his career. On the other, this association suggests how much Emerson's faith in "the infinitude of the private man" (*JMN*, 7:342) was intertwined with his performance as an orator. In terms of his rhetorical program, self-reliance meant more than just believing in his own ideas so much that he would dare to speak them out, no matter how unpopular or heterodox they might seem. It also meant relying on the power of the speaking self to bend the audience to its vision. The sovereignty of the imperial self that he celebrated depended, in his mind, on his mastery of the audience in front of him.

"Taking sovereign possession of the audience" was the end to which eloquence was the means.[17] If we look back at the passage from "The American Scholar" quoted earlier, we can note that it describes the orator's reunion with the society from which he has been estranged less like the prodigal's homecoming (though that paradigm is certainly present) than like an exiled king's return to power: "he who has mastered any law in his private thoughts, is master to that extent of all men whose language he speaks." This quest for power underlies nearly all of Emerson's celebrations of eloquence, including those already cited. Every heart will be thankful "for a master." "To be eloquent" means one can make an audience "saints or scoffers at his will." In his essay "Eloquence," the triumph of the orator's will is explicitly affirmed: "the highest bribes of society are at the feet of the successful orator. He has his audience at his devotion. . . . He is the true potentate; for they are not kings who sit on thrones, but they who know how to govern."[18] Thus while the thematic goal of Emerson's oratory was to announce the omnipotence of each listener's self, the dramatic goal of each such performance was to confirm his own. The little man bereaved of organs could become the illimitable master of all who heard him. If he could utter the right words well, he and his audience would "be of one mind" (*JMN*, 7:40), and that one mind would be his.

I suspect that many performers who have to keep defining themselves in the presence of a live audience share this need, which can be traced to the stage in earliest childhood when the unshaped ego first realizes that it does not create the world it perceives. By putting themselves at the center of an audience's attention, and then willing its unanimous approval of them, they keep seeking to triumph over their knowledge of the dividedness of the human condition. By reestablishing themselves as the center and creator of the world around them, they can recover the seamless kingdom that is lost when one falls into self-consciousness. On the stage, at least for the successful performer, is perpetual youth. Thus Emerson felt that his "best self" was in the lectures. If he could utter "what all must receive," the world would be the realized double of his will.

In lectures like "The American Scholar," "The Divinity School Address," and "The Transcendentalist," he privileged public speaking as the one mode of acting in the world that does not fatally compromise the self's infinitude. Only in words—not in deeds, and definitely not in institutions or causes—can the divine self be incarnated without betraying its divinity. But words in turn had their master. They had to gain every ear, make all other hearts vibrate. Restoring himself to a sense of his own omnipotence meant that Emerson had to keep "gazing into the looking-glass of men's opinion" (*JMN*, 7:400). The image here is exactly right: throughout his career the audience in front of him served as the mirror in which he sought to see the best of himself, his imperial selfhood, reflected. That is why his rhetorical strategy was to "assume an identity of sentiment" with his audience, even though he knew that his views were often in "straight antagonism" to theirs. Confronting them directly would have meant drawing a line between his will and their consciousness, reestablishing the boundary that his valuation of style as eloquence, his transformation of truth into rhetoric, was intended to transcend. Confronting them would have cracked the mirror, as the following journal entry makes plain:

> never compare your generalization with your neighbor's. Speak now, & let him hear you & go his way. Tomorrow, or next year, let him speak, & answer thou not. So shall you both speak truth & be of one mind; but insist on comparing your two thoughts . . . & instantly you are struck with blindness, & will grope & stagger like a drunken man. (*JMN*, 7:40)

So Emerson wrote in the early summer of 1838. At the time he was preparing the address that he was scheduled to read to the seniors at Harvard's Divinity School on 15 July. To develop the relationship between his private investment in oratory and his public work, I want to look closely at this one performance. Such a textual analysis enables us to study the strategies he evolved to bring his audience round to him in the immediate context from which it is crucial not to abstract them, the context of a live performance. The performance I have chosen was the most dramatic of his career.

"The Divinity School Address" is an intricate performance. In one respect it is orthodox early Emerson. It is the post-Kantian, post-Romantic descendant of the traditional jeremiad that had been preached from New England pulpits since the second half of the seventeenth century.[19] Like the Puritan Jeremiahs, Emerson laments the faith that "is passing away" (88) "in these desponding days" (89), and calls the "decaying church" and "wasting unbelief" a "calamity" that has befallen the "nation" (88). These are the clichés of the genre. Yet characteristically he turns the conventional jeremiad inside out. He does not rebuke the congregation for having strayed from the established path of righteousness, but rather blames the church for defrauding the individual worshipper:

> it is still true that tradition characterizes the preaching of this country; that it comes out of the memory, and not out of the soul; . . . thus historical Christianity destroys the power of preaching, by withdrawing it from the exploration of the moral nature of man. . . . And for want of this culture the soul of the community is sick and faithless. (87–88)

In one eloquently simple sentence near the end he describes the remedy as well as the disease and confirms the truth he had already announced in *Nature* and "The American Scholar": men and women "think society wiser than their soul, and know not that one soul, and their soul, is wiser than the whole world" (89).

The address acquired its public prominence from the conjunction of what Emerson said with where he said it. Forty-six years later Elizabeth Peabody, who had been in Divinity Chapel when Emerson read it, called it "the apocalypse of our Transcendental era in Boston."[20] Because it registered the differences between the "new views" and "historical Christianity" in the very citadel of Unitarianism, the address drew a line down the middle of the Unitarian Association, hastening the conservative, like Andrews Norton, back toward the Calvinist orthodoxy, and inspiring the liberal, like Theodore Parker, to more outspoken forms of dissent. When Norton's anger at the address led him to carry the issues that these two camps had been debating for several years out of *The Christian Examiner* and into the daily newspapers, he unwittingly gave the new movement—which only began to be called Transcendentalism after the public was thus alerted to it—a visibility it could not otherwise easily have achieved. For the next two years, during which the address was heatedly attacked and defended in sermons, articles, and pamphlets, it provided a means to mark the choices of faith and philosophy that were available to

New England's community of thought.[21] In the minds of all those interested, it established Emerson as the central figure among the Transcendentalists.

Emerson himself, by refusing publicly to acknowledge, much less to
participate in, the controversy, sought to minimize the significance of the
address. His journals, however, tell a very different story. To judge from
how often and how intensely he struggled over the next two years to di-
gest the reaction he had aroused, this public controversy was the most
traumatic episode in his life. Not even the deaths of his first wife, beloved
brother, or oldest son disturbed him more deeply. Then again, the address itself already sought to minimize its significance, to disguise the
drama of its performance. At the very end of it, Emerson asks the graduating ministers a blithe question: "What hinders that now, everywhere, in
pulpits, in lecture-rooms, in houses, in fields, wherever the invitation of
men or your own occasions lead you, you speak the very truth, as your life
and conscience teach it, and cheer the waiting, fainting hearts of men
with new hope and new revelation?" (92). As a benediction on what he
has just finished doing, this is both much too modest and much too sly.
Of course, by "now" the question has become a rhetorical one, for Emerson has succeeded in turning "the invitation of men" into his own occasion to speak the truth. But his journals from the time he left the ministry
to the moment he gave the address testify very powerfully to how much
is hidden behind that phrase "what hinders."

As early as 1832 Emerson was clear in his own mind, and in the pages
of his journal, about his errand as a prophet to Jacksonian America: "Has
the doctrine ever been fairly preached of man's moral nature? The world
holds on to formal Christianity, & nobody teaches the essential truth, the
heart of Christianity, for fear of shocking &c" (*JMN*, 4:45). Like Jesus or
Luther or Fox, he would call the established church of his day to account
for its apostasies and awaken his contemporaries to a new revelation.
Over the next six years, still in the pages of his journal, he grew more and
more impatient with the "nightmare preaching" that he mutely heard in
the Unitarian services he continued to attend (*JMN*, 5:502) and equally
impatient with his own silence.[22] "Is it not time," he asked himself in
1834, "to present this matter of Christianity exactly as it is . . . ?" (*JMN*,
4:309).

At the same time, this was the heart of his rhetorical problem, for he
knew that he and his audience were nowhere further apart than on "this
matter of Christianity": "In all my lectures, I have taught one doctrine,
namely, the infinitude of the private man. This, the people accept readily
enough, & even with loud commendation, as long as I call the lecture,
Art; or Politics; or Literature; or the Household; but the moment I call

it Religion, —they are shocked" (*JMN*, 7:342). In January 1835 he began giving his "winter courses," a series of lyceum lectures that he scheduled annually in Boston for the next half dozen years. In those lectures he was free to decide the topics for himself, but reading them alongside the journals he kept during those years reveals Emerson continually verging toward the new revelation he kept privately recommitting himself to, and continually retreating from it. He lectured *about* Luther and Fox, for instance, instead of following their example. The closest he came to tackling the religious issue directly was "Holiness," the eighth lecture in the 1837–1838 winter series. "Holiness" is a particularly evasive performance. Ellis Gray Loring, a young Bostonian who heard it, was left confused and uneasy about its theological assumptions—until the Reverend Convers Francis, who also heard it, reassured him that it did depict "God" as a "personal" Deity; still unsure, Loring asked Emerson himself about it and discovered that if he had been confused, Francis had been misled.[23]

Such misunderstandings, doubtless common among Emerson's listeners, suggest how cautiously he felt his way toward expressing his new revelation. At the start of "Holiness" he betrays the anxiety that had deflected his public utterance away from the topic that kept growing more urgent in his journals: "In approaching this subject I feel very sensibly its difficulty. Beside its own intrinsic subtlety it is surrounded and encumbered by armed prejudices."[24] Interestingly, the largest single section in "Holiness" is a 1,300-word extract from *I Promessi Sposi* that recounts how a man who has greatly offended another begs pardon of him publicly in such an eloquent manner that "with one voice," "all" his audience forgive him.[25] Emerson cites this lengthy episode as an illustration of humility, but biographically it tells a different story: instead of presenting the matter of Christianity exactly as it is, Emerson vicariously anticipates the offense he is unwilling to commit, substituting his need of his audience's acceptance for the crime of shocking them.

"If utterance is denied, the thought lies like a burden on the man" (84): this bland truism is one of the many ways that "The Divinity School Address" obliquely betrays how much psychological pressure had accumulated behind it. For by the end of the 1837–1838 series Emerson had worn through his tolerance for this pattern of substitutions and evasions. On 5 March 1838 he lectured himself about his lack of rhetorical self-reliance:

> We acquire courage from our success daily, & have a daring from experience which we had not from genius. I regret one thing omitted in my late Course of Lectures; that I did not state with distinctness & conspicuously the great error of Modern Society in respect to religion & say, You can never

come to peace or power until you put your whole religion in the moral con-
stitution of man & not at all in a historical Christianity. (*JMN*, 5:459)

Heartened by the success of the winter course—"a very gratifying interest
on the part of the audience was evinced to the views offered" (*JMN*,
5:451)—he decided to overcome his hesitations. "There is no better subject for effective writing," he wrote on 18 March, "than the Clergy. I
ought to sit & think & then write a discourse to the American clergy
showing them the ugliness & unprofitableness of theology & churches at
this day & the glory & sweetness of the Moral Nature out of whose pale
they are almost wholly shut" (*JMN*, 5:464). By coincidence, a few weeks
later he was asked by the graduating class at the Divinity School to speak
at their commencement.

This invitation Emerson turned into his own occasion in more ways
than one. As yet, he knew, he had balked at the prophetic identity to
which he had aspired. Although he had spoken to men, he knew he had
failed as yet to become a man himself. We can tell he knew by the address's extraordinary pattern of references to becoming a man. Using the
graduating preachers in his audience, Emerson exhorts himself to fulfill
his own ambitions: "But speak the truth . . . Speak the truth . . ." (78);
"Always the seer is a sayer. Somehow his dream is told" (84); "But say,
'I also am a man' . . . Be to them a man . . . Be to them a divine man"
(90). What he claims for Jesus overlaps the dramatic rite of passage being
enacted within Divinity Chapel through his own performance: "He felt
respect for Moses and the prophets, but no unfit tenderness at postpon-
ing their initial revelations, to the hour and the man that now is; to the
eternal revelation in the heart. Thus was he a true man. . . . Thus was he
a true man" (81).[26] Jesus earned his manhood by displacing the patriarchs
of the Old Testament, just as this evening Emerson—the hour and the
man that *now* is—earns his by displacing Jesus, the New Testament, and
the fathers of Unitarianism seated directly in front of him. How dramatic
his performance was is revealed by the fact that he decided at the last
possible moment, while reading his manuscript aloud, to leave out a con-
ciliatory paragraph disparaging those thinkers who had too little reverence for Jesus. He left it out, he told Elizabeth Peabody, because the
address "was getting too long," but since the paragraph came in the first
half of the oration, it seems likely that he omitted it for a more coura-
geous reason.[27] More than once since 1832 he had privately criticized the
teachers who fell back upon "the life & teachings of Jesus" to prop up
their own "great truth[s] . . . Well this cripples [their] teaching." On this
occasion he wanted his words to "stand alone" (*JMN*, 4:45). By letting
go of "formal Christianity," by confronting those Unitarian faculty members (some of whom had taught him a decade earlier) with his own vision,

Emerson took possession of his birthright as a man. Giving "The Divinity School Address" enabled him to preside over his own *delivery* as "a new-born bard of the Holy Ghost" (90).

Yet if, as Joel Porte also implies, a part of Emerson's motivation was Oedipal, shocking his audience was not the ultimate goal of the address.[28] Emerson's rebellion against the fathers of American culture, declared more directly on this occasion than on any other, always had to compete with his more deeply rooted narcissistic needs. As I have tried to show, his quest for identity depended not only on displacing tradition but also on compelling his audience's consent to his new revelations. "We shun to say that which shocks the religious ear of the people," he wrote in his journal a week before giving the address, indicating exactly why he had deferred his prophetic errand so long. The note on which the entry ends, where he declares his faith in the power of eloquence to bring the audience in Divinity Chapel home to a blessed unity, bears repeating: "if I can so imbibe that wisdom as to utter it well, instantly love & awe take place." Even in "The Divinity School Address," his largest ambition was to convert his listeners, to deliver his newborn bard into welcoming arms.

It did not quite work. Instead of love and awe, Andrews Norton's reaction was shock and outrage. Yet this one man's response should not dictate our sense of what Emerson had hoped to achieve. Norton's spluttering anger makes for a vivid moment in the history of the mind in America, but to appreciate the way Emerson addressed himself to the task of converting his America from a faith in Jesus to a faith in their own instincts it would be more accurate to emphasize the reaction of a different faculty member. Two months after Emerson, Henry Ware, Jr., spoke at the Divinity School, reading the devoutly unspeculative sermon on "The Personality of the Deity" that the Unitarians hurriedly printed to dissociate themselves from Emerson's heterodoxy. The day after Emerson's address, Ware wrote to his friend in obvious discomfort to say that, after further thought, its leading ideas now "appear to me more than doubtful." But what made Ware's letter necessary was that, immediately after the address, he had been mostly persuaded by it: "I said to you last night I should probably assent to your unqualified statements if I could take your qualifications with them."[29] The address is a brilliant rhetorical achievement. It would have been a far different work, however, and Emerson would have played a far different role in the history of American thought, if its purpose had been to shock its audience.

One of the most familiar points about Emerson's prose is that he was incapable of or uninterested in structuring a coherent argument. While it may seem easier to accuse him of an endearing disorderliness than to suggest that for him choices about structure were rhetorical strategies, the intricate subtlety of the address reveals how shrewdly he could plot. It must be recognized that the "plot" of an Emerson text was against his audience's assumptions. His utterances, that is, are not organized around a topic so much as around the audience they were aimed at. The structure of his discourse is another way to measure "the distance of thought between the speaker & the hearer."[30] In this instance Emerson knew he had to bridge a chasm.

His goal was to give his faith a home among an audience of Unitarian clergymen. His first strategic choice was to reverse the outline in the journal entry in which he announced his desire to "write a discourse to the American clergy showing them the ugliness & unprofitableness of theology & churches at this day & the glory & sweetness of the Moral Nature." This locates the real, thematic, contextual genesis of his address. But when he came to write it, he moved this beginning to the middle: "it is my duty to say to you, that the need was never greater of new revelation than now. From the views I have already expressed, you will infer the sad conviction, which I share, I believe, with numbers, of the universal decay and now almost total death of faith in society" (84). From this midpoint he proceeds to his "complaint of the Church" (89), drawing from the reservoir of passages about bad preaching and boring sermons that had accumulated in his journal. Two sentences in the first half about the monstrous way "Miracle" is mispronounced by the "Christian churches" had anticipated his complaint emphatically, but briefly (81). The four paragraphs on uninspired preaching were, Emerson knew, potentially the most divisive, offensive words he had to utter. Although he censored the most acerbic remarks in his journals, although he makes his audience his accomplices ("you will infer"), although he falls back momentarily on that politic reference to "numbers" (an authority almost as potent as Jehovah in a republic), he nonetheless does his duty by the occasion, confronting an audience of ministers with the sickness of their church.

This is the one instance in his career when Emerson verged on directly attacking his immediate listeners. Given his temperamental aversion to upsetting an audience, we must respect the courage he displays here. Think how easily he might have omitted one or more of these paragraphs with the rationalization that the address was getting too long. Yet we can also note that he had already rehearsed this topic on part of his audience. Twice during the spring of 1838 he had met informally with the divinity students; his journal entry for 1 April includes his account of the second meeting:

The Divinity School students wished to talk with me concerning theism. I went rather heavy-hearted for I always find that my views chill or shock people at the first opening. But the conversation went well & I came away cheered. I told them that the preacher should be a poet smit with love of the

harmonies of moral nature: and yet look at the Unitarian Association & see
if its aspect is poetic. They all smiled No. (*JMN*, 5:471)

This encounter betrays how reluctantly Emerson nailed his theses to the
church door, and also how sensitive he was to the reactions of an audience. Those students' smiles were very encouraging to the prophet who
needed to believe that "his privatest, secretest presentiment" was equally
"the most acceptable." As it turned out, after encountering their teachers' frowns, the students who had invited Emerson later sought to distance themselves from his address. Yet as he was writing and delivering
it, he must have felt he could count on them to smile again. More important, I think this vignette suggests how he hoped the whole address might be received. Although he replied to Ware's letter that he
"could not but feel pain in saying some things in that place and presence
which I supposed might meet dissent,"[31] the organization of the address
goes to considerable lengths to preclude dissent, to create a context for
agreement.

Its serene first paragraph not only finds a mutual topic in the weather—
perhaps the most elegant advantage anyone has ever taken of this familiar
way to break the ice; it is also deliberately couched in the language of the
Lockeans who dominated Harvard and Unitarianism: "this world in
which our senses converse . . . what invitation from every property it gives
to every faculty of man!" (76). Of course the "faculty" that Emerson
wants to address—the Reason—is one that the Lockeans in the room
would repudiate, yet as he moves in the opening paragraphs from "this
world" to "the mind" to the "sentiment of virtue" that is "the essence of
all religion" (76-77) he crosses the disputed ground as casually as if it
were a common. The first third of the address is actually its conclusion.
Although Emerson misleads his listeners at the end of the third paragraph
by assuring them that "God is well pleased" whenever someone takes
possession of this "sentiment of virtue" (77), in the fifth and sixth paragraphs "God" drops out of the cosmos. The deity's role is entirely taken
over by the creative "energy" intrinsic to the soul: "By it a man is made
the Providence to himself" (78). Thus when Emerson says "If a man is at
heart just, then in so far is he God" (78), "in so far" is a purely rhetorical
qualification. The man he describes *is* God. The Unitarians had already
stripped Jesus of his divinity and his office as a mediator, but in the ninth,
tenth, and eleventh paragraphs Emerson surreptitiously denies him the
one role they had left him to play in the historic drama of human salvation: that of the inspired teacher whose lessons had to be accepted as
divine on the external authority of the miracles he performed. All truth,
Emerson says instead, is an intuition: "It cannot be received at second
hand. Truly speaking, it is not instruction, but provocation, that I can

receive from another soul. What he announces, I must find true in me, or reject; and on his word, or as his second, be he who he may, I can accept nothing" (80). What we can never know about "The Divinity School Address" is whether, for example, Emerson chose to italicize "be he who he may" in his reading of it. The odds are he did not. Otherwise he would have mentioned Jesus by name.

At the end of the eleventh paragraph Emerson cancels out his Lockean beginning—it is only when "the doctrine of inspiration is lost" that "man becomes near-sighted, and can only attend to what addresses the senses" (80)—but still, at the start of the twelfth, he insists that the circle he has drawn around himself and his audience remains unbroken. "These general views, which, whilst they are general, none will contest" (80) is the accommodating way he sums up the first third of the oration, thus claiming the right to use the plural pronoun when he blandly refers back to this sweepingly radical set of assertions as "the point of view we have just now taken" (81). Yet of course if his audience does not contest these general views, they have to ride the winged horse of Emerson's eloquence all the way to the last stop. When the next portion of his argument goes on to explore the defects of historical Christianity (82), he simply develops the implications of the points he has already made, replacing abstractions like "another soul" with proper names like "Jesus Christ." Even then Emerson insists that he and his audience are still of one mind: "All who hear me, feel that the language that describes Christ to Europe and America . . . is appropriated and formal" (82).

That they already agree, that "all who hear me, feel" the same way, is the rhetorical stance that governs the entire address. It is Emerson's greatest single declaration of his faith. Yet it is most unlike Ripley's "Jesus Christ, the Same Yesterday, Today, and Forever" (1834) or Parker's "Discourse on the Transient and Permanent in Christianity" (1841), comparable manifestos by the other two leaders of the transcendentalist movement, in its refusal anywhere to acknowledge that there were, or could be, vast disagreements among contemporary believers. No wonder Ware was tempted to consent. What is most characteristically Emersonian about the address is his attempt to co-opt instead of confront the Unitarians' convictions. Emerson knew there were profound disagreements. Just three weeks before he spoke, he drew the line clearly in his journal: "They call it Christianity, I call it Consciousness" (*JMN*, 7:28). When he came to write the words he would read out loud, however, he found a linguistic means to blur that line, attacking historical Christianity, but in the name of "the true Christianity" (89), "the faith of Christ" (85).

"This problem of a vocabulary," Emerson told the journal, was one that "I would solve if I could" (*JMN*, 7:149). Words were a continual reminder of the distance that divided his message from his audience's opinions. He could hardly call it "Consciousness" without shutting most ears against him. His calculated solution to the problem involved a kind of dialectic: putting his truths in their words, and thus implicitly redefining the language of the tribe. As Quentin Anderson puts it, "To appropriate the language of politics or poetry or conventional morality was to set up a tension between the expectations that language gave rise to in Emerson's audience and the voice of the self, which devoted all these terms to the use of the inward empire."[32] Yet while this tension is there for the critic to note (in his newspaper attack on the address Norton objected specifically to its "abuse" of "words" like "God, Religion, Christianity"[33]), the intention of this lexical maneuvering was to preclude any tension between himself and his contemporary audience. To take a particularly striking example, the fifth sentence of *Nature* syntactically turns a pair of antonyms into synonyms: "Why should we not have a poetry and philosophy of insight and not of tradition, and a religion by revelation to us, and not the history of theirs?" A thesaurus would endorse the way Emerson matches tradition and history, but to pause over his marriage of insight with revelation is to marvel at how much he tried to get away with linguistically. Emerson knew, and after the address had put him at odds with the religious establishment he could acknowledge that he knew, what "revelation" meant: "the idea of a revelation which obtains in modern Christendom . . . see how degraded it is."[34] His own prophetic project could be summed up by saying that he sought to convince his contemporaries that their allegiance to revelation (what God had enjoined from without) had to be replaced by an utter faith in their insights (what the godhead within reveals). But Emerson would not have been Emerson had he been this explicit. His rhetorical project meant redefining his listeners' vocabulary covertly. In a sentence like this one, or in pleading for a "true Christianity," he tries to stretch the meaning of words far enough to include both his truth and his audience under their spell.

This manipulation of diction and his structural strategy are, respectively, the most local and the most inclusive reflections of his desire always to carry his audience with him. Between these extremes lie the other rhetorical resources he employed. One bond he did have in common with his audience was their identity as Americans. At the end of the address, he aligns his modernist assault on historical Christianity with a cherished paradigm: "A whole popedom of forms, one pulsation of virtue can uplift and vivify" (92). This reminds the audience of the Reformation that had led their ancestors to settle Boston and found Harvard in the first place. Earlier he types the idolatry of Jesus as "this eastern monarchy of a Christianity" (82), which may have reminded them of the Revolution their grandfathers had fought. By thus merging his images with familiar American motifs, he found quick access to the sympathies of his audience, although the Old World he urged his listeners to renounce was hardly Europe. Instead, although he hesitated to say so explicitly, he was asking them to leave behind the world of assumptions they had grown up in, to claim their birthright, as men, as souls, in a new world, a metaphysical America, the true land of individual opportunity:

> Accept the injurious impositions of our early catechetical instruction, and even honesty and self-denial were but splendid sins, if they did not wear the Christian name. One would rather be
>
> 'A pagan suckled in a creed outworn,'
>
> than to be defrauded of his manly right in coming into nature, and finding not names and places, not land and professions, but even virtue and truth foreclosed and monopolized. You shall not be a man even. (82)

This extremely resonant passage, which appropriates Wordsworth while holding out the exemplary economic promise of the American frontier, which subverts the very instruction offered at the Divinity School while its maneuvered pronouns enable Emerson to speak for rather than against his listeners, seems to me to epitomize the prophetic stance he found for himself.

Note how he imitates "scripture phraseology" (*JMN*, 5:471) at precisely those points in the address where his thought is most unbiblical: "See how this rapid intrinsic energy worketh everywhere" (78); "the very words it [primary intuition] spake" (80); "all that man doth" is a miracle (81). Note too how a radical assertion is followed by a retreat to common ground on which he and his listeners could feel equally comfortable: "By it a man is made the Providence to himself, dispensing good to his goodness, and evil to his sin. Character is always known. Thefts never enrich; alms never impoverish; murder will speak out of stone walls" (78). These four homely proverbs barely have to move over to make room for Emerson's dismissal of the Christian God. The rhythm here is a familiar one in his prose; this mélange of revolutionary truth and conventional truism is another of the rhetorical means on which he regularly relied to popularize his profundities and to reconcile his insights with his audience's preconceptions. If his platform style combines solemn factual instruction with poetic rhapsodies, ingratiating references to vernacular life with exhortations toward the empyrean, whimsical humor with earnest entreaty, echoes of the revivalist's tent and the political rally, the Bible and the columns of the daily paper—if in short it seems a remarkably well-blended mix of equal parts Poor Richard, John Wesley, Horace Greeley, and Plotinus, that is because it is the best style with which Emerson could hope to reach out to all his congregation and try to recreate their sense of reality without disturbing their composure.

"The Divinity School Address" was the most daring trial he ever made of his eloquence. Despite his desire to disguise the drama, one cannot easily exaggerate how much he had staked upon it. His private goals were divided, and not entirely compatible. The address is punctuated by two climaxes of self-assertion: the attacks on the doctrine of miracles and on traditional preaching. By thus speaking like "a man," he compensated for his previous evasions and silences. "Scarcely in a thousand years," he says, again bringing his own exigencies to the surface of the address, "does any man dare to be wise and good"—but now he dares. This sentence, however, goes on to include the ultimate return that he also sought: "and so draw after him the tears and blessings of his kind" (88). A thorough subversion of the values of its immediate audience, the address nonetheless seeks a home among the "brothers" (89) and "friends" (88, 91) to whom it rhetorically gestures. Although he admonishes the students "to go alone" (90), he promises that such a path will bring the world to their door: "Discharge to men the priestly office, and, present or absent, you shall be followed with their love" (90).

The primacy of these narcissistic longings explains why, after the address, Emerson was so staggered by the controversy he aroused ("Steady, steady," he coached himself at the end of August [*JMN*, 7:60]), and why he groped for so many months in his journal to discover its meaning for his career. At his darkest moments, Norton's "angry paragraph" in the newspaper seemed "the voice of the world," changing his "entire relations to society": "What was yesterday a warm, convenient, hospitable world soliciting all the talents of all its children looks bleak & hostile & our native tendency to complete any view we take carries the imagination out at once to images of persecution, hatred, & want" (*JMN*, 7:101). His "stern ambition to be the Self of the nation" (89) depended upon the presence of a receptive audience, and that was precisely what he feared the address had cost him. In September, for example, he wrote his brother William that he was apprehensive about scheduling a new course of lectures: "perhaps the people scared by the newspapers will not come."[35] As he later admitted to Carlyle, he overreacted to the controversy; his 1838–1839 winter course, once he'd decided to give it, "prospered very well."[36] But there was a reason why he "overvalue[d]" Norton's anger (*JMN*, 7:101). Threatened by his failure to convert that audience in Divinity Chapel was his deepest need: to believe he could create the world he perceived by bringing his audience's consciousness into unity with his own.

The most audible public echo of "The Divinity School Address" is "Self-Reliance," which he published in his 1841 *Essays*. Although it has never been read as such, "Self-Reliance"—the first three-fourths of it at least—is the oblique autobiography of his career as an orator. In keeping with his methods of composition, the essay was compiled from many journal entries, a few of which dated back six years. Most of it, however, came directly from the numerous entries in 1838 and 1839 dealing with the reaction the address had stirred up, in his own mind as well as the community's. Like "The American Scholar," it represents "self-trust" as the special concern of the man who speaks to men, but the rhetorical situation in which that man finds himself seems to have become considerably more "bleak & hostile." The speaker who had earlier distrusted himself now seems to have grown scornful of his public: "Let us stun and astonish the intruding rabble of men and books and institutions by a simple declaration of the divine fact" (2:41). Reunion with society has apparently given way to rebellion; nourishing music to "hard words" (2:33). The divine facts no longer seem synonymous with "the most acceptable," and the man speaking, though "his voice" remains "as sweet as the murmur of the brook" (2:39), does not use it to "complement his hearers." He has apparently been driven instead into an adversary relation with a society defined by its deafness.

Among the stances Emerson tested out in his journal in the wake of the address, he several times considered the alternative of rhetorically breaking with his audience:

> And whilst I see this that you must have been shocked & must cry out at what I said I see too that we cannot easily be reconciled for I have a great deal more to say that will shock you out of all patience. Every day I am struck with new particulars of the antagonism between your habits of thought & action & the divine law of your being & as fast as these become clear to me you may depend on my proclaiming them. (*JMN*, 7:105)

In this mood Emerson sounds very much like Thoreau. But he never put this edge on his speaking voice. He never used this journal entry, and the difference between it and the strategy of "Self-Reliance" is absolutely symptomatic. Instead of this explicitly antagonistic "I" and "you," in the essay he consistently substitutes the hostility between "us"—him and his audience—and "society" as an abstract force: "Let us affront and reprimand" (2:35), "Let us stun and astonish." As in the address, he maneuvers his quarrel with his culture in a way that enables him to argue for instead of with his readers. His words, unlike Thoreau's, could be absorbed so easily by that culture because of his rhetorical determination, even while declaiming against "society," to assume an identity of sentiment with every one of its members, with every mind in his audience.

The reaction to the address did, however, introduce a new element into his sense of the relationship between man speaking and his listeners. Even in "Self-Reliance" the end of nonconformity remains narcissistic reunion: "Speak your latent conviction, and it shall be the universal sense; for the inmost in due time becomes the outmost" (2:27). Yet this is not

quite the encounter described in "The American Scholar," where the orator discovers "to his wonder" that his listeners "delight in" and "drink his
words"—for now "time" has entered into the account. His earlier faith in
imminency, in the instant of performance itself, gives way throughout
"Self-Reliance" to a dependency on the "course of time" (2:38) to reconcile the orator's perceptions with his audience's acceptance. In this respect, "Self-Reliance" anticipates the revision of Emerson's program that
became more obvious during the 1840s, as time, history, progress, and
compensation played increasingly prominent roles in his thought. I don't
think I overstate the case I'm trying to make for the centrality of Emerson's preoccupation with his audience to suggest that behind this change
lay the rhetorical failure of "The Divinity School Address." Its reception
chilled his hopes for an instant "conversion of the world" (69).

It did not, however, change the terms of his largest ambition, or the
need he had invested in speaking to others. Eloquence's failure on this
occasion led to a prolonged period of self-doubt, cadenced by manic intervals of self-assertion, but in nearly all the journal entries dealing with
the controversy, Emerson cannot stop until he arrives at a redeclaration
of his belief in eloquence's promise:

> Society has no bribe for me, neither in politics, nor church, nor college, nor
> city. My resources are far from exhausted. If they will not hear me lecture,
> I shall have leisure for my book which wants me. Beside, it is an universal
> maxim worthy of all acceptation that a man may have that allowance which
> he takes. Take the place & attitude to which you see your unquestionable
> right, & all men acquiesce. Who are these mourners, these haters, these
> revilers? Men of no knowledge, & therefore no stability. The scholar on the
> contrary is sure of his point, is fast-rooted, & can securely predict the hour
> when all this roaring multitude shall roar *for* him. (*JMN*, 7:60–61)

The end of this passage refutes its self-reliant, indeed solipsistic beginning. It was not mere popularity that Emerson sought from this multitude, but a confirmation of his right to the place and attitude that he saw
in his visionary moments, and that he claimed as the birthright of the self.
The podium was his throne, and his audience the mirror in which he
looked to see his sovereignty reflected.

Thus his books remained secondary to the resources of art and energy
that he invested in his live performances. And the people would hear him
lecture. Much in his contemporary culture displayed the same fascination
with roaring multitudes: politics, reform movements, evangelical religion. The lyceum network was born out of Jacksonian America's com-
bined faith in self-improvement and love of public assembly. Other writers, including Thoreau, Poe, and Melville, tried out their voices as lyceum
lecturers. But no other writer, and very few lecturers of any kind, could

match Emerson's success. Beyond question he was a beautiful speaker. He relied on no platform mannerisms; he would stand still, read his manuscript without raising his voice, and seldom depart from the text he had prepared. Yet his voice, his voice alone carried his words to the edge of the hall, and a number of his contemporaries describe it as the voice that found them in the American wilderness. James Russell Lowell, who by no means belongs to the camp of Emerson's followers, said he spoke for his whole generation in saying that, in his lectures, "Emerson awakened us, saved us from the body of this death."[37] "My special parish," Emerson told Elizabeth Peabody, "is young men inquiring their way of life."[38] Yet Lowell, reporting firsthand on his observations in various halls where Emerson spoke, reminds us that Emerson's success was general, that he did gain almost every ear: "No doubt Emerson, like all original men, has his peculiar audience, and yet I know none that can hold a promiscuous crowd in pleased attention so long as he."[39]

Because Emerson's voice remained committed to the quest for this "blessed" unity, because he was bound, both as a matter of principle and as the deepest need of his temperament, to "assume an identity of sentiment" with his audience, it is harder than we have generally recognized to assess his role as a figure in American culture. Although "The Divinity School Address" resulted in his being banned from speaking at Harvard for over twenty years as a "radical," he eventually sat on the Harvard board of overseers. Yet neither his rejection of historical Christianity nor Victorian America's allegiance to it had changed a bit. He never recanted his central article of faith, that the one soul is wiser than the world. Yet when, in 1877, Mark Twain spoke at the Whittier Birthday Dinner and, according to the newspaper paragraphs of that day, delivered the very latest form of infidelity (forty years after Emerson's address, it seems, the most unforgivable heresy was against cultural decorum, not ecclesiastical institutions!), Emerson's place was on the dias with Whittier, Holmes, and Longfellow, and in the other speeches on that occasion he was revered as one of the guardians of American society.[40]

This is why, to me, the best of Emerson has to be sought in his journals.[41] Of his published work, only "Experience" bears witness with anything like the journals' candor to the humanness of his condition as a man who has been vouchsafed glimpses of his own infinitude, but who must consistently struggle to reconcile that vision with the doubts and frustrations that circumstance and temperament have given him as his portion of life—and "Experience" is atypical in that it was never delivered as an oration. That is a very telling fact. In "The Divinity School Address" Emerson insists that the "capital secret" of preaching is "to convert life into truth" (86), but whenever he addressed his listeners from the platform of his eloquence, he was more likely to convert truth into rhetoric.

Precisely because his private needs, the most urgent questions of his life, were so bound up in the quest for his public's consent, the "I" of his experience disappears behind the "we" that his oratory seems to take for granted while working so hard to create.

And when we read the journals, it is hard to escape the conviction that taking sides with his audience carried him too far away from his own life. In the 1838–1839 winter course, for example, Emerson delivered "The Protest." Like "Self-Reliance," it is full of echoes of the controversy his recent address had stirred up. But even on this occasion Emerson could not protest directly. To keep on the right side of his audience's assumptions, he quoted his own anguished words from the journal as those of "a youth," "our young Hamlet," and then, with the disingenuousness that is all too typical of his public voice, suggested to his listeners that such "a fantastic young person might find a friend in each one of us."[42] When one realizes how profoundly he edited his own thoughts before allowing his audience to overhear them, one may even be tempted to accuse him of hypocrisy[43]—but nothing in Emerson was more sincere than the desire to anneal the alienated, hesitant particularities acknowledged in the journals in the aphoristic universalities of his public expression. It was not an act of bad faith; it was a deeply earnest effort to keep the faith. It is in the gap between the man he was in the journals and the self he announced in his lectures that one can find the path Emerson was compelled to follow in his quest for identity. The journals record his needs: the struggle to get to, even to see steadily that kingdom of the will that his best moments had revealed to him. The way he spoke to others was his attempt to satisfy those needs: to create, to be in that kingdom, "that were indeed life." On the platform he spoke from the promised land of unity, of a self reunited with and master of its world, which he could only attain glimpses of from the Pisgah where he, like the rest of us, had to live. By using the resources of eloquence to gain every ear, he sought to carry himself into that promised land. By taking possession of his audience's rapt attention, he sought to make reality the realized double of his will.

What Emerson's whole career reveals is the paradox of the prophet as performer. To take possession of his audience, he must "assume an identity" with them. It is impossible to avoid thinking that, if he began by anxiously seeking to appropriate their assumptions, they concluded by appropriating his. Americans heard him, gratefully, and went their way. Whitman was simmering, simmering, and Emerson brought him to a boil. But Jane Addams could equally assume that Emerson was speaking to her. His aphorisms became a mirror in which almost any ambition could find itself reflected. According to Thomas Pittman, a Gilded Age lawyer speaking in 1871 to a reporter for the New York *Herald*, "the innocent little boy in Yankee land, with his stomach full of beans and his head full of Ralph Waldo Emerson, wants to go and do likewise, and become another Jim Fisk or a 'Prince Erie' or an 'Admiral of the Sound Steamboats.'"[44] To the man who wanted to "destroy the old" and "build the new" (61), the need to court the assent of his audience was an expensive one. This was the high price of eloquence.

Chapter III

"HE DID NOT FEEL HIMSELF
EXCEPT IN OPPOSITION":
THOREAU'S *WALDEN*

WALDEN BEGAN as a performance too. I am not thinking of Thoreau's life at the pond, although in so small a community as Concord his decision to move out to the woods, on the Fourth of July, carrying his personal belongings in a wheelbarrow, had its unmistakably theatrical aspects. I mean that Thoreau's first written account of his experiment at Walden was a script. On 10 February 1847 he came into the village to read a lecture titled "A History of Myself" to the Concord lyceum. This was the first draft of *Walden*, and as he says in his journal, what precipitated the lecture was the expectation of "some of my townsmen" that he should give them "some account of my life at the pond."[1] There was so much interest in the lecture that he read it at the lyceum again a week later, "to a very full audience."[2] According to Walter Harding, it was Concord's "favorable reactions" to these performances that "persuaded Thoreau that it would be worthwhile to write a book-length account of his life at the pond."[3] As he worked during the next seven years to revise the lecture, first to read it again in Salem, Portland, and Worcester, then with publication in mind, the next title he gave it was: "Walden or Life in the Woods by Henry Thoreau Addressed to my Townsmen."[4] All of this only begins to indicate the part Thoreau's audience played in the creation of his masterpiece. In the book he explicitly asserts and defends his use of "I": "We commonly do not remember that it is, after all, always the first person that is speaking."[5] Just as crucial to the text, however, is his use of the second person, "you," the reader who is also invariably present.[6]

Walden's first sentence asserts that he wrote the book "alone, in the woods, a mile from any neighbor" (3). But the first thing to notice about the book he wrote is that in its words he is never alone. Immediately after claiming all that solitary space, in the second paragraph he crowds himself dramatically by introducing his audience into the text. He justifies "obtrud[ing]" his self "on the notice of [his] readers" by recalling the "very particular inquiries" of his "townsmen concerning [his] mode of life." By adding that he is writing "to answer some of these questions," he makes his audience, and not his life in the woods, the specific occasion for the book. There is a good deal of confusion in the opening paragraphs about both the "circumstances" of Thoreau's relationship to these neighbors, and the "theme" of his book. It is impossible to determine whether their "very particular inquiries" are "impertinent" or "pertinent," or to know whether he intends to offer "a simple and sincere account of his own life" (3) or to "say something . . . concerning . . . you who read these pages, . . . something about your condition" (4). There are even some outright contradictions. Within the space of seven sentences he says that he is "confined" to the theme of his own life "by the narrowness of my experience" and that he is entitled to write about his readers because "I have traveled a good deal in Concord" (3–4). It is just these tensions, however, that shape *Walden*'s structure and style, and that give it much of its power.

In his third chapter, "Reading," Thoreau contrasts "written words" and "spoken language" (102). Unlike Emerson, he claims to despise "the orator's eloquence" because the orator finds his occasion in the audience "before him," while the writer's "more equable life is his occasion" (102). Yet these distinctions—between written and spoken, between the different occasions for telling the truth—are destroyed by the book itself. By his third paragraph Thoreau conclusively identifies his reader, "you who read these pages," with his townsmen, "my neighbors" (4–5). Thus although he worked on *Walden* for nine years, through seven drafts, he chose to preserve the dynamic of that evening at the Concord lyceum in his text.[7] He treats his audience very much as a live one, even though the basis of his complaint about their condition is that they can only be "said to live" (4). Indeed, Thoreau's treatment makes his audience much livelier than any we can imagine in the staid atmosphere of the lyceum; at a number of points his readers interrupt his text as scoffers and hecklers: " 'But,' says one, 'you do not mean that . . .' " (51); " 'Sir, if I may be so bold, what do you mean by . . .' " (66); in the middle of one paragraph, "a million Irishmen" start up to exclaim " 'What!' " in reply to Thoreau's remarks about the railroad (54).

"You who read these pages" are cast by these lines into a role that is unmistakably an adversary one. Thoreau's audience not only crowds him, it confronts him. Actually, of course, it is he who stages the confrontation. According to all the evidence, the townspeople to whom he addressed himself were genuinely curious about his experiment. It was their receptivity to the lecture that prompted him to start revising it as a book. Yet he explicitly assumes a hostile reader and treats us accordingly, bent on defining himself in an antithetical relationship to his audience. "The greater part of what my neighbors call good," he states early on, "I believe in my soul to be bad, and if I repent of anything, it is very likely to be my good behavior" (10). He could hardly have found a sentence that puts more distance between his readers' sympathies and his own values, nor have put himself rhetorically in a tighter spot. For Thoreau was not writing merely *pour épater le bourgeois*. He aspired to be a prophet of joy, one of those "who by their lives and works are a blessing to mankind" (76). His stance and tone, however, exacerbate the traditional problem of the prophet: by rejecting his audience's definition of "good" so emphatically right at the start, he almost invites them in return to dismiss what *he* believes in his soul. "If I seem to boast more than is becoming, my excuse is that I brag for humanity rather than for myself" (49), he writes, but this generosity is complicated by the way throughout the opening chapters he keeps defining his "I" in opposition to "many," or "most men," or "the mass of men." Thoreau does conceive his audience as democratically as Emerson did: "I would gladly tell all that I know . . . and never paint 'No Admittance' on my gate" (17). Even this image, though, underscores the way *Walden* begins by setting up a fence between Thoreau and his readers.

Emerson, who began by drawing a circle around himself and his audience, confessed in his journal that reading Thoreau often made him feel "nervous & wretched" because of his friend's "old fault of unlimited contradiction."[8] In the eulogy he read at Thoreau's funeral he toned down his dismay but nonetheless declared that this "habit of antagonism defaced" Thoreau's writings.[9] Yet while Emerson never appreciated Thoreau's intransigence, his recognition of this "habit" gives us the clue to how *Walden* works: Thoreau "did not feel himself," Emerson added in the eulogy, "except in opposition."[10] Thoreau would have agreed with this assessment. In 1852 he told H.G.O. Blake, a contemporary from Worcester who had sought out Thoreau in 1848, and who remained until the end of Thoreau's life his most ardent admirer, that he could not write Blake often or easily: "you have not cornered me up, and I enjoy such large liberty in writing to you that I feel as vague as the air."[11]

Nearly every aspect of *Walden* is informed by this need for antagonism. Structurally, the dialectical arrangement of the chapters—"Reading" followed by "Sounds," "Solitude" followed by "Visitors," and so on—gives the whole book a tautness approaching that of Thoreau's best aphorisms. Even his punning keeps opposing his use of a word to a more familiar one.[12] But the book's most dramatic "opposition" or "antagonism" (here they mean the same thing) is the one he creates from the outset between "I" and "you." Probably the clearest difference between these two Concord Transcendentalists is just this diametrically opposed rhetorical strategy: where Emerson courts his audience's assent, Thoreau confronts them with his separateness.

The text reveals this habit but cannot account for it. If Thoreau felt himself in opposition to the public for whom he was writing *Walden*, the first place to seek an explanation would be his experience with that public. In this he was also very different from Emerson, who doubtless would be astonished to learn that these days Thoreau's major work is at least as well known and highly regarded as any of his own orations and essays.[13] As an aspirant for literary fame, Thoreau had to live with rejection and failure, or, to use the terms he picked to sum up his career just after *Walden* was published, "obscurity and poverty" (*J*, 7:46). A decisive event was the failure of the book he had moved out to Walden in the first place to write, *A Week on the Concord and Merrimack Rivers*. After a fruitless search for a publisher, he paid for its publication himself in 1849; that less than a quarter of the one thousand copies he had printed were sold cost Thoreau a lot, in both dollars and dreams. *Walden* omits almost all mention of this episode. Though he goes into detail about other aspects of his routine at the pond, he says nothing about when or how or why or what he wrote; he says, for example, that his only lock was "for the desk which held my papers" (172), but he does not say that it guarded his growing manuscript of *A Week*. *Walden*'s only reference to *A Week* is a passage he added after the 750 unsold copies of his first book were returned to him as tangible proof of its failure. After describing a hapless Indian who could not persuade Concord to buy his baskets, Thoreau adds: "I too had woven a kind of basket of a delicate texture, but I had not made it worth anyone's while to buy them. Yet not the less, in my case, did I think it worth my while to weave them, and instead of studying how to make it worth men's while to buy my baskets, I studied rather how to avoid the necessity of selling them" (19). This locks up the story of *A Week* in a different way. It not only hides a crucial part of Thoreau's life at the pond behind a private allegory; it also suppresses the ambition he had cherished as the maker of that basket. Only the passage's poignant iterations of "worth while" betray how disappointed he was.

Thoreau's secretiveness about *A Week* raises a set of issues to which I want to return, but the reception of his first book cannot account for *Walden*'s antagonism to its reader. Aggressively confronting a hostile audience is already his stance in the first version of *Walden*, which he wrote before *A Week* was even finished. At the time he started his "History of Myself" he had had little encouragement as a writer, but neither had he suffered any traumatic frustration. To explain why he organizes the story of his success as an attack on others' failures, it helps to put *Walden* back into its immediate dramatic context: to consider his relationship to his "neighbors," the originals on whom his sense of his "readers" was based.

Probably only a novelist with Stendhal's genius for the conflict between an individual's inner longings and a particular cultural environment could do justice to the complexity of Thoreau's lifelong engagement with Concord. The available evidence points in two directions. In his biography Walter Harding persuasively concludes that by 1850

"Thoreau was in general accepted by his townsmen. If they did not praise him, they no longer paused to condemn him as a college graduate too indifferent to his opportunities."[14] Thoreau, on the other hand, saw Concord's opinion of him in much harsher terms. He was "the humblest, cheapest, least dignified man in the village" (*J*, 2:285). What must concern us are Thoreau's own perceptions: the way he saw his neighbors seeing him. Invariably when he looked in their eyes he saw himself as a pariah. "I see," he noted in 1856, "that my neighbors look with compassion on me, that they think it is a mean and unfortunate destiny which makes me to walk in these fields and woods so much and sail on this river alone" (*J*, 9:121). Wherever he walked in the village he felt compelled to wear the epithets "idler" and "loafer" pinned to him like Hester's *A* by his neighbors' judgment. Even Emerson, the one neighbor who might have been expected to endorse the unconventional destiny to which Thoreau consecrated himself, felt compelled to say in his eulogy that "I cannot help counting it a fault in him that he had no ambition" and to concede that Thoreau had "disappoint[ed] the natural expectations of his family and friends."[15] This is certainly among the most egregious of all the instances in which Emerson echoes his audience's assumptions.

No ambition! when how extravagantly ambitious Thoreau was appears in almost everything he wrote. Most nakedly in his journal, where in 1841, for example, he could assert that "my future deeds bestir themselves within me and move grandly towards a consummation, as ships go down the Thames" (*J*, 1:225). This image of the British fleet setting out to conquer the world is a good reminder that his quest was not merely private, "not [to] walk in procession with pomp and parade, in a conspicuous place, but to walk even with the Builder of the universe" (329); it also had designs on history. He did want to "engineer for all America." In "Walking," for instance, he converts the destiny that took him through fields and woods into epic heroism: "For every walk is a sort of crusade, preached by some Peter the Hermit in us, to go forth and reconquer this Holy Land from the hands of the Infidels."[16] Yet even in that essay, originally a lecture written while he was still revising *Walden*, he concedes that "the hero is commonly the simplest and obscurest of men."[17]

This huge disparity between his ego ideal and his village reputation explains why, when he walked, he was anxious to "make a hill or wood screen [him from every house he had to pass]—to shut every window with an apple tree" (*J*, 4:118). Whenever he actually ran into any of his neighbors on those walks, he felt bitterly sure of their thoughts: "They think I'm loafing" (*J*, 3:193). Writing to Blake only weeks before sending *Walden* to the publisher, he gives an affecting glimpse of his estrangement from the people with whom he shared the world, and of his sensitivity to them:

> Ah! what foreign countries there are, greater in extent than the U.S. or Russia, and with no more souls to a square mile—stretching away on every side from every human being with whom you have no sympathy. Their humanity affects me as simply monstrous. Rocks —earth—brute beasts comparatively are not so strange to me. When I sit in the parlors and kitchens of some with whom my business brings me—I was going to say in contact— . . . I feel a sort of awe and as forlorn as if I were cast away on a desolate shore. . . . You who soared like a merlin with your mate through the realms of ether—in the presence of the unlike drop at once to earth a mere amorphous squab—divested of your air inflated pinions.[18]

This passage reflects *Walden* the way Walden reflects the trees on its shore, inversely. In this mood Thoreau admits that his isolation is not the solitude he has chosen but the alienation he cannot escape. And the unfledged, crippled nestling at the end of the passage is the antithesis of the image with which he victoriously concludes his narrative of the year at the pond: the "Merlin" hawk, with its "ethereal flight" and "proud reliance," with its invulnerable, transcendent autonomy: "It appeared to have no companion in the universe—sporting there alone—and to need none. . . . It was not lonely, but made all the earth lonely beneath it. Where was the parent which hatched it, its kindred, and its father in the heavens? The tenant of the air, it seemed . . ." (316–17).

Thoreau, however, was a child of Concord, wingless except in his imaginings, unable to soar beyond the eyeshot of his neighbors. Despite *Walden*'s repeated claims to the contrary, he was very vulnerable to the opinions of those others. This anxiety even haunted his dreams, as one of his most intimate journal entries reveals. On the morning of 16 November 1851 he "had a thought . . . before [he] awoke," which he "endeavored to retain [and] to express." It concerned the way the world "hates like virtue" "any direct revelation, any original thoughts": "The fathers and the mothers of the town would rather hear the young man or young woman at their table express reverence for some old statement of the truth than utter a direct revelation themselves. They don't want to have any prophets born into their families—damn them!" (*J*, 3:119, 121). He aspired to be a prophet of renewal and joy, but as this entry suggests, he was often brought to the sour verge of despair by "the town's" lack of recognition, which he identified as "the world's" response as well. Giving in to such a mood at the end of 1853, he railed as a wrathful, self-righteous prophet of doom against the neighbors who hired him to survey their land but would not invite him to lecture:

they who do not make the highest demand on you shall rue it. . . . All the while that they use only your humbler faculties, your higher unemployed faculties, like an invisible cimetar, are cutting them in twain. Woe be to the generation that lets any higher faculty in its midst go unemployed! That is to deny God and know him not, and he, accordingly, will not know it of them. (*J*, 6:21–22)

As a prophet without a shred of honor in his own village, Thoreau came to feel that all his gestures were excruciatingly public ones. His naked vulnerability to the eyes of the hostile audience before which his life was enacted is indicated by the startling violence of this entry from 1851, which begins by admitting that the problem was one he could not escape by ducking behind apple trees, because he had internalized it:

In roads the obstructions are not under my feet, . . . but they are in my vision and in the thoughts or associations which I am compelled to entertain. I must be fancy-free. . . . Where I can sit by the wall-side and not be peered at by any old ladies going a-shopping, not have to bow to one whom I may have seen in my youth, —at least, not more than once. I am engaged and cannot be polite. Did you ever hear of such a thing as a man sitting in the road, and then have four eyes levelled at you? Have we any more right sometimes to look at one than to point a revolver at him; it might go off . . . ? (*J*, 2:326)

Given such acute self-consciousness, and the narrow circumference of his life as a son of the village, it is no wonder that he could confess to himself that "I almost shrink from the arduousness of meeting men erectly day by day" (*J*, 1:174). Nor is it surprising that he wound up conceiving life in military terms, as a marching to a drummer. As he walked around Concord, his eyes were "invisible cimetars" cutting his neighbors "in twain"; their eyes were loaded pistols pointed at him; going near places where "houses are thick" meant "pass[ing] the enemy's lines" (*J*, 4:118). Concord's two best-known sites, the "Battle Ground" (86) and Walden Pond, obviously have a lot in common.

For although the pose that Thoreau tries to adopt in *Walden* is that of the swaggering conqueror returning in triumph with the spoils of the kingdom he has won, the book's style and structure are defined as sharply and self-consciously as the movements of a soldier alone in enemy territory. The image Thoreau gives is that of a prisoner running a gauntlet (168–69). Either metaphor suggests his state of mind when he sat down to write "A History of Myself" for an audience of his neighbors. In what must be the earliest rehearsal of that lecture, Thoreau thought of beginning this way: "I expect of any lecturer that he will read me a more or less simple and sincere account of his life, of what he has done and thought. . . . We want a man to give us that which was most precious to him, —not his life's blood but even that for which his life's blood circulated" (*J*, 1:484). Here blood does not imply warfare, but communion. In Thoreau's writings there are many other passages that indicate how hungry he was for such an open, unguarded, mutually sustaining, indeed life-giving relationship to his contemporaries.[19] But stronger than that desire were his doubts about whether they could appreciate what "was most precious to him."

The expository situation in which he found himself when he wrote *Walden* to answer his neighbors' questions is summed up, paradigmatically, by his hesitation about responding to a questionnaire from the Association for the Advancement of Science. He would "be rejoiced," he says, if he could tell them, simply and sincerely, about his own pursuits; "yet a true account of my relation to nature should excite their ridicule only!" To avoid being a "laughing-stock," he feels instead "obliged to speak to their condition" (*J*, 5:4–5). This is exactly what happens, as I noted, in the beginning he finally wrote for *Walden*, where he quickly changes the subject from "a true account" of himself to "something" he would say about his readers' "condition." Instead of sharing his life's blood with us, he goes on the attack: "It is very evident what mean and sneaking lives many of you live, for my sight has been whetted by experience" (6). These sharpened eyes make this attack on our lives almost too literal, but he is determined to put us on the defensive. There is nothing at all "simple" about *Walden* as an account of his life, and it is at least as stagily rhetorical as it is "sincere," but the complexity of its strategic maneuverings are the guage of Thoreau's own defensive anxieties. In "Winter Animals" he boasts that once he made his way to Lincoln to lecture, "traveling in no road and passing no house between my own hut and the lecture room" (271). When he stood up in the Concord lyceum, however, to talk about that most intimate of subjects, "The History of Myself," his path was more crowded, and hazardous: he felt he had to fight his way past everyone in his audience before he could get to his "Life in the Woods."

I want to look at how *Walden* was built around Thoreau's sense of himself as beleaguered by his audience, at his need to justify his ways to men. We have to go further, however, to try to answer the question implicit in Emerson's assessment. Why did Thoreau only feel *himself* in opposition? Behind his attitude toward his reader, as he tells us himself, are the figures of his neighbors. But "here," he also tells us, is not "all the world" (320). He could have moved away from Concord,[20] he could have met his readers on less contested ground. To understand his performance either before his townsmen or for his audience, we should look at the pattern of his relationship with his family. This is the aspect of

Thoreau's life about which the commentators have said the least, probably because he himself said so little about it.[21] A striking fact about his
published works is that they are all based on the comparatively brief time
he spent away from his parents' house. His trips to Cape Cod, Maine, and
Canada, a week on the rivers, two years at the pond, even the one night
he spent in jail—these are the experiences he writes about, although most
of his adult life was spent living with, and often working for, his family.
His life at home is rarely mentioned even in the thousands of pages of his
journals, which follow the pattern of his published works in finding the
occasions for writing outside the family, mainly, of course, in the three or
four hours a day he spent walking. Thoreau made the most of these occasions, mastered the art of symbolic action so well that moving to the
pond and being thrown in jail stand in many people's minds for the whole
of his life. Emily Dickinson's inability to leave home calls itself to everyone's attention, but Thoreau can seem to be a world traveler. Yet one
surely has to wonder at this disparity between Thoreau's life as he lived it
and as he chose to record it. Like Emerson, he believed that the prophet
should convert his own life into truth. Yet the largest single element in his
experience, even as an adult—his relationship with his family—was almost
entirely excluded from his writing.

I do not intend to explore this most suppressed side of Thoreau at
length, nor to analyze it clinically. If it calls for a Stendhal to render
Thoreau's anguished relationship to the society immediately around him,
it would probably take a novelist with Faulkner's brilliant instinct for
what Freud calls "the family romance" to do justice to the complexity of
Thoreau's entanglements with mother and father, brother, sisters, and
resident aunts. But we are concerned with his "habit of antagonism," and
it is clear that (to quote *Walden*) his "stiff neck is of older date" (241)
than his relationship to the village. At issue in *Walden* is why he repudi-
ated his neighbors yet continually defined himself against them, or, to put
it another way, why he confronted his readers so vehemently while nonetheless writing to convert them. The patterns here, I want to suggest, are
those of his life at home. There the figure that looms largest is his
mother's. He never outgrew his need for her love, never broke away from
his place as her son, never left her home for long.[22] Yet he was never sure
she loved him for himself, and so—although apparently he never once
argued with or confronted her directly[23]—by steadily refusing to meet her
expectations, he kept demanding to be loved on his own terms. In his life
he kept those terms in implicit opposition to his family's expectations. In
Walden, using his readers' expectations instead, he makes the opposition
explicit. But in both cases he is determined to force home the difference
between who he is and who he is supposed to be. The prodigal son rejects
his inheritance as a child of Victorian America, of the village, and ulti-

mately of his parents, then, rather than repent, he demands that those he has rejected come and admire his prodigality. This is neither freedom, however, nor autonomy, because success still depends on proving to the fathers and mothers that a prophet had been born among them.

"Parents," wrote Thoreau four years after returning home from Harvard and four before moving out to Walden, "and relations but entertain the youth; they cannot stand between him and his destiny" (*J*, 1:231). He was ten years older in 1851, when he began taking some of his walks after midnight during the warmest weeks of the summer. The phenomenon that seized his attention—"the great story of the night" (*J*, 4:145) he recounts in a number of entries—was the moon "waging continual war with the clouds," fighting "her way through all the squadrons of her foes," trying to keep a clear heavenly field in order to "ride majestic" and "shine unobstructedly" (*J*, 2:383–84). As he writes in "Autumnal Tints" about the study of nature: "A man sees only what concerns him."[24] Why his thoughts were preoccupied with the drama of the moon and the smothering clouds is made clear by the beginning of this entry, which specifies the foes and obstructions *he* had to contend with: "*1.30 A.M.—* Full moon. Arose and went to the river and bathed, stepping very carefully not to disturb the household, and still carefully in the street not to disturb the neighbors. I did not walk naturally and freely till I had got over the wall" (*J*, 2:383). His destiny was a heavenly one, but instead of riding to it majestically, he had to tiptoe toward it through his own house like a child sneaking out.

"It is such a relief," he writes in *Walden*, to "breathe freely and stretch myself" (49–50). There is no question of how emotionally cooped up he felt at home. When his sister Helen went to Taunton, he wrote to explain his "long silence":

> You know we have hardly done our own deeds, thought our own thoughts, or lived our own lives, hitherto. For a man to act himself, he must be perfectly free; otherwise, he is in danger of losing all sense of responsibility or self-respect. Now when such a state of things exists, that the sacred opinions one advances in argument are apologized for by his friends, before his face, lest his hearers receive a wrong impression of the man, —when such gross injustice is of frequent occurrence, where shall we look, & not in vain, for men, deeds, thoughts?[25]

Although he says "friends," he is surely referring to parents and relations, especially (since his father by all accounts was an uncommonly quiet man) his mother, probably also the various spinster aunts who often resided with the family, all of whom were just this outspoken, none of whom could understand the choices, "the sacred opinions," on which Thoreau's life was based.[26] His freedom, his self-respect, his masculinity,

even his "own thoughts" were threatened. Surely, he is telling Helen, you
know I cannot be myself at home.

Yet he was no more comfortable away from home either. The furthest
he got was Staten Island, where he went in 1843, when he was twenty-
six, to tutor Emerson's nephews and to launch his literary career among
the editors and publishers in New York City. He stayed for eight months
but was miserably homesick the whole time. His letters home are full of
longing for the same family that gave him claustrophobia both before and
after this aborted attempt to define himself on his own.[27] Severe home-
sickness can have many causes, but I think that Thoreau's problem was
essentially that, at this distance, he had no way to know if his mother
missed him. One letter he wrote near the end of his stay, for example, is
clearly an attempt to convince himself that at that very moment she was
in sympathy with him: "I fancy that this Sunday evening you are poring
over some select book almost transcendental perchance." "Methinks," he
adds, "I should be content to sit at the back-door in Concord, under the
poplar-tree, henceforth forever."[28] In his writings the longing for communion with a sympathetic, sustaining family is expressed as profoundly
as the more conspicuous desire for self-reliance and independence.[29]
Could he have taken his mother's love for granted, he would not have
needed to "turn [his] face more exclusively . . . to the woods, where [he]
was better known" (19). Alone at the pond, in the chapter called "The
Ponds," he carefully studies the surface of the water and is rewarded by
proof that he is not alone: "I can see by its face that it is visited by the
same reflection; and I can almost say, Walden, is it you?" (193). Pleasure
in the pun on "reflection" should not distract one from the depth of the
need revealed here: to see himself, his own hopes and values, in another's
face.

The most obvious source of his uncertainty about the way he was
known at home was his status as a younger brother, his mother's second
son. There is no doubt that while both brothers lived, the people of Concord thought much more highly and fondly of John than of Henry.[30]
Their mother's preference, if she had one, cannot be known, but as
Thoreau said, some circumstantial evidence is very strong. His life indicates how much he felt he had to compete with his more popular, easy-
going older brother. He worked hard in school to be the one son chosen
to go to college, yet being sent away to Harvard was an ambiguous reward; while living in Cambridge, Henry went home as often as he could.
He proposed marriage to Ellen Sewall a week after John had been rejected by her, as if the only place to look for love was where John had
been first. And the most incredible event in Thoreau's psychic life shows
the same need to measure himself against his older brother's image: a
month after John died of tetanus, Henry himself apparently came close to

dying of the same disease; that is, the symptoms were the same, although as Thoreau himself admitted, his illness was purely psychosomatic. Thoreau's biographers have agreed that in this incident he was "punishing himself" for surviving the beloved brother with whom he had competed.[31] Guilt certainly would have been a factor. But no one seems to have considered how Henry's coming down with the symptoms of the disease that had just killed John would have struck the rest of the family. They must have been horrified. Were they, however, as overwhelmed by the thought of losing Henry as they had been by John's death? Henry's psychosomatic mirroring of John may have been a test of their reactions, an extreme attempt to find out how much *he* was loved.

This is a very schematic account, but I hope I have said enough to suggest a reason why Thoreau could feel himself *only* in opposition—that is, neither in solitude nor in conformity to others. The most enviable thing about the hawk that reigns in the sky at the end of *Walden* is that it betrays no signs of dependency; "the parent which hatched it" has completely disappeared. Thoreau, however, remained a son. Throughout his adult life, he kept trying the family he could never leave. He stayed home, but without surrendering to their expectations. He needed to feel loved, but he had to be sure he was loved for himself, not as a younger brother. His insecurity is revealed most clearly, perhaps, in his belief that nearly everyone in the village pitied or mocked him. At home he lived a life of quiet defiance, affronting the ambitions and values of the family that had sent him to college, that expected him to go to church, that defined success by the standards of Concord.[32] "I am perhaps more willful than others," he noted, "and make enormous sacrifices, even of others' happiness, it may be, to gain my ends" (*J*, 7:48). Under such circumstances, "living erectly day by day" demanded the ardor of a soldier. Yet the ultimate victory he was fighting for, we must remember, was not freedom; it was love, recognition, approval—on the terms he himself had laid down.

This is the quest of *Walden*. Although in its myth of self-creation Thoreau tries to erase almost all traces of his identity as a son, the book enacts the same drama as his life in the family. The spot he chose on which to build a cabin and assert a self was just far enough away from home for him to keep looking back at the world he claims to have escaped.[33] His meditation as the "Hermit" at the start of "Brute Neighbors" begins this way: "I wonder what the world is doing now." And though as a hermit he is absolutely alone, his thoughts remain full of "farmers" and "hands," "house-keeping" and "dinner-parties" (223). Including these among his "brute" neighbors may be a clever linguistic victory over conventional society, but what emerges undisguised in such a passage is his preoccupation with other people. Indeed, throughout

Walden Thoreau's definition of himself depends on them. The way he sets life at the pond in such direct opposition to the village is, of course, what makes *Walden* such a good introduction to the historical time and place. Whereas Emerson tends to deal with "society" as a timeless abstraction, *Walden* goes into detail about exactly what was happening in the 1840s: slavery and the Fugitive Slave Law, the Mexican War and expansion across the continent, technological changes like the railroad and telegraph, "our factory system" in places like Lowell and the capitalist exploitation of labor, Irish immigration and the rate at which farms and businesses fail, the ways that people decorate their houses and the things they do with their leisure time, the sounds of village days and holidays. What seems paradoxical—that this book about life in the woods tells more about contemporary American society than almost any other major work from its period—makes perfect sense once one realizes how dependent its "I" is on the "they" of the village and the "you" of its contemporary reader.

We cannot appreciate how *Walden* works until we see it as a response to this conflicted dramatic situation. Thoreau's symbiotic relationship to others shows up in many ways. There is, for example, his regular practice of seeing things from two points of view: his and Concord's. About the prospect of a farm he writes, "some might have thought [it] too far from the village, but to my eyes the village was too far from it" (81). To him the "value even of the smallest well" is that it helps the imagination to "float the earth"; "This is as important as that it keeps butter cool" (87). The cranberries he admires, "the farmer plucks with an ugly rake" (238). Even in such trivial descriptions—and a complete list of examples would cover several pages—Thoreau is not alone. His point of reference, his angle of vision, is in constant competition with the eyes through which others see the world.

His aphorisms, at least in the book's first half, are also molded by the pattern of this drama. They delight in simultaneously acknowledging and confounding the conventional perceptions with which Thoreau competes. "For a man is rich in proportion to the number of things he can afford"—so far his Yankee readers would have followed him, probably with a gleam in their eyes—"he can afford to let alone" (82): with these last three words Thoreau stands those readers' assumptions on their head. In the age of the railroad he insists that "the swiftest traveller is he that goes afoot" (53), then proves it with an eye for the best swap that turns out to be as keen as any Yankee peddler's. On second thought, these aphorisms turn out to be strictly logical, but Thoreau stubbornly parades his logic as paradox. In *Walden*'s "Conclusion," he ridicules common sense and all who "demand" that "you shall speak so that they can understand you" (324). When the seer whom Plato describes in the parable of the cave comes back into the darkness after seeing the sun, none of the benighted prisoners of the shadows can understand him; "The light which puts out our eyes is darkness to us" (333) Thoreau writes three lines from the book's end, thus admitting the proverbial problem prophets have with their immediate audience. As a transcendentalist, he has every right to warn his readers: "You will pardon some obscurities, for there are more secrets in my trade than in most men's, and yet not voluntarily kept, but inseparable from its very nature" (17). Yet the volley of economic aphorisms with which *Walden* begins are not concerned with the mysteries of the spirit. They deal with the material facts of life, but in a way that disguises Thoreau's desire to enlighten his readers behind his determination to bewilder and confront them. How he tells the truth is decided not by "*its* very nature" but rather by his attitude toward the audience to whom he is telling it.

"My trade": there is no clearer evidence of his self-consciousness than his choice of words in *Walden*'s first half. "Economy," in particular, is full of beautifully sustained raids on the language of capitalism and the marketplace, the language of the tribe he keeps claiming to have put behind him:

> My purpose in going to Walden Pond was not to live cheaply nor to live dearly there, but to transact some private business with the fewest obstacles; to be hindered from accomplishing which for want of a little common sense, a little enterprise and business talent, appeared not so sad as foolish.
>
> I have always endeavored to acquire strict business habits . . . (19–20)

The passage goes on in this idiom for another five hundred words. Like *Walden*'s other references to "business" and "trade," it is offered playfully, as a linguistic tour de force. But its mere presence in the book, not to mention its explicit references to "obstacles" and being "hindered," betrays the enormous amount of pressure that was exerted against almost every point of Thoreau's life, and that is resisted by the nervous tautness of his prose. Such virtuoso passages have little meaning except as performances. They display the resources of his imagination, flaunt his superiority to the shibboleths of the village, and announce his independence of conventional definitions. Yet if he had really felt this "fancy-free," he would hardly have needed to keep engaging and triumphing over the diction of the society he had rejected.

The seriousness of the stakes he is playing for emerges in "Baker Farm." This chapter rehearses both the rhetorical drama of *Walden* and the psychological drama of living at Walden. John Field plays the role of Thoreau's neighbors and readers; he may be just off the boat from Ireland, but his materialistic values and ambitions are those of the American audience Thoreau addresses. As in *Walden* as a whole, he shares his life with Field, trying "to help him with my experience," talking to him "as if he were a philosopher" (205). That this "audience" seems incapable of grasping the message would be discouraging enough, but Thoreau goes on, in a moment of real candor, to admit a more severe misgiving. Seeing how hard Field and his family are working forces him to wonder whether the relations and neighbors to whom he "looked like a loafer" (205) were not right:

> As I was leaving the Irishman's roof after the rain, bending my steps again to the pond, my haste to catch pickerel, wading in retired meadows, in sloughs and bogholes, in forlorn and savage places, appeared for an instant trivial to me who had been sent to school and college . . .

This rare use of the passive tense in regard to himself concedes what the rest of *Walden* denies: that he owed his life, at least in part, to others. In this painful "instant" he looks at himself *through* their eyes, and what he sees is the uncomprehending disappointment he must often have noticed *in* their eyes.

It is an instant that threatens his lifework profoundly. Although he resolves this crisis before the end of the sentence, which I'll finish quoting in a second, this moment of self-doubt makes *Walden* a much stronger book than it would have been if he had entirely suppressed the anxieties with which he never finished wrestling, just as he never left family and village behind. He reassures himself by appealing to a higher authority than that of those who sent him to college, as if to describe a chosen son being sent out to play in his kingdom; even here, however, one can sense the captive running the gauntlet:

> . . . but as I ran down the hill toward the reddening west, with the rainbow over my shoulder, and some faint tinkling sounds borne to my ear through the cleansed air, from I know not what quarter, my Good Genius seemed to say, Go fish and hunt far and wide day by day—farther and wider—and rest thee by many brooks and hearthsides without misgiving. Remember thy Creator in the days of thy youth. . . . Grow wild according to thy nature. . . . Through want of enterprise and faith men are where they are, buying and selling, and spending their lives like serfs. (207–8)

His truancy from others' expectations is blessed by his creator. He is cherished for his own nature. He is the lord, they are the serfs. But his consciousness of other eyes and his vulnerability to their judgments reappear in his need to appropriate the language of commerce and Christianity to assert his title to this joyous sovereignty. *His* want of conventional "enterprise and faith" was the tenderest point in his relationship to the people he met at those "hearthsides." He still needs to throw those words back in the faces of the people who have used them to accuse him. "Without misgiving," he demands to be accepted on his own terms—except that those terms turn out to be inextricably linked to the terms they laid down first.

The direct confrontations with his "nearest neighbors" (205) and with himself that Thoreau stages in "Baker Farm" bring to a climax the conflict that looms largest in the first two-thirds of *Walden*. Before he could get to his own life in the woods, he had to "walk over" his readers' "premises" (81); he had to evoke, indict, deny, and redefine their assumptions. His mode of affirmation is essentially negative: the basis for his claim to success is that the rest of us have been "such miserable failures" (9). Three times in the opening chapter he insists that he is not writing for anyone who is already perfectly happy with the status quo. To such a reader, if any exists, it would doubtless seem that he protests too much, both about others' "desperation" and his own self-satisfaction. Hearing his hoe "tinkl[ing] against the stones" in "The Bean-Field," he writes that "I remembered with as much pity as pride, if I remembered at all, my acquaintances who had gone to the city to attend the oratorios" (159). What gives him away is "if I remembered at all." Not only is he measuring his life against more conventionally successful ones (see 162); at the same time he is trying to get us to believe that he's not! The aggressive posture Thoreau adopts can seem poignantly self-defensive.

Yet *Walden* also thrives under the pressures that plagued Thoreau. He deploys his "habit of antagonism" strategically as the basis for a dialectic of change: "I do not wish to flatter my townsmen, nor to be flattered by them, for that will not advance either of us. We need to be provoked—goaded like oxen" (108).[34] He whetted his prose on his grudge against his place at home and in the village, improved the isolation he had been consigned to into a visionary vantage point, and disciplined his need to justify himself into a potent set of attacks on our self-complacent, slavish "prejudices" (8). For the reader who is prepared to let down his or her defenses, Thoreau's aggressions can be liberating. Whatever the source of his need to "stik[e] at the root" of conventional values (75), such a reader (and I am one, at least most of the time) is grateful for *Walden*'s enormous analytical and polemical power as a work of social criticism. His habit of antagonism can serve us as well as him; every rereading of *Walden* is a new occasion to reexamine one's own life. There is something inspirational just in the stance Thoreau takes so emphatically as a "man more right than his neighbors," in the way he takes on his whole culture as "a majority of one."[35] "In opposition" Thoreau became the prophet Emerson kept privately urging himself to be: the one who confronts "you" directly.

Yet while I would never question the moral incisiveness and imaginative heroism of the assault *Walden* mounts on conventionality, I think one must recognize the price it pays for being overdetermined by the demands of performing for an audience perceived as hostile.[36] I am not thinking of the obstacles Thoreau put between himself and such readers as were actually available to him in the mid-nineteenth century—though given his ambitions, including the desire to be an agent of social change, and given the amount of real good his uncommon sense might have done, had he made his truth more accessible to his contemporaries, one cannot leave that cost out. I am thinking instead of Thoreau's own definition of "the cost of a thing": "the amount . . . of life which is required to be exchanged for it" (31). We have to notice what the text itself omits or occludes about his own life: not just what he wanted to suppress, but what he was afraid to share. He is so busy fighting for the space he sought to occupy at the pond that he cannot really tell us who lived there, and why. The substitution of a chapter on "Reading," which again goes after his audience, for any discussion of "writing," which would have led much more directly into the meaning of his own life, is typical of the way that throughout much of the book he uses the follies and vices of the village as a sword that is actually a shield, behind which he shelters his own deepest aspirations, his own truest experiences. The pattern established in the first three paragraphs, of shifting his focus from "I" to "you," recurs over and over. Halfway through chapter 2, for example—"Where I Lived, and What I Lived For"—we finally get a paragraph that begins, "I went to the woods because . . ." (90). By the end of that paragraph, however, he is already talking about "most men," and for the next five pages his prose is once more preoccupied with the emptiness of *their* lives.

One can hardly say that the text gives no account of what he lived for, and we need not hold him to his standard of "simple and sincere." We need to note, however, that the history of his self is the subject he has the most difficulty writing about. Where his indictment of our delusions is razor-sharp, his references to himself tend to retreat into mystifications like baskets, bay horses, and turtle doves;[37] as he himself says in "Economy," "I will only hint at some of the enterprises which I have cherished" (16). There he also indicates why he could not bring himself to be more forthright: "If I should attempt to tell how I have desired to spend my life in years past, it would probably surprise those of my readers who are somewhat acquainted with its actual history" (16). Even in *Walden*, the constraints he felt on thinking his own thoughts (as he summed up his home life in that letter to his sister) are still active. As the reply he felt compelled to make to the Association for the Advancement of Science had revealed, he was reluctant to expose the most sacred parts of his life to heathen eyes. There is a beautiful passage at the start of "Sounds" about some of his best moments, when he sat "rapt in a revery," outside time, one with the harmonies around him. Such "seasons," "so much over and above my usual allowance," were a major part of what he lived for. But even here he cannot get outside his obsessive awareness of a critical audience: "This was sheer idleness to my fellow-townsmen, no doubt; but if the birds and flowers had tried me by their standard, I should not have been found wanting" (112).

As Thoreau reminded himself in a journal entry that switches the metaphor for his anxiety from the courtroom to the battlefield, the defensive attitude he adopts in *Walden* costs too much, though the entry reveals too how inevitably he felt driven into defensiveness:

> If you would really take a position outside the street and daily life of men, you must have deliberately planned your course, you must have business which is not your neighbors' business, which they cannot understand. For only absorbing employment prevails, succeeds, takes up space, occupies territory, determines the future of individuals and states, drives Kansas out of your head, and actually and permanently occupies the only desirable and free Kansas against all border ruffians. The attitude of resistance is one of weakness, inasmuch as it only faces an enemy; it has its back to all that is truly attractive. (*J*, 9:36)

Because the attitude of *Walden* is predominantly that of resistance, the reader who wants to know what Thoreau found most truly attractive about the life in which he lived and moved and had his being must read his journals. They leave out a lot too, but they not only help us understand why he had to keep fighting for the boundaries of his life; they also fill in its center, "that for which his life's blood circulated."[38]

The closest that *Walden* comes to doing this is his extended celebration of Walden Pond: "the gentle pulsing of its life" (188). This description is the only place in the first ten chapters where for any length of time Thoreau invites readers to share his perspective: "When you invert your head . . . You would think . . . As you look . . . You may often detect . . . You can see . . ." (186–87). We may have to begin by inverting our heads, but these locutions declare a truce between our point of view and his. Yet while this description comes at the center of the book's central chapter, there is still a center from which we are excluded. It is symptomatic that Thoreau projects the ultimate vision of the goal of his own life away from himself, onto the pond and its life; he will let us look there, but not at him; he leaves it up to us to find there this reflection of himself.

Nor could he sustain this openness, and the faith in our ability to "see" on which it depends, for long. "The Ponds" ends with some of *Walden*'s most spiteful passages. The furious attacks on Flint, "the unclean and stupid farmer" (195), and on a "model farm! . . . A great grease-spot" (196), lead to the chapter's despairingly bitter last paragraph: "Nature has no human inhabitant who appreciates her. . . . what youth or maiden conspires with the wild luxuriant beauty of Nature? She flourishes most alone, far from the towns where they reside. Talk of heaven! ye disgrace earth" (199–200). Having invited us close to the heart of his life in the woods, he here turns on us in disgust. These passages destroy the luminescent serenity of the chapter as effectively as finding a rotting corpse in the pond would ruin the charm of gazing at its surface. The abruptness of the chapter's concluding attack is unmotivated in the text, but we could explain it as his reaction to the intimacy he had verged on: he may be raging against his own desire to expose his "life's blood" to others' eyes. In any case, it is his own deepest hope that is left stranded here, for if there is *no one* who can appreciate nature, for whom is he writing *Walden?* Who could possibly appreciate him?

What Thoreau said explicitly about writing for an audience shows the same contradiction one finds in the remarks of most canonical nineteenth-century American writers. He complained when he was not asked to lecture; he felt he was "in danger of cheapening" himself when he was (*J*, 7:79). He wrote to Blake that "the value of literature" lies in what it communicates: "that it is not in vain that man speaks to man."[39] He wrote in his journal that he had nothing to say to "other men": "Though you should only speak to one kindred mind in all time, though you should not speak to one, but only utter aloud, that you may the more completely realize and live in the idea which contains the reason of your life" (*J*, 3:157). *Walden* is similarly divided. Although he announces in the epigraph that he is writing "to wake my neighbors up," the bitter sense of martyrdom that he succumbs to at the end of "The Ponds" often tempted him to conclude "that most that I am and value myself for is lost, or worse than lost, on my audience" (*J*, 7:79). When the unsold copies of *A Week* were delivered to him, Thoreau wryly noted that his book had apparently been addressed exclusively to himself:

> The unbound [copies] were tied up by the printer four years ago in stout paper wrappers, and inscribed, —
>
> H. D. Thoreau's
Concord River
50 cops.
>
> So Munroe had only to cross out "River" and write "Mass." and deliver them to the expressman at once. I can see now what I write for, the result of my labors. (*J*, 5:459–60)

As he revised his manuscript between 1847 and 1854, with plenty of reasons to conclude that great writers were invariably neglected, he came to feel at times that writing was a private end in itself: "To set down such choice experiences that my own writings may inspire me and at last I may make wholes of parts" (*J*, 3:217). One can see signs of this turning inward in the book itself, particularly if one compares the two quasioriental parables that he invented for *Walden*.[40] The first he added to chapter 2 in 1848–1849, the second he added to "Conclusion" in 1852–1853.[41] The first concerns the son of a king who lived in exile with a "barbarous race" until a "holy teacher" "revealed to him what he was" (96). As a man, of course, Thoreau identifies with the unappreciated "*Brahme.*" As a writer, however, he sees his role as that of the teacher, whose expression is a means to a larger, social end. The second of the parables Thoreau wrote, on the other hand, is about the "artist in the city of Kouroo" who turns his back on everyone else—on friends, society, history—"to strive after perfection" in his art (326–27). After the failure of *A Week* forced him to postpone *Walden*'s publication, which led to the process of revising and re-revising the manuscript, one of Thoreau's goals was to make it whole and perfect, an autonomous achievement in itself.[42] To the extent that he despaired about being appreciated or even read by an audience, he came to see *Walden* as a private compensation for the absence of a public role to fill.

He was clearly tempted to put literature outside the conflicted world he inhabited as a man speaking to men. But *Walden* remains a performance. Even through all the revisions, he defined it foremost in terms of the drama that initially inspired it: sharing his self with the townspeople to whom he "addressed" the book. As a writer, he remained faithful to his ambitions as a prophet, a holy teacher. And as a son, he had too much invested in his hope of being appreciated. Despite all the anxieties it involved, he continued to write with his reader in the front of his mind. Despite bouts with despair, he was unwilling to renounce the quest for sympathy. He wanted to be appreciated for himself, so he begins by rejecting his readers' values, asserting himself as an act of defiance. We would, however, misread *Walden* as a whole if we overlooked its larger design: to be reunited with those readers. In the last third of the book he moves back toward his audience as well as toward the village. Having fought for the space his life occupies, he takes on a new rhetorical task in the last part of *Walden*: to get readers to surrender to his vision.

Except for "Spring" and "Conclusion," the last seven chapters of *Walden* have never attracted as much attention as the rest.[43] Any doubts about how well Thoreau was served by his habit of antagonism would be put aside when one sees how much power goes out of his prose as he relaxes his rhetorical stance.[44] Given how strenuously he had felt compelled to fight to get into the woods, we should be glad he can finally write about his life there—warming his house, studying the animals, conjuring up former inhabitants, sounding the pond—without flashing his eyes like scimitars or clenching his writing hand into a fist. We may even be impressed with the stylistic virtuosity he displays; who would have guessed he could imitate the elegant sentimentality of Irving's or Hawthorne's sketches as he does in much of "Former Inhabitants"? But most readers simply see these chapters, which were largely written after the first drafts, as the book's dullest stretches. Part of the problem is that Thoreau still needs to shelter his "inmost Me" from readers' eyes, and thus his details about squirrels and ants and so on are arranged around a missing center. But if we keep in mind the dramatic context I have tried to define, there is a new reason to read these chapters carefully, even compassionately. In them Thoreau is striving to put his life at Walden (and in *Walden*) on common ground.

Let me briefly outline some of the ways these chapters change the patterns of *Walden*. Gone is the pressure on his diction and style to strain against conventional usage and expectations. In place of the opposition between "most men" and "I," Thoreau begins to talk in terms of "all men" and "every man," "the villagers" and "I too" (252). In 1850 or 1851 he added most of the quotations from oriental scriptures;[45] these mainly went into the book's first half. In its last third, however, instead of these obtrusive references to books whose titles "most men in this town" have never even heard of (106–7), he supplements his own vision with a host of anecdotes about hunting and fishing that he picked up from those very neighbors. The most conspicuous instance of this new deference to the oral culture of the village—which he had previously scorned as "gossip" (94, 167–68) and "*parlaver*" (244)—comes on *Walden*'s very last page, where he gratefully uses "the story" about the bug coming out of the table, the story that "everyone has heard," "which has gone the rounds of New England," as his ultimate symbol for regeneration, for his book's central theme (333). And it is not just the mood of the chapters that is more hospitable to other people; what he says about "Winter Visitors," for instance, acknowledges the pleasure he finds in others' company much more openly than anything in the first part of the book, even "Visitors," which emphasizes the need to put the largest possible distance between himself and even his friendliest guests (140–41). Most unguarded of all is the last paragraph of "Winter Visitors." One of the questions his neighbors ask him at the start is if he "did not feel lonesome" (3). In "Solitude" he says, yes, once, "for an hour," but then this "slight insanity" passed and left him indifferent to any "person" or "villager" (131–32). This is part of the pose of perfect self-sufficiency that he strives to maintain at first. But the end of "Winter Visitors" admits that at Walden, "as everywhere, I sometimes expected the Visitor who never comes . . . but did not see the man approaching from the town" (270).

"Thaw with his gentle persuasion," he decides in "Spring," "is more powerful than Thor with his hammer" (309). In his efforts to relax the mood of *Walden*, however, to make himself and us feel equally at home in the woods, Thoreau is a much less impressive figure (though it is worth remembering that it was this "Thoreau," the genial lover of nature, who first gained acceptance from American readers). And at points he still reverts to antagonism—"when the frost had smitten me on one cheek, heathen as I was, I turned to it the other also" (266); this is as calculated to annoy a conventional Victorian reader as his reference to the Bible as merely "an old book" on *Walden*'s third page (5). But in both what they say and how they say it, these winter chapters are implicitly moving toward the reunion with neighbors and readers that is explicitly announced in "Spring":

> In a pleasant spring morning all men's sins are forgiven. Such a day is a truce to vice. While such a sun holds out to burn, the vilest sinner may return. Through our own recovered innocence we discern the innocence of our neighbors. You may have known your neighbor yesterday for a thief, a drunkard, or a sensualist, and merely pitied or despised him, and despaired of the world; but the sun shines bright and warm this first spring morning, re-creating the world, and you meet him at some serene work, and see how his exhausted and debauched veins expand with still joy and bless the new day, feel the spring influence with the innocence of infancy, and all his faults are forgotten. There is not only an atmosphere of good will about him, but even a savor of holiness groping for expression, blindly and ineffectually perhaps, like a newborn instinct . . . (314–15)

Of course, under the cover of this truce Thoreau is still pushing his dialectic into hostile territory. The diction of this passage is taken from his neighbors' Christian catechisms, but the words have been redefined by Thoreau's newer testament of nature's joy. The "expression" Concord is groping for turns out to be *Walden*. The father and mothers of the town turn out to be lost children whom Thoreau can lead home. He is not surrendering to his readers. He is, however, formalizing the offer to make peace with them—on his terms, yet the terms are very generous. So are the pronouns in this passage: "I" do not despair of "you," "you" may have despaired of "your" neighbors, but "we" can "all" be saved.

He has redrawn the lines of *Walden* as a circle that now includes us inside it. This rhetorical mood lasts through "Conclusion," which he wrote very late in the process of the book's composition.[46] This last chapter understandably strikes readers as the most Emersonian part of *Walden*. It is Emersonian both in what Thoreau says about the infinitude of man, and in how he says it; unlike the paradoxes of "Economy," the aphorisms of "Conclusion" seek to inspire readers rather than confront and challenge them. "I" and "you" merge in the "we" Thoreau privileges throughout the chapter. Having fought his way past our expectations and judgments, he now throws open the gate to the kingdom he has won. That he wrote "Conclusion" long after the failure of *A Week*, that he speaks there on behalf of his audience, that he is less interested in blowing his own horn than in summoning them to their own glorious destinies—all of this seems to prove that he had not abandoned any of his prophetic ambitions.

We can call "Conclusion" Thoreau's leap of faith. The faith is in Emerson's Over-Soul, but, just as important, it is also in his readers' receptivity. He could not transcend all his doubts: "I do not say that John or Jonathan will realize all this" he writes five sentences from the end (333). But he has returned to the village, he looks to human nature rather than to nature as the source of his inspiration, and he writes for people who are prepared to entertain his vision. The celebratory tone of "Conclusion" is based not just on his success at Walden, or in *Walden*; it also seems to anticipate success *for Walden*. There is evidence of this hope in the journals too, including a passage written a month after the book's publication in which he prepares to bid goodbye to "obscurity and poverty" with some reluctance: "I do not see how I could have enjoyed it, if the public had been expecting as much of me as there is danger now that they will" (*J*, 7:46). Certainly he had every right to expect that publishing *Walden* would change his life. He had written a great book. He had defeated his defeats. Although he would never have mentioned this fact, that hawk that plays so triumphantly in the sky at the end of "Spring" is defying gravity all the time; its apparent freedom is earned by a continuous struggle, an unremitting effort. In *Walden* Thoreau earns his triumph the same way.

Yet while *Walden* did comparatively better than *A Week*, selling close to eighteen hundred copies in the first year, there was no need to reprint it until shortly before Thoreau's death, and the few additional lectures he was invited to give in the wake of its appearance left him just as frustrated with his audience as ever. "The public" still did not expect the right things from him. He had written one of the masterpieces of American prose without measurably changing his status in the village or at his parents' home. It is easy to understand why, at the very end of his life, Thoreau devoted himself to studying "The Dispersion of Seeds."[47] As he said at the end of "The Succession of Forest Trees," the last lecture he ever gave, "I have great faith in a seed. . . . Convince me that you have a seed there, and I am prepared to expect wonders."[48] Perhaps he knew that *Walden* was such a seed, that one day his life in the woods would flourish in the sun of the recognition it deserved.

Yet the relative failure of *Walden* in its own time is not surprising. Nor is it grounds for indicting the taste of the contemporary reading public. As a performance *Walden* is too complex and divided in the attitude it adopts toward its audience ever to be popular. It simply makes too many demands—rhetorical demands, not intellectual ones—on the patience, the negative capability, even the humility of the readers it begins by assaulting so aggressively. Readers who are cast at once and unequivocally into the role of antagonist can be forgiven their hostility to the book. Those of us who teach it to modern readers should keep in mind the way *Walden* treats "you who read these pages." Seeing the book as a performance does not diminish its moral and imaginative achievement. Indeed, helping readers get on the other side of the way it confronts and coerces them can make *Walden*'s greatness more accessible. We have to have sympathy for what Thoreau was up against day by day and sentence by sentence, feeling like "a king's son" unrecognized in the midst of "the barbarous race with which he lived" (349). He wanted to write "the record of my love" (*J*, 2:101)—"When I am condemned, and condemn myself utterly, I think straightway, 'But I rely on my love for some things'" (*J*, 1:296)—without ever seeing the love he felt reflected in a pair of human eyes. But we can also sympathize with the reactions of "the fathers and the mothers of the town" to his defiant quest for love. Thoreau was one of the most brilliant children of Jacksonian America. He was also among the most difficult. It is always from the difficult children that we learn the most about ourselves.

Chapter IV

MOTHERS, HUSBANDS, AND AN UNCLE: STOWE'S *UNCLE TOM'S CABIN*

THERE ARE still two good reasons to read *Uncle Tom's Cabin*: for its radicalism, and for its conventionality. As a novel of social protest, it generates so much passion within its own pages that, although the particular evil it indicts has given way to other forms of injustice, its power remains largely intact. In this respect it is like *The Grapes of Wrath*, which is deeply indebted to Stowe's archetypal work. As one of the three best-selling novels of mid-nineteenth-century America, it is also a perfect mirror of genteel Victorian preconceptions, a wide-ranging guide to the tastes and values of the audience for which contemporaries like Hawthorne and Melville, as struggling professional novelists, tried to write. Powerfully radical and perfectly conventional: it might sound as if I mean two different books. But while Stowe does not finally manage to reconcile these antithetical qualities, in *Uncle Tom's Cabin* she does enable them to live together—as husband and wife.

Stowe's work first appeared serially, between June 1851 and April 1852, in *The National Era*, a weekly abolitionist paper. Almost exactly in the middle of its run, *Moby-Dick* was published in New York. It took about a decade to sell the first printing of Melville's book; just over three-fourths of those two thousand copies were sold within a year. By comparison, Hawthorne's *House of the Seven Gables*, also published in 1851, did better: it sold about seven thousand copies its first year. According to her own subsequent account of writing the novel, Stowe felt the same anxiety of performance that all writers experience. "A feeling of profound discouragement came over her," she says about the moment when the manuscript was finished, but not yet published as a book; "Would anybody read it?"[1] She did not have to worry for long. Appearing in two volumes in 1852, *Uncle Tom's Cabin* sold five thousand copies in two days, fifty thousand in six weeks, well over three hundred thousand by the end of the year, and more than half a million before the panic of 1857 depressed the book market.[2] Her novel may not ultimately have done quite as well as Susan Warner's *Wide, Wide World* (1850) or Maria Cummins's *Lamplighter* (1854)—probably the most popular of all nineteenth-century American novels—but as the first novel that Stowe ever wrote, it was an inspired work. She liked to suggest that God had inspired it and dictated it to her scene by scene, but the wondrous way her novel worked on its contemporary audience is not as mysterious as that. Stowe had great gifts as a novelist; they were, however, those of a Victorian American woman who knew her reading public.

The National Era's subtitle promised "Original Sketches and Tales for Home Reading," a phrase that locates that public very accurately. But Stowe herself regularly addresses her readers, and two of her formulas are equally revealing: "my lady readers" and "our refined and Christian readers."[3] As Ann Douglas and Henry Nash Smith have recently reminded us, the audience for fiction in Stowe's America was broadly middle class, at least nominally Christian, and overwhelmingly female.[4] It is hard to say precisely how female, but since more than thirty copies of Warner's novel were sold for every one, say, of *Some Adventures of Captain Simon Suggs* (1845), among the most successful of the books by the Southwestern Humorists who wrote for male readers, it is clear that "Home Reading" almost invariably meant the parlor, not the den. And adjectives like *lady*, *refined*, and *Christian* point to the needlepoint mottoes that were likely to be hanging on those parlor walls, the pieties by which the female American novel reader understood the world, and her place in it.

Harriet Beecher Stowe believed in those pieties. Her novel about slavery professes to realism; on her first pages she announces "the desire to be graphic in our account" (11), in her last chapter she iterates her "desire to exhibit [slavery] in a *living dramatic reality*" (513), and when introducing her titular character, she does so in the guise of a nineteenth-century realist: "At this table was seated Uncle Tom . . . who, as he is to be the hero of our story, we must daguerreotype for our readers" (34).[5] Contemporary Southern critics accused her of lying, but more conspicuous is the pervasive way her vision of "reality" was determined by the assumptions about the world she shared with her American readers. The subtitle of her novel, for example, is "Life Among the Lowly," a phrase that sufficiently indicates the class-conscious perspective within which all the characters of the novel are placed. While as a Christian she believes in the equality of every soul before God, and as an opponent of slavery she insists that the slave is endowed with a fully human capacity to love and suffer ("For, sir, he was a man, —and you are but another man" [55]), as a dramatic novelist she preserves the social distinctions between her characters as carefully as Fielding or Austen ever did. In fact, Stowe displays even more firmness on this point, for the American bourgeoisie can never take its status for granted. Haley, the slave trader, is not just morally evil; socially, he is an affront to the "well-furnished dining parlor" in which he sits: "He was a short, thick-set man, with coarse, commonplace features, and that swaggering air of pretension which marks a low man who is trying to elbow his way upward in the world" (11). Treating coarse and commonplace as synonyms is hardly democratic, but if sainthood is a role all have an equal opportunity to apply for, "gentleman" is a title Stowe explicitly reserves for men of property and manners.

Stowe's ear for dialect was almost as fine as Mark Twain's. But Murray's Grammar, which Haley defies, was one of her fixed points of cultural reference, and she never allows her narrator's voice to speak in any but the most refined accents. The linguistic line between genteel whites and lowly blacks is held in place through all her attempts to expand the boundaries of middle-class sympathy to include the slave. At times there is a noticeable schizophrenia in this mixture of egalitarian intentions and snobbish means, as in this passage that treats all races as one, but not all modes of speech: "Black Sam, upon this, scratched his woolly pate, which, if it did not contain very profound wisdom, still contained a great deal of a particular species much in demand among politicians of all complexions and countries, and vulgarly denominated 'knowing which side the bread is buttered'" (61). The need for quotation marks here to preserve her distance from the vernacular is symptomatic of the aesthetic way she treats the "vulgar" throughout. Like Jay Gatsby, Fitzgerald's parvenu, she picks her words with a care that betrays the anxiety as well as the allegiance she and her readers shared as a class.

Two of her allegiances, however, inform the novel still more fundamentally than class. These are anchored to a pair of comparably sacred, omnipotent authorities: mothers and the New Testament. Indeed, often it is impossible to tell them apart. "*She* was *divine!*" is what Augustine St. Clare says about his mother; "She was a direct embodiment and personification of the New Testament" (263). St. Clare, Tom's master during the novel's middle portions, is a middle-aged, well-traveled sophisticate whom worldly experience has turned into a cynical aesthete. But Tom's faith, coupled to the example of his own little daughter, brings him home to Christianity, and in this Victorian version of the parable of the prodigal son, home is presided over by a doting mother—and so, apparently, is heaven, as we learn at St. Clare's death bed:

> "His mind is wandering," said the doctor.
> "No! it is coming HOME, at last!" said St. Clare. . . .
> So he lay for a few moments. They saw that the mighty hand was on him. Just before the spirit parted, he opened his eyes, with a sudden light, as of joy and recognition, and said "*Mother!*" and then he was gone. (370)

The might of a mother's hand is underscored by Simon Legree's bad dreams, which are haunted by the holy ghost of his doting mother. Evil, Stowe reminds her readers, is an alchemist that can convert "things sweetest and holiest to phantoms of horror and affright." To Legree's "demoniac heart of sin," his mother's "forgiving love" becomes the "fiery" proof of his damnation (434); he is as terrified of a lock of golden hair that recalls his mother as a vampire is of the Cross. At night, it seems, grown men go back to that state St. Clare arrives at on the verge of death: "that of a wearied child who sleeps" (370). The way Legree's Victorian mother, American ancestor of Portnoy's Jewish one, reigns over his pre-Freudian nightmares makes him pathetic rather than villainous, but Stowe cannot imagine an adversary more potent than mother love. Tom's parting advice to George Shelby, young son of his first master, is Stowe's revision of the first commandment: "Don't be gettin' into any of them foolish ways boys has of gettin' too big to mind their mothers" (124). As a means of salvation, minding your mother almost makes God and the Bible superfluous.

This idolatry of motherhood might seem out of place in a devoutly Protestant novel, but the thematic prominence Stowe gives mothers and the way she regularly treats "maternal love" as a "supernatural power" (67) are not the consequences of her theology. They are the first principles of her cultural faith.[6] Stowe and her readers were nowhere more deeply in agreement, nor more apparently sure of themselves, than in their assumptions about the way the hand that rocked the cradle did indeed rule the world. As the recent feminist revisioning of the genteel tradition has noted, this belief can be seen as a fantasy by which women sought to compensate for the changing patterns of nineteenth-century American life; as the growth of a capitalist marketplace economy marginalized women, as they felt increasingly excluded from socially productive roles, they converted their place in the home's domestic "economy" into a moral and emotional throne. Maternal "power" was "supernatural" precisely because it was not political, or even real.[7] That this was a form of fantasy, however, just increased the need middle-class women felt to insist on it, especially in the pages of the books, magazines, and annuals that were admitted into the home.

What kind of reverence and respect was due to mothers is what we hear in the archly smug tone of Stowe's voice when she talks about Rachel Halliday, the woman whose "face and form . . . made 'mother' seem the most natural word in the world" (163): "Bards have written of the cestus of Venus, that turned the heads of all the world in successive generations. We had rather, for our part, have the cestus of Rachel Halliday, that kept heads from being turned, and made everything go on harmoniously. We think it is more suited to our modern days, decidedly" (169). *Eros* is thus replaced by mother love, and even *caritas* is made to wear Rachel's apron. As Rachel's son says, "Mother can do almost everything" (170); when she presides over breakfast, not only do the chicken and ham seem glad to be sizzling in the pan ("as if they rather enjoyed being cooked than otherwise"!), but also the "dark, misanthropic, pining, atheistic doubts" of George Harris, an embittered runaway slave, "melt away" before the unction of her "motherliness" (170). No scene in *Uncle Tom's Cabin* is set in a church, but there are many that take place in various kitchens, where the table supplants the altar, and a mother's cooking becomes the eucharist. At Rachel's table this is made explicit: "There was so much motherliness and full-heartedness even in the way she passed a plate of cakes or poured a cup of coffee, that it seemed to put a spirit into the food and drink she offered" (170). Where institutional Christianity puts the wine and wafer, where Emerson put instead the orator's eloquence, Stowe (and her readers) put homemade cakes and coffee.

Stowe's self-gratulatory celebration of home and mother does serve her polemical purpose. The most persistent way she dramatizes the evil of slavery is to describe its brutal impact on family life; there are only a few chapters that do not at least refer to the forced separation of mother and child by the slave trader or on the auction block, and more than a few times that rending is described in detail. In that famous scene when Eliza flees across the ice on the Ohio River, she is presented not as a woman escaping the personal horror or injustice of slavery but as a mother desperately trying to keep her child. One lesson that Stowe learned from Charles Dickens was that the mass audience could be made to feel an injustice more readily than it could be logically convinced of one. Given her audience of "home readers," the most effective heartstring for her to tug at was the maternal one. Susan Warner had already demonstrated the potency of this motif: in *The Wide, Wide World* all the emotional urgency of the story derives from the fact that little Ellen Montgomery is forced to leave her mother. They are separated by an act of God—Mrs. Montgomery's failing health. Stowe's novel, while often fully as sentimental, deserves credit for exploiting this motif for socially redeeming purposes. In her novel, mothers and children are separated by the remediable acts of men.

Yet if motherhood as an abstract value dominates Stowe's portrayal of slavery, so does Christianity. That modicum of romantic love that has not been displaced onto maternal instinct, for instance, is transposed into the all-inclusive terms of the New Testament: "And your loving me," George Harris tells his wife, "why, it was almost like raising one from the dead! I've been a new man ever since!" (225) Throughout the novel Stowe keeps two plot lines in motion; both begin in Kentucky, then move in opposite directions. The Harrises head north, to Canada, freedom, and family reunion; Tom is carried south, to a lonely death at Legree's hands. It would, however, be heretical to decide that Tom's story ends any less happily than Eliza and George's. Here is Stowe's own coercive synopsis of that story, offered just before Tom is killed:

The longest way must have its close, —the gloomiest night will wear on to a morning. An eternal, inexorable lapse of moments is ever hurrying the day of the evil to an eternal night, and the night of the just to an eternal day. We have walked with our humble friend thus far in the valley of slavery; first through flowery fields of ease and indulgence, then through heart-breaking separation from all that man holds dear. Again, we have waited with him in a sunny island, where generous hands concealed his chains with flowers; and, lastly, we have followed him when the last rays of earthly hope went out in the night, and seen how, in the blackness of earthly darkness, the firmament of the unseen has blazed with stars of new and significant lustre. (474)

It is fair to say that Tom's movement southward does work to initiate Stowe's readers into the true horror of slavery, the institutional realities that always underlay the benign appearance slavery assumed at the Shelby plantation. As a secular movement, Tom's journey is a fall: from a type of paradise to an unmistakable inferno; in her descriptions of Legree's plantation, Stowe uses the whole glossary of Christian melodrama: "sooty," "diabolical," "fiendish," and so on.

But at the same time, when we consider the journey of Tom's soul through that emblematic valley, we see that he has not been moving downward at all, but upward, to heaven. And the diction and imagery of Stowe's synopsis require us to set his story in this allegorical context, where worldly night translates as eternal day. Four times in her novel she specifically mentions *Pilgrim's Progress*, the definitive Protestant account of a soul's pilgrimage to salvation. There were probably almost as many copies of Bunyan's book in Victorian America as there were parlors; it is the book that Huck Finn, unacculturated as he is, tries to read at the Grangerford plantation on the Mississippi just about the time that Tom would have passed by on his way south. Brought up outside the pale of genteel Christianity, Huck does not know how to interpret the allegory: it was "about a man that left his family it didn't say why." But Stowe's readers knew why: because in the Gospels Jesus had said that to be worthy of the kingdom of heaven, a man must leave everything, even sons and daughters, to follow him. Because it dramatized the precepts of the New Testament so vividly, and thus made theology entertaining to the mass public that read novels, Bunyan's allegory supplied the popular writers of mid-nineteenth-century America with their essential plot. Homelessness, pilgrimage, suffering, trial, growing through adversity toward God—these are the basics of Uncle Tom's story, and Ellen Montgomery's, and Gerty Flint's, the central character of *The Lamplighter*.

Ellen and Gerty are young, female, white, Anglo-Saxon Protestants. Certainly Stowe displays a large amount of sociological courage in stepping outside this pattern of narcissistic self-reinforcement to put a black male slave at the center of her novel. The most daring aspect of the novel, probably, is the way that in the central chapters she spiritually "marries" Tom to the book's heroine, Eva St. Clare, who is young, female, white, and so on. As Stowe points out through the character of Miss Ophelia, even in the free North the prejudice against blacks was deeply rooted. And as she reminds us many times, the official attitude toward Tom labeled him "chattel property." To refute both private prejudices and legalistic dehumanization, she gives Tom not just an immortal soul but a beautiful, redemptive one. By the end he becomes a black Christ, crucified by Legree yet able to forgive his oppressors. We may feel, however, that it would have been better for the cause of the slaves she is pleading so earnestly if she had made less of Tom as a Christian and more of him as a man, because the terrible paradox of Christianity is that it is precisely through suffering and submission that one earns immortal glory. Each third of her novel contains a character who resists or even rebels against fate. George Harris is prepared to kill for his and his family's freedom. Augustine St. Clare cannot accept the death of his daughter. Cassy—to the modern reader probably the most compelling character in the book— is Stowe's version of the Romantic dark heroine, within whose black eyes can be read a history of sexual oppression and abuse (which, needless to say, Stowe leaves largely unwritten) and fierce contempt for both her master and for the God who permits a man like Legree to exist. Cassy, as we first meet her, belongs in the company of Hawthorne's Hester Prynne and Melville's Ahab and Pierre. But doctrinally, resisting fate is rejecting Providence. "Bitter" is the adjective Stowe repeatedly, even obsessively, uses to describe these characters, all of whom must finally be soothed and tamed;[8] the only response to personal suffering that Stowe's Christianity permits is the posture of resignation that has made Tom infamous:

> "O, Mas'r [he tells St. Clare], when I was sold away from my old woman and the children, I was jest a'most broke up. I felt as if there warn't nothin' left; and then the good Lord, he stood by me, and he says, 'Fear not, Tom;' and he brings light and joy into a poor feller's soul, —makes all peace; and I's so happy, and loves everybody, and feels willin' jest to be the Lord's, and have the Lord's will done, and be put jest where the Lord wants to put me."
> (352–53)

Uncle Tom does not actually deserve the particular reputation that he has. Although he is willing to be a good and faithful servant wherever the Lord puts him, he never ceases to want his own freedom; he tells Cassy that she should escape from Legree because her soul is imperiled; and in fact he dies because he will not betray where she and a fellow slave are hiding. The quarrel with Tom as a stereotype of the happy darky should more properly be with Stowe's Victorian Christianity, which thematically subordinates her concern with this life to the next. This might even seem to imply that slavery, by institutionalizing suffering and submission, is good for the slave's salvation, just as in Warner's novel several people point out to Ellen that it is for the best that she has been separated from her mother, else she might not have come to Him on whom her eternal happiness depends. "It is through suffering only," Cummins insists in *The Lamplighter*, that "we are made perfect."[9] Like Bunyan's Christian, Tom attains a "Victory" within the novel, but it is not over slavery. It is over religious doubt and his stubbornly human heart. Stowe's valuations become particularly problematic at the end of Tom's life, when he instructs young George Shelby, the son of his first master who finds Tom dying at Legree's, to tell his family and fellow slaves back in Kentucky "'to follow me—follow me!'" (486). He even rebukes George's moral rage against Legree: "'He an't done me no real harm, —only opened the gate of the kingdom for me; that's all!'" (487) This missionary zeal for martyrdom seems to put much too high a price on the next world, and to sell one's claims in this world much too cheaply.[10] As a protest novel designed to indict the "living dramatic reality" of slavery, *Uncle Tom's Cabin* is undermined by its other identity as an allegory about "a Christian soul goin' to glory," for there living realities are referred to higher, scriptural meanings. But of course, although she is writing on their behalf, Stowe is not writing for the slaves.

Her literary priorities—seeing reality through the eyes of a mother who cherishes the New Testament—reach a quintessentially Victorian-American apotheosis in the figure of Evangeline St. Clare, the blue-eyed, blond-haired little girl whose exemplary life and death define the spiritual dimensions that even a character like Cassy must be humanly diminished to fit. Eva is an impossible child, more attractive than Ellen or Gerty only because, though the daughter of slaveholders, she nonetheless feels deeply the wrongs of slavery. Yet what is most amazing about her is that, while Stowe and her readers agreed that Eva was too good, too innocent, too saintly to live very long in this polluted world, they would have been astounded at the thought that little Eva is too good to be true.[11] To realize how thoroughly conditioned *Uncle Tom's Cabin* is by genteel ideals, we need only quote Stowe's first description of Eva, which doubtless was intended to "daguerreotype" her as well:

> Her face was remarkable less for its perfect beauty of feature than for a singular and dreamy earnestness of expression, which made the ideal start when they looked at her, and by which the dullest and most literal were impressed, without exactly knowing why. The shape of her head and the turn of her

neck and bust was peculiarly noble, and the long golden-brown hair that floated like a cloud around it, the deep spiritual gravity of her violent blue eyes, shaded by heavy fringes of golden brown —— (175)

Enough. No picture emerges from this mélange of euphemism (bust), cliché (like a cloud), Sunday school eloquence (spiritual gravity), and abstraction (noble, beauty), but then again, the passage explicitly devalues a literal sensibility. Stowe and her readers united in prizing the ability to see the reality that was not there, whether that was the hand of Providence, maternal sovereignty, or little Eva. They read this passage and *saw* someone, but only because they had agreed beforehand on the meaning and validity of these terms. We read this passage, and all we can see is the pattern of pieties by which they understood reality.[12]

This description is typical of Stowe's diction throughout, which linguistically leaves the ideals of her refined, Christian, lady readers snugly in place. Yet those contemporary readers were unaware of the way Stowe reconfirms their preconceptions, were instead roused by her book to a passionate conviction that something had to be changed. What remains for us to note is the equally consistent way Stowe puts her novel in opposition to American culture. In this context, even diction becomes a polemical resource. We could look, for example, at the dialogue in chapter 9, "In Which It Appears That a Senator Is But a Man." That title itself suggests one of Stowe's most incisive moral arguments: that man's existence in society is a fallen one, that the social roles he plays alienate him from his individual humanity. This was one of the cardinal points Emerson made in his transcendentalist attack on society: "Whoso would be a man, must be a nonconformist." The conversation Stowe records between Senator Bird and his wife further measures the distance between the statehouse, where laws are enacted, and a mother's home, where life is lived, and shows as clearly as Orwell would how the official language of politics serves to obscure the truth. The husband has just returned from Columbus, where he has helped pass a law " 'forbidding people to help off the slaves' " as a means of " 'quieting the excitement' " stirred up by " 'these reckless Abolitionists' " and reassuring " 'our brethren in Kentucky.' " The verbal distinctions here between slaves and people, reckless and brotherly, were exactly the ones by which politicians sought to preserve the status quo. Mrs. Bird sees through them in eloquently plain language:

> "And what is the law? It don't forbid us to shelter these poor creatures a night, does it, and to give 'em something comfortable to eat, and a few old clothes, and send them quietly about their business."
>
> "Why, yes, my dear; that would be aiding and abetting, you know." (99)

"Aiding and abetting" is the legal abstraction Bird relies on to obfuscate the Christian virtues of love and charity. Stowe's contempt for the politic desire to play this game with matters of conscience is no mere liberal one. By the end of the chapter, after Senator Bird, brought face to face with the breathing reality of slavery, has helped Eliza to evade Haley's pursuit, he has become more than a man, more even than a nonconformist. He is now an outlaw.

As an exhortation toward "Civil Disobedience," Stowe's novel is as radical as Thoreau's essay. Her desire to write it may have been initially prompted by the passage of the Fugitive Slave Law, which made the North an accomplice in the business of catching and keeping slaves. But her indictment of American society—North and South—is far more sweeping. Again and again she attacks and subverts the "constitutional relations" (80) of the United States. Alongside her consoling Christian moralism one finds her scathing treatment of institutional Christianity in America: "the dead sea of respectable churches" (214) in which the values of the New Testament are disgraced by the very "ministers of Christianity" (158). Every figure in the novel is defined by his or her relationship to Jesus, but the only white Christians about whom Stowe has no reservations are the Quakers, a group that has embraced St. Clare's subversive conclusion about the antisocial consequences of true Christianity: "'My view of Christianity is such,' he added, 'that I think no man can consistently profess it without throwing the whole weight of his being against this monstrous system of injustice that lies at the foundation of all our society'" (365). The foundation of *all* society: St. Clare includes the wage relations between employer and laborer in exactly the same moral category as the chattel relationship between master and slave, thus lining Stowe's novel up with the *Communist Manifesto* Marx had published three years earlier.

Indeed, the business of catching slaves is only the most visible part of the complicity that, in Stowe's account, despite the protestations of her southern critics, binds North and South together in a monstrous system of evil—the very "business" of slavery. Perhaps her most radical, most tough-minded assault is the case she draws up against "business" itself, though that too is certainly a cherished American piety. She uses the word repeatedly. Aptly, it is spoken first in the novel by Haley, the slave trader: "Well, I've got just as much conscience as any man in business can afford to keep" (12). It is mentioned frequently in a later conversation between him and two other slave traders as they draw up a contract for running down Eliza and her son. Stowe expands her use of the word until one begins to feel that business in America is inseparable from this trade in human flesh. When, for instance, the steamboat carrying Tom to market in New Orleans and proudly flying the American flag reaches the Mississippi, Stowe offers a culturally panoramic view:

> What other river of the world bears on its bosom to the ocean the wealth
> and enterprise of such another country? —a country whose products em-
> brace all between the tropics and the poles! Those turbid waters, hurrying,
> foaming, tearing along, an apt resemblance of that headlong tide of business
> which is poured along its wave by a race more vehement and energetic than
> any the old world ever saw. . . .

These sentences are further proof of Stowe's brilliant ear for dialect, in this case the tub-thumping bombast of America's chambers of commerce. But with one sentence more she erases this materialist complacency; precisely because of its produce, the Mississippi is a river of tears that may yet be a river of fire:

> Ah! would that they did not also bear along a more fearful sight, —the tears
> of the oppressed, the sighs of the helpless, the bitter prayers of poor, igno-
> rant hearts to an unknown God—unknown, unseen and silent, but who will
> yet "come out of his place to save all the poor of the earth!" (172)

And when still later she recounts how a young quadroon named Emmeline is sold away from her mother to Simon Legree to satisfy her owner's creditor, "the respectable firm of B. & Co., in New York," Stowe pointedly establishes the economic bond between business offices and Legree's plantation in the swamp. Like the slave trader, Brother B. has just as much conscience as any man in business can afford: "He didn't like trading in slaves . . . but, then, there were thirty thousand dollars in the case; and that was rather too much money to be lost for a principle" (383).

As Stowe continues, through forty-five chapters, to point with irony and indignation at such "Select Incidents of Lawful Trade," her book gathers enormous moral force. It becomes a jeremiad as rhetorically compelling as any ever preached. The expression she puts on her prose evokes the look that Moses must have had on his face, fresh from his communion with God, holding the Ten Commandments in his hand and watching Israel worshipping the golden calf. The America she observes every day, in its constitutional relations, in its business affairs, from its legislatures and pulpits as well as on its plantations, damns itself. It is found in default of its political principles, as embodied in the Declaration of Independence, and its professed moral laws, as laid down in the New Testament. Like a swollen river, it is rushing toward Armageddon, for the New Testament whose values she defers to is a gospel of wrath as well as love. Even little Eva's favorite chapter is the Book of Revelation, and it is on a sustained note of apocalyptic urgency, a kind of moral wail, that Stowe ends her own "Concluding Remarks." "Christians!" she cries, leaving her audience without a shred of complacency to consider the last judgment of the new world, "every time that you pray that the kingdom of Christ may come, can you forget that prophecy associates, in dread fellowship, the *day of vengeance* with the year of his redeemed?" (519)

Thus this book is split right down the middle between confirming and condemning Victorian America. Stowe hangs "God will damn our country" right next to the sampler that says "God bless our home." It is time to note where she draws the line. While her critique of capitalism, like her portrayal of Tom's journey as a pilgrimage, is made sub specie aeternitatis, there is a still more striking dichotomy in the novel than the one between secular and spiritual realms. Unconsciously, Stowe segregates the culture she reflects into two worlds. As in that conversation between Mr. and Mrs. Bird, what is smugly affirmed throughout the novel is the world of women—home, mothers, gentility. What is radically attacked is the world of men—business, law, politics. Even Christianity is divided between the domestic and the institutional, the kitchen table and the pulpit, where the crucial but unacknowledged distinction is again the sexual one. It is frustrating to realize that Stowe, despite her moral clarity and sheer brilliance as a polemicist, never notices this split. There is one sentence in her last chapter that tries to make a connection: "If the mothers of the free states had all felt as they should, in times past, the sons of the free states would not have been the holders, and, proverbially, the hardest masters of slaves" (515). Potentially this taps a reservoir of maternal guilt at least as vast as that of maternal love she had drawn on so often earlier, but it alone cannot reconcile the two halves of the book.

Nowhere is this split clearer than at the end of the plot line that follows the Harrises to Canada. There the tone is very different from the fury Stowe whips up in her concluding exhortation; warmth and coziness prevail:

> The scene now changes to a small, neat tenement, in the outskirts of Montreal; the time, evening. A cheerful fire blazes on the hearth; a tea-table, covered with a snowy cloth, stands prepared for the evening meal. In one corner of the room was a table covered with a green cloth, where was an open writing-desk, pens, paper, and over it a shelf of well-selected books.
>
> This was George's study. . . .
>
> At this present time, he is seated at the table, making notes from a volume of the family library he has been reading.
>
> "Come, George," says Eliza, "you've been gone all day. Do put down that book, and let's talk, while I'm getting tea, —do."
>
> And little Eliza seconds the effort, by toddling up to her father, and trying to pull the book out of his hand, and install herself on his knee as a substitute.

"O, you little witch!" says George, yielding, as, in such circumstances, man always must. (497–98)

To Stowe and her readers this genteel setting, complete with cheerful hearth, tea-table and well-selected books, presided over by women, regulated by what Hawthorne called "homely witchcraft,"[13] was the full secular equivalent to the heaven that Tom attains in death. To be sure, there is one sharp irony in Stowe's account of it: only in Canada can these Americans be free to be a family; in a stunning reversal of America's self-serving mythology, she had earlier described the joy with which the Harrises had hailed "the blessed English shores" (451). But the more urgent irony Stowe wholly misses. To be genteel, tea–tables must be covered with a snowy cloth; study tables, with a green one. And where did the cloths that Eliza doubtless washes and irons and keeps very neat come from? Perhaps the very cotton field where Uncle Tom died.

This is the point that Thoreau makes in *Walden*, his antislavery work. John Field, an Irish immigrant struggling toward gentility through his own Slough of Despond,

> rated it as a gain in coming to America, that here you could get tea, and coffee, and meat every day. But the only true America is that country where you are at liberty to pursue such a mode of life as may enable you to do without these, and where the state does not endeavor to compel you to sustain the slavery and war and other superfluous expenses which directly or indirectly result from the use of such things.[14]

What Thoreau saw, but Stowe remains blind to, is that it was Victorian habits of consumption as much as male business practices that caused the economic and moral injustices she protests.[15] *Walden* has many affinities with *Uncle Tom's Cabin*, including a narrative reliance on the plot of *Pilgrim's Progress* (though Thoreau applies the terms of Christianity to what Carlyle called natural supernaturalism). But Thoreau's emphasis is on white slavery, on how an individual's mind is trapped by the dominant prejudices of his culture. Harriet Beecher Stowe is a case in point. Making money is tainted, but spending it tastefully on decorous superfluities is a sacramental act.[16] Little Eva must be daintily dressed—"always in white" (176)—though it never occurs to Stowe, as it would to Thoreau, to count the number of slave hours that were spent picking the cotton to make her wardrobe. The "graceful," "beautiful," "elegant," "exquisite" furnishings in Eva's bedroom are described with a lavish and doting detail that is the narrative equivalent to a shopping spree (333–34). Rachel's table must groan with food. Even an ex-slave like Eliza needs an elaborate set of cotton tablecloths. These are the feminine pieties her book never challenges.[17] Indeed, her tribute to them is as heartfelt as any part of her protest.

When Stowe's novel was published, its immediate popularity alarmed the guardians of the status quo because it seemed like a wedge driven between the North and the South. To anyone interested in American culture it is still a disconcerting document for the way it reflects a kind of Mason-Dixon line between the sexes. By the mid-nineteenth century, apparently, American husbands and American wives lived culturally at such extremes that "home" and "the wide, wide world" might as well have been located on two different planets. The only link between them, it seems, was the relationship between mothers and sons, which was consequently made to bear a huge and suffocating burden.[18] To the student of American literature, however, there is one further consequence to note. If Stowe's endorsement of conventional gentility hobbled her as a social critic, it nonetheless gave her great freedom as a novelist. Because unconsciously she could divorce the essentially male evil she was attacking from the essentially female audience she was addressing, she felt invited to use all her powers as a writer, all the resources of popular fiction. That is why *Uncle Tom's Cabin* is the most Dickensian of all Victorian American novels. For Dickens identified the social evils he wanted to attack chiefly with the neofeudal aristocracy of rank and wealth; thus he could use his genius to entertain as well as instruct his middle-class reading public without feeling as though he were violating his integrity either as a writer or as a critic. The gender division served Stowe the same way this class division served Dickens: she and her home readers were on the same side.

This was an encouragement to expression that her male contemporaries never felt. Hawthorne's work makes a number of concessions to Victorian appetites and expectations. His light heroines—Phoebe, Priscilla, Hilda—resemble Eva, Ellen, and Gerty in ways that often make modern readers wince; two of the twenty-four chapters in *The Scarlet Letter* dramatically recount the threat of the Puritan patriarchs to separate Hester and her little daughter Pearl; his most popular story, "The Gentle Boy" (1832), is unfortunately one that Susan Warner would have been proud to have written herself. On the whole, though, as I shall discuss later, Hawthorne managed brilliantly to write for his audience without sacrificing his vision and to enjoy at least a moderate degree of success. Yet it did not seem so to him. In 1855, while everyone around him was reading *The Lamplighter*, he wrote a friend to complain bitterly about "that damned mob of scribbling women" who wrote the most popular stories of his time. "I should have no chance of success," he went on, "while the public taste is preoccupied with their trash—and I should be ashamed of myself if I did succeed."[19]

Melville's fate reveals still more poignantly the cost of a novelist's ambivalence toward his or her prospective audience and misgivings about potential success. In the middle of his short, anguished career, Melville wrote "Hawthorne and His Mosses" (1850) to plead with the American public to nurture the American writer, and the audience to whom he looks is, like Stowe's, an explicitly maternal one: "Let America then prize and cherish her writers . . . she has good kith and kin of her own, to take to her bosom."[20] Yet for Melville, as for Thoreau, this audience defined reality by the very preconceptions from which he was trying to struggle free. Thus Melville could not decide whether to write *for* or *at* those readers with whom Stowe felt so much at home; any desire to please them seemed to him a temptation to betray himself. His works too are split down the middle, but we have to draw the line in a different place— where Melville did: between himself and his only available audience. "What I feel most moved to write," he told Hawthorne, "that is banned, —it will not pay. Yet, altogether, write the *other* way I cannot. So the product is a final hash, and all my books are botches."[21] He began *Pierre* (1852) determined to bridge these two extremes, and he began aptly, telling how Pierre Glendenning was driven away from his mother into the wider world. But as he narrated the tragedy of Pierre's naive attempt to be a writer, all his own accumulated resentments returned. Near the end, just before Pierre spits on his manuscript, Melville disgustedly repudiates his responsibilities as a narrator: "Nor does any canting showman here stand by."[22] This is a rejection of more than the culture. It dismisses the very role that Dickens and Stowe could play as novelists. Any attempt to communicate with, much less to entertain the public, turns language into cant, and the writer into a debased showman.

Thoreau came to the same disgusted conclusion: "If you would get money as a writer or lecturer, you must be popular, which is to go down perpendicularly."[23] Yet there is a better reason than money to seek popularity. In keeping with Romantic and Victorian notions of aesthetics, both Stowe and Melville gave the novelist a prophetic office. Fiction was a means, not an end; ultimately, it was a way to tell the truth. Pierre speaks for both when he declares that his ambition as a writer is to "gospelize the world anew!"[24] But the Old Testament prophets were commissioned directly by God. Stowe put in a claim for that sanction, yet finally, of course, the novelist as prophet—if her words are to have any larger authority, if his vision is to matter in the world—has to depend upon the appreciation of an audience. In his unwillingness to concede to the expectations of the American public, Melville lost, though just as unwillingly, his chance to arouse or redeem them, to tell them anything at all. Thoreau similarly sacrificed any opportunity to reach his contemporaries to his need to define himself. He could jokingly refer to the "mothers" in the audience of *Walden*,[25] but he could only write for them by casting them into a role they could never have been expected to accept. In her first novel, on the other hand, Stowe became the only American novelist of her generation to cross the gap between great and popular fiction, although she was able to do so only because of the other great divide in her culture. What she felt moved to write was a vehement condemnation of American society. No one can doubt her sincerity, or her book's literary and moral power. But at the same time she wrote a best-selling novel that paid very well and deeply satisfied its readers' tastes—because the society she attacked was off at the office, while the one that bought books stayed home to read them.

Chapter V

THE DEMOCRATIC NONESUCH:
SOUTHWESTERN HUMOR

> . . . he rolled up the curtain, and the next minute the
> king come a-prancing out on all fours, naked; and
> he was painted all over, ring-streaked-and-striped, all
> sorts of colors, as splendid as a rainbow. And—but never
> mind the rest of his outfit, it was just wild, but it was
> awful funny. The people most killed themselves laugh-
> ing; and when the king got done capering, and ca-
> pered off behind the scenes, they roared and clapped
> and stormed and haw-hawed till he come back and
> done it over again; and after that, they made him do
> it another time.
> —Mark Twain, *Adventures of Huckleberry Finn*

WHAT ABOUT the husbands of Stowe's home readers? What contemporary American literature were they reading? Obviously, there is no precise
answer to so large a question.[1] Given the stir the book was making, they
would certainly have read *Uncle Tom's Cabin*. For the same reason, a
great many men doubtless read such best-selling novels as *The Wide,
Wide World* and *The Lamplighter*.[2] During the 1850s the best-selling
male American writers were essayists. Emerson's revised and collected
lectures on *Representative Men* (1850), *English Traits* (1856), and *The
Conduct of Life* (1860) did well, but the decade's most popular male essayists were "Ik Marvel" (Donald Mitchell), who published *Reveries of a
Bachelor* in 1850, Henry Tuckerman, author of *The Optimist* (1850), and
George William Curtis, who wrote *Prue and I* (1856).[3] Yet as Ann
Douglas has shown, these essayists owed their popularity mainly to
women readers; their stances, voices, and concerns were defined by the
tastes and assumptions of the audience that subscribed to *Godey's Lady
Book* and bought domestic fiction.[4] Although we can assume that men
also read these works, they can't really give us access to the audience that
Melville, for example, had in mind when he instructed a woman friend to
warn all women (and gentle fastidious people) away from *Moby-Dick*[5]: the
audience, in other words, of male readers in a "feminized" culture.

Probably the best place to look for the reflection of that audience is the body of texts that are collectively referred to as Southwestern Humor. The earliest text in this tradition is, by most accounts, A. B. Longstreet's *Georgia Scenes*, which was published in Augusta, Georgia, in 1835 and reprinted in New York in 1840. Southwestern Humor, however, flourished as a popular genre during the 1840s and 1850s primarily through the agency of a New York weekly periodical called the *Spirit of the Times;* edited by a former New Englander named William T. Porter, the *Spirit* was aimed exclusively at a male readership. By the early 1840s, a staple of its pages were letters from gentlemen of the Southwest—especially Arkansas, Alabama, Mississippi, Kentucky, and Louisiana—about local manners, customs, and characters. These letters proved so popular that Porter kept calling on his subscribers to send more, and published two anthologies of them as *The Big Bear of Arkansas and Other Sketches* (1845) and *A Quarter Race in Kentucky* (1847). Other anthologies followed, and individual authors collected and published their works separately; among these the most popular were Johnson Jones Hooper's *Some Adventures of Simon Suggs* (1845), Thomas Bangs Thorpe's *Mysteries of the Backwoods* (1846), Henry Clay Lewis's *Odd Leaves from the Life of a Louisiana "Swamp Doctor"* (1850), and Joseph G. Baldwin's *Flush Times of Alabama and Mississippi* (1853). George Washington Harris could not persuade anyone to publish a collection of his tales until after the Civil War, but Sut Lovingood, Harris's long-legged protagonist, first appeared in Porter's *Spirit* in 1854, and *Sut Lovingood's Yarns* (1867) has to be included among these other works from the 1840s and 1850s.[6]

Popularity here is a relative term. Only two works from this body of texts make it onto Frank Luther Mott's list of American "better sellers"—Longstreet's and Baldwin's.[7] E. Douglas Branch, Fred Lewis Patee, and Carl Bode do not mention Southwestern Humor at all in their cultural histories of mid-nineteenth-century America.[8] In his study of *The Popular Book* in America, James D. Hart devotes only one paragraph to it.[9] While Porter optimistically boasted about forty thousand subscribers in 1856, the separately published volumes of Southwestern Humor usually sold between fifteen and twenty-five thousand copies. They sold better than, say, *The Scarlet Letter* and Melville's most successful books, but did not command anything like the sales figures of the best-selling women writers. After Longstreet's first edition of *Georgia Scenes*, however, these books almost all appeared from the country's major publishing centers of New York and Philadelphia, and were read by a national audience.

A national audience of men. The subtitle of Porter's journal—"A Chronicle of the Turf, Agriculture, Field Sports, Literature, and the Stage"—warned women readers away, and the writers took advantage of this exclusion to treat in excess and detail the kind of material that was scrupulously unmentioned in genteel literature. In particular, the body and its various urges and appetites govern many of the sketches. In the pages of middle-class domestic fiction, bodies get sick and waste away from decorous diseases like consumption. In the pages of these humorists, the body gets drunk, gets horny, gets violent, and gets gouged, kicked, and often bounced across the landscape.

The Civil War destroyed the national audience's interest in the humor of the Old Southwest, and the texts in this tradition were largely neglected until the twentieth century. They were first rediscovered by the powers that shape the American canon by means of the critical interest in Mark Twain and William Faulkner, who were both clearly indebted to the techniques and situations developed by these humorists. Since then, most research and analysis of the genre has been done by scholars who are essentially folklorists in their orientation, and they have laid claim to these works as one of the clearest points of intersection between America's oral and written cultures. The kind of etiology evoked by Hennig Cohen and William B. Dillingham in their introduction to the standard modern anthology of the genre, *Humor of the Old Southwest*, is typical:

> By the 1830's the region was saturated with tall tales and comic stories that were laughed at over campfires, aboard rafts floating slowly under the stars, or in villages wherever men gathered. Then all over the South men, many of whom never thought of themselves principally as writers, began to compose humorous sketches for publication.[10]

True, the people on America's frontier did develop rich imaginative traditions of their own. But one of the most striking things about American culture is that, until the frontier was practically "closed," no American equivalents to the Grimm brothers appeared to sit down with the folk and transcribe the stories they invented and told each other.[11] What the kind of account that Cohen and Dillingham provide ignores is not so much the difference between oral and written storytelling, but the difference that audience makes. The works of the Southwestern Humorists were not written to be read around campfires or on board rafts. They were written to be read in the dens, the clubs, or the barbershops where their national male audience, the gentlemen on Porter's subscription list, were to be found.[12] The oral culture of the frontier was shaped by the experiences of the frontier, but it by no means follows, as James M. Cox has suggested, that "the ultimate power of Southwestern Humor lay in discovering through dialect the direct experience of the frontier."[13] The humorists did appropriate motifs from the oral culture, just as they imported local dialects and vernacular diction into their tales and sketches. The work of these writers, however, was shaped far more profoundly by the experience, the conscious and unconscious concerns, of the audience that read Southwestern Humor, and from which the writers themselves directly sprang. In other words, their texts should not be identified with the folk they wrote *about*, but rather, as I will try to show, with the gentlemen they were writing *for*.

It was Ernest Hemingway who said that "all modern American literature comes from one book by Mark Twain." If he meant this (he may have been trying to disguise his own deeper indebtedness to Henry James's thematic preoccupations and formal strategies), Hemingway must have been thinking of style: of the way that Mark Twain, by allowing Huck Finn to narrate his story in his own voice, opened the pages of American fiction to the language and perspective of American vernacular speech. Because Huck is barely literate, and culturally illiterate, his voice puts us in direct contact with the world of his experience, as opposed to the "world" that books, Sunday school teachers, and other agents of acculturation have preconceived. One of the great goals of modern literature is certainly to present, as Ezra Pound put it, "reality as never before." Southwestern Humor, it is often argued, deserves a place near the start of the path that leads through Huck to the culturally impoverished protagonists of Hemingway's fictions and to the other radically disillusioned characters of modernism. As Larzer Ziff writes about George Washington Harris, "decades before Mark Twain attempted through the concrete, nature-bound diction of Huck Finn to elicit a feeling larger than the homely details in which it was expressed, Harris, whose work Twain knew well, was experimenting with shabby American circumstances."[14] Ziff then cites the following description of Sicily Burns, in which Sut Lovingood's unmistakably vernacular voice is allowed to create its own version of the world:

> "She shows amung wimen like a sunflower amung dorg fennil, ur a hollyhawk in a patch ove smartweed. Sich a buzzim! Jis' think ove two snow balls wif a strawberry stuck but-ainded intu bof on em. She takes adzactly fifteen inches ove garter clar ove the knot, stans sixteen an' a 'alf hans hi, an' weighs one hundred an' twenty-six in her petticoatail afore brekfus'. She cudent crawl thru a whisky barrel wif bof heads stove out . . ."[15]

To compare this with descriptions of women in most other Victorian American fiction, including Poe's, Hawthorne's, or Melville's, is to be graphically reminded of how artificial and formal novelistic diction had become. Sut's use of "buzzim" subverts even as it evokes the pattern of euphemism by which the popular feminine writers idealized physical realities. Still more impressively, there is no other abstraction or literary cliché in Sut's vocabulary. All his points of reference, from the smartweed to the whisky barrel, derive immediately from his own experience. Since Sut's experience is clearly American, while mid-nineteenth-century linguistic conventions were based on British models, it is easy to understand why critics would want to claim for Harris and the other humorists a part in the development of "modern American literature." Here, for example, is how Jake Barnes describes Brett Ashley in *The Sun Also Rises*; although his voice is grammatically correct, in its use of firsthand experience and colloquial style it seems directly descended from Sut's: "Brett was damned good-looking. She wore a slipover jersey sweater and a tweed skirt, and her hair was brushed back like a boy's. . . . She was built with curves like the hull of a racing yacht, and you missed none of it with that wool jersey."

Yet there is a crucial difference. Brett is Lady Ashley, and while thematically "Lady" has a purely ironic resonance in Hemingway's novel (like "king" in *Huckleberry Finn*), it does help measure how antidemocratic, how inversely exclusive, is the reach of Sut's vernacular. Sicily Burns belongs to the lowest class of white property owners. The kinds of concrete details that give Sut's speech its stylistic vividness are not sociologically unloaded, for throughout the *Yarns* Harris is determined to keep Sut and his racy vernacular among the dog fennel and the whisky barrels. Mark Twain uses Huck's voice to record the lives of "quality" people like the Widow Douglas and the Grangerfords. Sut plays his pranks at home, where his "poor white" family is too poor to buy a plough horse, or at Negro revivals, lower-class sewing bees, or backwoods camp meetings where even the "passun" (parson) is barely literate, but Sut is never allowed to cross the class line that separates the Sicilys of his milieu from the ladies of Harris's. George, the laconic narrator who listens to and transcribes the yarns, encounters Sut only when business takes him out into the hills around Knoxville. In one of the tales, Sut asks him what would happen if he ever came into town, ever presumed to meet George in *his* world, while wearing the tow-linen gown he grew up in, and that establishes his place in the social order:

> "Say, George, wudn't yu like tu see me into one 'bout haf fadid, slit, an' a-walkin jis' so, up the middil street ove yure city church, a-aimin fur yure pew pen, an' hit chock full ove yure fine city gal friends, jis' arter the peopil hed sot down frum the fust prayer, an' the orgin beginnin tu groan; what wud yu du in sich a marigncy? Say hoss?"
>
> "Why, I'd shoot you dead, Monday morning before eight o'clock," was my reply.[16]

George's prim response makes explicit the gap that characterizes almost all of this "humor": the gap between the culturally privileged writers and the audience they wrote for, on the one hand, and the vernacular figures they wrote about, on the other. Actually, "vernacular" is a much more ceremonious epithet than any that would have been used at the time. When Poe reviewed Longstreet's *Georgia Scenes* in 1835, he praised it as "a portraiture of the manners of our South-Western peasantry."[17] Longstreet's work draws a different kind of line than Harris's narrator's threat, but it too is intended to keep the "peasantry" in its place; each portrait of backwoods society is framed by Longstreet's Addisonian prose, which, as Kenneth Lynn has said, draws "a *cordon sanitaire*, so to speak, between the morally irreproachable Gentleman and the tainted life he described."[18] The human landscape the humorists depicted is seldom allowed to escape this frame. Sometimes the gentlemanly frame dominates the text, as in Longstreet's book and Baldwin's *Flush Times*. Sometimes it recedes, as in Hooper's *Simon Suggs*. Sometimes it seems almost entirely absent, so that the rustic's vernacular speech and point of view are not immediately controlled by a genteel narrator, as in many of Sut's *Yarns* or in "Pete Whetstone's" letters from Arkansas. But here the texts will mislead us, unless we recall the context in which Southwestern Humor originally appeared.

"Whetstone's" letters, like the majority of works in this genre, were first published in the *Spirit of the Times*. This weekly paper was deliberately modeled after aristocratic British sporting magazines. Porter, its editor, did not hesitate to announce that it was "designed to promote the views and interests of but an infinitesimal division of those classes of society composing the great mass . . . we are addressing ourselves to gentlemen of standing, wealth and intelligence—the very corinthian columns of the community."[19] Harris's first Sut story, for instance, appeared in the *Spirit* on 4 November 1854, where it was surrounded by elegant reports on the racing season in London and Paris, scores from a New Jersey cricket club, advertisements for yachts, carriages, and thoroughbred horses, and a glowing account of the first medieval tournament in Kentucky, where "knights . . . clad in costly costume" chivalrously competed for the honor of naming "the Queen of Love and Beauty." This larger context, even more than Harris's condescendingly proper prose, helps us understand how his readers would have regarded Sut's story of his "'spectabil white famerly,'" with its hovel in the woods full of kids ("an' Catherin Second, an' Cleopatry Anthony, an' Jane Barnum Lind," and so on) and its "dad," Sut's father, who strips naked and impersonates a horse, pulling the plough across the field until he runs into a hornets nest and the real fun begins. No sketch of "peasant manners" published in the *Spirit* needed a specific frame to segregate its tattered characters from its well-dressed readers. It is interesting to note, though, that when Porter decided to republish fifty-three of the best sketches in his two anthologies, he was clearly anxious that "each story should be introduced with some appropriate remarks."[20] In these brief introductions he is mainly concerned to establish for a wider audience what readers of the *Spirit* would have taken for granted: the gentlemanly class standing of the various authors.[21] Choosing the epigraph for *The Big Bear*, the first anthology, from Shakespeare, Porter even encouraged his general readers to put the same distance between themselves and the shiftless Petes and Chunkeys of the tales: "This is your charge; you shall comprehend all vagrom men."

There is little to be gained by another simplification as vast as Hemingway's. Doubtless in some respects these humorists, to quote Porter's preface to *The Big Bear*, "conferred signal honour on the rising literature of America."[22] In their representations of frontier and village life they did develop a number of national resources—most notably, back country speech, character types, and customs. Yet if what they wrote about, to quote Porter again, opened "a new vein of literature . . . in this country,"[23] how they wrote about it only complicated, in fact probably hurt the efforts of contemporary American writers who had much more invested in the cause of the nation's literature. Southwestern Humor attained its popularity at exactly the time when authors like Melville and Whitman were self-consciously trying "to carry republican progressiveness into Literature."[24] The phrase is Melville's, from the essay on "Hawthorne and His Mosses" in which he pleads for an enlightened recognition of the prospects of American literature. Looking southwesterly himself, as well as toward the promise of democracy, Melville declares that "men not very much inferior to Shakespeare are this day being born on the banks of the Ohio."[25] Shakespeare was on Melville's mind because of the novel he had just begun; his ambition in *Moby-Dick* was to write the American equivalent of a Shakespearian tragedy. Thus he invokes as his Muse "thou great democratic God" who carried Andrew Jackson from the backwoods of Tennessee to the White House, the "just Spirit of Equality" that always locates the greatest men "among the kingly commons."[26] He claims for Ahab—"in all his Nantucket grimness and shagginess"—the aesthetic stature that Shakespeare reserved for "Emperors and Kings," the Old World's tragic heroes, and he writes in a prose that tries to erase the distinction between colloquial and literary diction. Similarly Whitman, in "Song of Myself," claims for his "barbaric yawp" and for the vernacular experience it celebrates the stature of sacred poetry; he promotes his representative American self, a dizzying conflation of backwoods roarer, urban rowdy, and revivalist preacher, to the rank of epic hero. In these unequivocally New World works, which seem to catch up all the grasping energy of frontier life, Melville and Whitman try to redefine European literary categories in terms of democratic values. As both would say, that is how American literature should reflect "the spirit of the times," and of the place.

The masculine audience to which Porter's *Spirit* was addressed was precisely that part of the reading public most likely to appreciate Melville's and Whitman's work. Indeed, Porter printed one of the few highly favorable American reviews of *Moby-Dick*. In his readers' minds, however, Southwestern Humor, much like a squatter despoiling a homesite, had already preempted the ground these works laid claim to. Because its governing assumption was that the men who lived in cabins along the riverbanks or in the backwoods were not at all superior to Shakespeare's clowns, it effectively made the idea of a noble tragedy or a heroic poetry of vernacular life unthinkable. By and large it practically insists that there is only one appropriate mode for portraying characters and events among the "commons": the mode of comedy, or humor, or, to speak most accurately—since comedy and humor as literary modes still depend, however subtly, on some sort of sympathetic identification between the reader and the characters he or she overlooks—the *mood* of ludicrousness.

For what is funny in the works of these "humorists"? Many of the sketches do work up recognizably comic situations, but most mainly depend on what the authors and readers alike perceive as the inherent ridiculousness of "life and manners" outside the pale of aristocratic or bourgeois culture.[27] In that 1854 number of the *Spirit* in which Sut first appeared, for instance, there is a letter from a gentleman recently arrived in California who travels into the local back country. He shares with the *Spirit*'s subscribers the amusement of "my first introduction into the real genuine Simonpure 'Pike County' society." He describes a wedding between two raw-knuckled yokels, arriving at his punch line when, at the wedding dinner, the bride reached for the grapes, and "her husband, with a look of horror, cried out, 'Ma-ry, don't eat any o' them grapes, cos you've had the diaree!'" This letter, which in its next paragraph talks respectfully about theatrical events in San Francisco, will never be reprinted in the anthologies of the genre. It makes no attempt to develop this incident into a sketch or tale. But the *Spirit* printed hundreds of letters like it, and in fact most southwestern "sketches" simply string together a series of paragraphs in this mood. In the basis of this writer's amusement, which he rightly presumes his readers will share, one gets a very frank sense of the class-bound ugliness that informs the genre as a whole.

"A Quarter Race in Kentucky," which was considered one of the best works in the genre, is entirely typical. Porter called it "perhaps the most humorous of its kind in the language,"[28] even though it contains only one joke—a cross-eyed judge at the finish line. Physical deformities play a prominent role in the genre, but of course that it has in common with a good deal of "humor." As Steve Martin has said, comedy is never pretty. What is generically characteristic about this sketch, however, is that its humor derives solely from class distinction: from the difference between a plough horse and a real thoroughbred, from the distance between the rituals of racing as "the sport of kings" and the crude way these Kentucky squatters desecrate them in their efforts to imitate their betters. It was written by Thomas Kirkman, who owned and raced thoroughbreds; he assumed that merely to expose the behavior of these uncouth frontiersmen is to be funny. In most of the sketches reprinted in Porter's two anthologies, in "That Big Dog Fight at Myers's," or "A Texan Joker 'In a Tight Place'," or "Billy Warrick's Courtship and Wedding," or "Life and Manners in Arkansas," or "Dick Harlan's Tennessee Frolic," or "A Day at Sol. Slice's," the writers expect to excite laughter simply by reporting rustic traits. Often they do not even bother to exaggerate them for comic effect; the sight of a hick wearing his first suit of store-bought clothes, or seeing a piano for the first time, or trying to waltz, or fighting, or courting, or preaching, was sufficiently hilarious. It is therefore not enough to say that these works discounted the possibility of a tragedy or poetry of the vernacular; even the implicit dignity that realism as an aesthetic bestows on everyday life was ruled out. In the boondocks, ostensibly, reality was comic; "their" everyday life, a source for "our" amusement.

There were, of course, exceptions to this patronizing attitude. The most notable is the work of Thomas Bangs Thorpe, who reveals a rare capacity to admire the backwoodsman. While most southwestern sketches are set in crudely social situations (camp meetings, dances, races, village "doggeries") and set their unmannered characters at odds with each other, Thorpe was one of the few writers who depicted the backwoodsman actually in the backwoods, where his ignorance of etiquette is less important than his knowledge of the wilderness. At the end of "Bob Herring, the Arkansas Bear Hunter" (reprinted in Porter's second anthology, A Quarter Race), Thorpe's citified narrator, who has gotten hopelessly tangled in the undergrowth while trying to catch up with the dogs and the bear, looks up to see Bob "stalking over the cane, like a colossus."[29] In Thorpe's best piece, "The Big Bear of Arkansas," Jim Doggett, another preemption squatter, tells another genteel narrator the story of his quest for "an *unhuntable bear*," and his tale develops the encounter between man and nature with a power and sense of awe that, as many critics have pointed out, anticipates *Moby-Dick* and Faulkner's "Bear." Yet if Thorpe clearly found much to value in the manliness of these figures, his work just as clearly betrays his anxiety about portraying them sympathetically. Doggett's tale veers abruptly toward burlesque at the end, when he recounts how he finally shot the bear one morning while literally "squatting" in the woods behind his cabin, tripping over the pants and underpants he had taken down from daily "habit." Thorpe closes the piece by firmly reasserting the narrator's cultured voice, in which he dissociates himself from the superstitions of Doggett and all other "children of the wood."[30] To call Bob Herring "a colossus" is to use an Old World standard to dignify him (a device Melville regularly uses in *Moby-Dick*), but in that sketch's opening paragraphs, Europe and the European haut monde with which readers of the *Spirit* identified serve to put all mere backwoodsmen in their place. Bob, for instance, has built his hut in a spot named "the Devil's Summer Retreat," and Thorpe begins by suavely contrasting this raw wilderness to "Brighton and Bath, Ballston or Saratoga." He quotes Milton and refers to Izaak Walton, and even his praise of the scene's natural sublimity imports a metaphor to disparage the squatter living there: "Associated with these scenes, they to him possess no sentiment; he builds his log cabin in a clearing made by his own hands, amid the surrounding grandeur, and it looks like a gipsy hut among the ruins of a Gothic cathedral."[31]

As nineteenth-century American literature struggled to define itself, this kind of neocolonial ambivalence took various forms. Washington Irving, widely admired and imitated by the Southwestern Humorists, only used the mock-heroic style in those of his works set on this side of the Atlantic. The way he uses it in a tale like "The Legend of Sleepy Hollow" betrays his anxiety about exposing American scenes and subjects to the eyes of the English-speaking reading public. Above all, he does not want to appear provincial, nor to be identified with the provincial characters he is writing about. The mock-heroic, which presumes a familiarity with the classics of European literature, nicely establishes his and his readers' superiority to the rustic material of his American tales—though it also, of course, diminishes the human meaning that can be attached to the lives his characters lead. Once Ichabod has been compared to a knight and his borrowed, broken-down nag to a charger, we can only be expected to laugh at him; nothing very serious can ever happen to him. Thorpe's uneasiness is similar, although provoked less by his ambivalence about nationality than by his anxiety about caste, as his analogy to gypsies indicates. By building cathedrals in the forests of Arkansas, by ultimately patting Jim Dog-gett on the head, he lets his contemporary audience know that, however attracted he may be to these shaggy protagonists, *his* world (like that audience's) remains larger, more refined, more cosmopolitan. Thorpe's attraction to these frontier "colossi" is undeniably sincere. If anything, he seems more reluctant to dissociate himself from them than to celebrate and enjoy them. But in the literary context created by the other Southwestern Humorists, and in the face of the still larger cultural context that governed their attitude, Thorpe dare not claim too much for Jim or Bob. Since he was not prepared to challenge the expectations of his audience, he ultimately had to confirm their prejudices.

Most of the other humorists show few signs of Thorpe's ambivalence. To them homespun or buckskin is just another form of motley. Their tales are an instance where American folklore and American literature intersect, but they do so at a right angle. Their intention was not to record the achievements of "peasant" culture but to mock and condemn its vulgarities: to attack the very assumption that it could be capable of cultural achievements. Thus they are less like the Grimm brothers than like Swift's Gulliver, that appalled anthropologist of Yahoo life and manners. On this point we can trust the judgment of Henry Watterson of Tennessee, who published the only anthology of Southwestern Humor that appeared between the Civil War and the end of the last century.[32] A man who served the Confederacy although he believed in the Union, who belonged to exactly the same class as most of the humorists and most of their audience, Watterson loved this literature. But he did not confuse it with folklore. In 1877 he read a lecture called "The South in Light and Shade" in which he attempted to reconstruct an audience for the humorists despite the hostility and distrust toward the South left over from the war. After reading appreciatively from Sut's adventure with "Parson John Bullen's Lizards," he summed up the intentions of the genre in this way: "It is not real life, indeed, but an attempt, in a rough way, to travesty the shams of the crude life sought to be portrayed and satirized."[33]

Travesty and satire are terms that come closer than "humor" to the writers' aesthetic. As in all satire, the crudities of the frontier are consistently measured against an implied or stated norm—though in this case the norm is not moral but cultural or, rather, a combination of these realms in which the manners of the gentleman are made synonymous with virtue, while the misbehavior of the locals is comically vicious. There is, as commentators have noted, a political side to this. The most specific analysis of the genre's politics is Kenneth Lynn's *Mark Twain and Southwestern Humor*, which establishes the southern Whig biases of the humorists and explores the Whig interests they sought to promote by showing northern readers how the southern commoner was a destructive force that could only be held in check by a politically strong southern aristocracy. Lynn's analysis is detailed and persuasive, but perhaps too specific. The political values at work in the tales were not just those of "southern Whiggery"; they were broadly shared by that much larger party that Emerson referred to as "the Establishment," "the Party of the Past": the many propertied conservatives (or men of the middle class who aspired to such rank) who distrusted American's experiment in egalitarianism.

Southwestern Humor was a counterattack upon the spirit of the times, a deeply motivated repudiation of the contemporary surge of democratic impulses most conveniently represented by Jacksonianism. When Henry Thoreau, that metaphysical Jacksonian, looked southwest (the direction, he said, in which he loved best to walk), he declared that "Adam in paradise was [not] more favorably situated on the whole than the backwoodsman in this country."[34] To him, and to many other eastern radicals, southwest was the direction of freedom and the future, from which would come "the helpful giant" that Emerson called for "to destroy the old or to build the new."[35] That, in fact, is exactly what the humorists feared. They saw the Southwest as an American dystopia. Their emphasis is not on individual freedom but on social chaos, moral anarchy, "vulgarity—ignorance—fussy and arrogant pretension—unmitigated rowdyism—bullying insolence."[36] This string of phrases from Baldwin's *Flush Times* makes explicit the judgment that the other humorists pass in their sketches. To them the backwoodsman was little more than a beast who revealed his true nature when (very much like Swift's Yahoos) he stripped and got down on all fours to act horse, or to fight the big dog at Myers's.

Although they lived and wrote on the edge of the frontier, as writers of fiction—unlike Poe or Hawthorne or Melville, the great romancers of this period—the humorists' paramount concern is with society. But instead of the European novel of manners, they wrote in the mode that, from Brackenridge to Irving to Cooper's testy late books, dominated early American depictions of society: the antirepublican, quasisatiric fiction of *bad* manners. While the social novelists of Europe were skeptically exploring the patterns of middle- and upper-class life and testing the adequacy of civilized manners to human needs, the writing of these humorists valorizes bourgeois conventions, the more aristocratic the better, as the ultimate authority. Their conscious allegiance was to the old order, the restraints of law, property, caste, religion, and institutions—all of which seemed threatened by the energies and possibilities of the rawly democratic frontier. To Porter, for instance, the "characteristics of the 'squatters' and early settlers" were not only "strange" and "peculiar," but also "fearful."[37] Both to travesty and disarm this dangerously inverted society, humorists turned the giants of the frontiersmen's own tall tales into clowns. Although they never had the literary courage of their convictions about the superiority of caste, never allowed their Suts and Chunkeys directly to confront and challenge the genteel order, but kept them confined in their own crude milieu like cocks fighting each other in a pit, repeatedly they reassured their readers that the growth of refinement— and the domestication of the brutes—was historically inevitable. While the eastern radicals saw the West as the future, the humorists wanted the frontier to keep receding into the past, and to take the backwoodsmen with it.

Yet there is more to say about the way Southwestern Humor, as a popular genre, served the needs of the audience for which it was written. Politics, even construed broadly as a self-serving or reflex contempt for egalitarian tendencies, cannot wholly explain its appeal. It cannot account for the sheer number of sketches submitted year after year to Porter's journal and to the other papers, usually in southern cities, that quickly began to mine this vein, nor for the obvious relish with which the writers detail the misadventures of their frontier characters. It cannot explain the enormous vogue of the sketches, despite their repetitiousness of setting and event, with Porter's subscribers and with the national audience that bought out the volumes that he (and Hooper and Baldwin and so on) published. Anti-Jacksonian politics defined the public side of the genre—and for the men who wrote and read it, their public role mattered enormously. Being an American gentleman, however, also caused them a lot of uneasiness.

The mirror in which one can still see reflected their ambitions and anxieties is the *Spirit* itself, with its staple of reports on fashionable masculine society abroad and the founding of cricket and hunt clubs at home, with its advertisements for custom-made carriages and guns and the other accoutrements of elegance, with its pervasive concern about measuring up to the aristocratic model to which its readership aspired. Behaving with the decorum expected of the kind of gentleman who could serve as a frame narrator for a southwestern sketch required a vast expenditure: of money obviously, but most especially of temperament. In our democracy birth alone cannot establish caste status, and in any case few of the humorists could claim unequivocal pedigrees. Most of them, in fact, had much in common with Faulkner's Thomas Sutpen, who arrived in Mississippi during the "flush times" that Baldwin writes about determined to shinny his way up the slippery "corinthian columns of the community." For the New World's arrivées, being a gentleman meant acting like one, which imposed on their behavior a complex, severe network of repressions.[38] George tells Sut that he would wait until *Monday* morning to shoot him; even in this outrageously hypothetical instance, he defers his anger to the conventions of honor, religion, and gentility that he is bound to respect. Their addiction to Southwestern Humor, however, reveals more than these gentlemen could ever have acknowledged, even to themselves, about the psychic underside of their public selves. Simply put, it reveals their instinctual doubts about the sacrifices that the role of gentleman in a democracy exacted of them.

Rousseau had posed this question about civilization and its discontents more openly, and for a number of representative American writers it was among the most compelling issues of the time. Doctrinally, consciously, the humorists scoffed at the notion of natural freedom and saw society's artificial refinements and institutional conventions as both necessary and attractive, the antidote to the ills of freedom. Yet their clownish vernacular characters nonetheless resemble two of the period's most resonant types: the child who (as Emerson said) has not yet been clapped into jail by his consciousness, and the savage who (as Melville described him in

Typee) has escaped the penalties of the Fall into civilization. In a sense, this is where most southwestern sketches are actually set: not on the frontier, for the work and hardships of pioneering go entirely unrecorded, but rather in a kind of psychological fairyland where the restless self-centeredness of childhood and the muscular and emotional liberties that civilization projects onto savagism are allowed full play. The character types they depict are monstrously overgrown children and strangely Anglo-Saxon savages whose incredible selfishness and excesses of appetite writers and readers alike found perversely fascinating, because they act out, without a moment's hesitation, without a twinge of regret or embarrassment, the presocial impulses that an American gentleman was forced to repress.[39]

Thus "religion" appears in Southwestern Humor as a succession of circuit riders and camp meetings set up as targets for practical jokers like Sut to ravage. No frontal attack is made on genteel ecclesiastics or fashionable churches or Christianity; the same men who savored Simon Suggs's subversion of a camp meeting would have agreed with the editor at *Putnam*'s who refused Melville's story, "The Two Temples," because its satire on the new Grace Church in New York City was bound to offend "some of our church readers."[40] Instead, the spitefulness of Sut's pranks or of "A Millerite Miracle" (reprinted in *A Quarter Race*) reflects the actual powerlessness with which contemporary males submitted to the tightening hold that Victorian Christianity had on the official culture; they dutifully went to church in the city, then turned Sut or Simon loose in the woods. These men saw nothing to laugh at or resent in Kentucky's first medieval tournament, in which young gentlemen ceremoniously dedicated themselves to the ideals of chivalry and beauty and turned their prowess as horsemen into a strained and expensive display of the sacrifices they were willing to make to femininity. But they exempted their uncouth protagonists from that debt. "Courtesy" gives way to an explicit hostility between the sexes, so that, along with parsons, women typically figure as victims—and anger is a much more prevalent emotion than desire. Most typically, however, women do not even figure at all, making Southwestern Humor the telling counterpart to a best-selling feminine work like *The Wide, Wide World*, a depiction of middle-class family life in which the world is presided over by a dead mother and an intangible God, while the male head of household, though alive, is throughout conspicuous by his absence, his utter irrelevance. The feminist revision of Victorian American society that is currently underway has attuned us to the sense of exclusion, marginalization, and powerlessness felt by women—but this analysis almost invariably proceeds on the assumption that men controlled the center, enjoyed the power, felt like masters in the house of culture. The fantasy life men created for each other in these sketches, however, belies that. On the evidence it offers, we have to conclude that they too felt excluded and powerless, victimized by the cultural patterns that also dictated their place to them. If he felt impotent and even invisible in the home that he paid for but did not run, the gentleman could find vicarious compensation in the rough world of the humorists, where it is women who do not matter, except as occasional objects of unfrustrated resentment.

Southwestern Humor is often given credit for its representation of sex, for bringing back toward consciousness the facts of life that so much in Victorian American culture sought to deny. The human body is given a prominent part in these works, as prominent as that given the soul in contemporary genteel fiction. At times the frankness of the humorists does seem directly subversive of Victorian idealizations. "Somebody in My Bed" (also reprinted in *A Quarter Race*) is a clever tale told by a man who once returned late to his tavern to find a luscious young woman already sleeping in his room. Taking advantage of her unconsciousness, he pulls down the covers and proceeds slowly to unbutton her nightdress. As he draws out his account for his impatient listeners, he brilliantly plays off the descriptive euphemisms of gentility—"an angel," "rivalling the snow in whiteness," "a stray ringlet," "shoulders of alabaster," even "bust"—against the brutishly human desires he is arousing.[41] It is as though one of Alcott's "little women" were suddenly posing for a centerfold. It would be hard to say, however, that the fundamentally adolescent attitude of Southwestern Humor—sex as smut—made it any easier for a writer like Hawthorne to treat sexuality as an inevitable and serious aspect of adult life, or for Whitman to treat body *and* soul as equally sacred. And what is most characteristic about "Somebody in My Bed," what it has in common with Sut's relationship with Sicily or a host of sketches about sleeping in one-room cabins with bevies of "poor white" girls, is that it is not finally about sex, but about sexual frustration. It forces a laugh out of the disparity between aroused expectations and literal anticlimax. Here again one can see the way unconscious resentments fueled the energies of the genre, for in these sketches readers were looking for a defense against their own frustrations in the compensation of humor.[42] Yet you pay a price when you try to deal with the needs of your body by treating them as exclusively comic. Norris Yates, the most diligent historian of the *Spirit*, expresses surprise that alongside the often bawdy southwestern tales Porter regularly printed "conventionally sentimental pieces praising woman for her purity and nobility."[43] There is really nothing to wonder at. The humorists' mode of representing sex, and all physical appetites, effectively completed the program of genteel denial. In one case the body was excluded; in the other, ironically denigrated. In either case, the high culture's idealizations were reinforced.

Although Southwestern Humor may look like a vigorous assault on convention, its actual achievement for its contemporary readers (as one would expect from a popular genre) was to reaffirm the preconceptions of their culture. Its ultimate consequence was to reconcile readers to the place convention marked out for them to aspire to. In these sketches the instinctual life that a gentleman was forced to repress was allowed to disport itself. Drunkenness, rage, violence, cruelty, greed, selfishness: the aboriginal pleasure-seeking self was allowed to come out of hiding. But it remained always behind the intricate barriers that the conventions and assumptions of the genre interposed between it and the gentleman's public identity, and not only because the right to look down on these "peasants" was the one clear privilege that their sacrifices at the altar of propriety had gained them. It was only because they felt secure in the knowledge that they were writing for fellow gentlemen about a world set apart from themselves in time and place and caste that these writers could hoodwink the censor who guarded their own language, gestures, and cultural loyalties, and imaginatively participate in the earthy, unrestrained antics of their backwoodsmen. By keeping the tales' poor white "neutral territory" so remote from the circles in which they and their readers moved, they could attack such values as religion, matrimony, chivalry, and "honour"—for although those values defined their conscious allegiance, they could not win their unconscious consent. What runs amuck in the genre is the unrepression of instinct, dressed in motley and let loose upon the circumscribed landscape of the tales.

It is dressed in motley because "humor" served as the chief expedient by which this ragtag cultural rebellion was permitted. Whatever happens in the tales is presumed by the terms of the genre to be funny. The comic perspective was made possible by the genre's invariable class-consciousness. But that comicality in turn made possible the simultaneous indulgence and repudiation of the readers' hidden selves. Between gentlemen it was agreed that no one in the audience could possibly be identified with anyone in the sketches (except, of course, the irreproachable narrator). This enabled them to laugh, and laughing was a way to exorcise their own uneasiness, to disown the frankly ungentlemanlike urges that the sketches thrust into sight. If modern readers do not laugh as much, it is because we are not so severely afflicted with the same pattern of repressions— which is not to say we are freer, just differently bound. Its contemporary masculine audience sought and found in Southwestern Humor a safe way momentarily to escape the chafing of their public selves. Yet by laughing at the lack of genteel manners they did more than dismiss the poetic or heroic potentialities of vernacular American life. Ultimately they denied the reality that a vernacular is always based upon: the truth of their own private experience. By laughing, they gave Victorian convention the last word. Though they did not seem to know it, it was the uncomfortable self inside their elegantly fashionable clothes that they tried to laugh away.

In the word processing program I am using to write the final drafts of this book, pressing the F3 function key "reveals" the "codes" by which the electronic memory of the computer keeps track of the wordless parameters of my text—margins, indentions, spacing, and so on. Literature works analogously. Especially for all the forms of popular literature, unrevealed, assumed codes—of meaning, expectation, value, and so on—control the relationship between what authors say and how readers respond. In these last two chapters I have tried to reveal, to make explicit, some of the basic cultural codes that organize Stowe's novel and the humorists' sketches, as a way of exploring the kind of performance a writer who shares the assumptions of her or his audience is engaged in. Both *Uncle Tom's Cabin* and Southwestern Humor, depending upon the point of view from which you look at them and the characteristics on which you choose to focus, can be seen as attacks upon the various complacencies of their era. And both are, up to a point. We can, however, locate that point very precisely by noting the terms of the relationship they presume with their respective contemporary audiences. In ways that were largely unspoken, because there was no need to bespeak them, both Stowe and the humorists can take for granted what Emerson worked so hard to preserve the illusion of: an "identity of sentiment" with their readers. In popular literature, what remains unspoken and thus unexamined is often the most determinant. Despite the way Stowe's novel is an act of witness to her moral horror at the sins of American society, she never turns on her refined, Christian, lady readers to challenge their way of life. Southwestern Humor lets loose an enormous amount of potentially subversive energy, both linguistic and physical, but no writer so much as disturbed the look of self-gratulatory composure on the faces of the genre's gentlemanly narrators; indeed, no writer ever turned the reader's attention to that gentlemanly presence as a subject for scrutiny. The readers of these tales and sketches, like the audience to whom Stowe addressed herself, were privileged to share the writers' outrage or amusement from within the network of values or preconceptions encoded in these texts. While some values were radically challenged, the implicit prejudices of the audience were confirmed at every point.

Chapter VI

"TO OPEN AN INTERCOURSE WITH THE WORLD": HAWTHORNE'S *SCARLET LETTER*

NATURE, *Moby-Dick, Walden, Leaves of Grass, The Scarlet Letter*—the five major works of the American Renaissance all get their titles from a central symbol. All have large rhetorical designs, for the act of reading them engages the reader in the more active task of interpretation. Much more than the meaning of a text is at stake, for correctly to understand any one of these symbols means seeing reality and one's self in new, more challenging ways. Where typical Victorian American readers sought recreation, especially when they picked up a novel, or at most a reassuring sense of edification, these writers seek instead to use reading as re-creation.

The ultimate model for all five works is unmistakably the Protestant sermon. Just as the minister chooses a passage from Scripture as the occasion for his exposition, these five writers begin with a particular piece of the phenomenological world: nature, a white whale, a pond, the grass, or a rag of scarlet cloth. In each case we are expected to accede to the very ambitious pun that Hawthorne makes when he calls his novel's penultimate chapter "The Revelation of the Scarlet Letter." He is not simply referring to what happens when Dimmesdale confesses his guilt and bares his breast; he is claiming that the scarlet letter as a symbol is a "revelation," has the same status, in other words, as the minister's Scripture. And just as the minister opens the text of his sermon to discover what God meant and what He wants from us, so these writers study nature, grapple with leviathan, sound the pond, observe the spear of grass, or try to solve the "riddle"[1] of the *A* as a means of gaining access to the highest laws, as a way of finding our place in the eternal scheme of things.

There is, however, a crucial difference between preaching a sermon to a congregation in a church and writing a work of literature for the American reading public. Rhetorically, whatever his topic, the minister could take a lot for granted. He and his congregation already agreed on the authority of the Bible that provided his occasion and on at least the basic articles of the faith that brought him and them together; his authority was bestowed by the institution to which he and they belonged, and attested by the pulpit from which he spoke to an audience that had to attend to what he said. They could reject or ignore his message, but they did so at their peril. Psychically as well as rhetorically, the minister was in charge of his occasion.[2] These five mid-nineteenth-century writers, on the other hand, were in a much more vulnerable position. From the sermon they inherited their deepest sense of what literature should be, but this legacy did not include any of the minister's traditional privileges. With no clear authority outside their own texts to which they could point to sanction their interpretations of the human condition, with neither institutional nor traditional common ground with their audience, they not only had to try to tell the truth in their works; they also had to create the context in which the truth they were trying to tell would be listened to and understood.

Of the authors who wrote the five undisputed masterpieces of the American Renaissance, Hawthorne's response to this set of rhetorical exigencies seems to me to have been the most exemplary. The strategies by which he sought to bridge the gap between his own vision and his audience's preconceptions were less radical than Emerson's or Thoreau's, Melville's or Whitman's, but they were also more mature. Whereas Melville, for instance, complained to Hawthorne that his books were botches because he could not write the way he wanted to, and would not write the way his audience expected him to, Hawthorne was willing to find a middle ground: to tell the truth "without violating either the reader's rights or his own" (4). In his quest "to open an intercourse with the world,"[3] he neither patronized his audience nor compromised his own integrity. His career was hardly free from the anxieties and ambivalences of performing, and it too was shaped by the private needs he brought to his public ambitions as a writer, but by trying to close the widening distance between the highest art and the middle-class culture, he wrote a book that can remind us that genius and the common reader are not invariably estranged from each other. There are already a good many reasons to admire the achievement of *The Scarlet Letter*, but not least among them should be the example it sets of how an American writer with a profound and unpopular vision can communicate with the largest possible audience.

We can begin to distinguish Hawthorne from the other four authors by noting the kind of symbol around which he organizes his work. Unlike the whale, the pond, or the grass, the *A* is not organic. The paradigm for the act of seeing and interpreting in the other four works is essentially the atemporal and unmediated two-term relationship that Emerson defines at the start of *Nature*, where he divides existence into the Me and the Not-Me, consciousness and nature. The perceptual modes Melville, Thoreau, and Whitman invest with significance are those that lead the reader beyond history or civilization; they choose natural phenomena for their central symbols because the mind alone in nature could aspire to what Emerson called "an original relation to the universe." From the start, on the other hand, Hawthorne's choice of a symbol denies such a possibility; to put it more positively, his choice of a symbol asserts by its very nature that one's relation to the universe is inescapably qualified by the existence of history and other people. As *an A* his symbol already exists on this side of the fall into language that the Romantics lamented. More particularly, *this A*—the one Hawthorne claims to have found as the inspiration for his novel—was sewn by a woman who was condemned to wear it by a group of magistrates who held office over two hundred years earlier. Even by itself Hawthorne's symbol, and whatever truth it embodies, already surrounds us with other human presences.

We see the same difference when we consider where he claims to have found his symbol. *Nature* begins with the quest for "solitude": "if a man would be alone, let him look at the stars." According to "Self-Reliance," the path to the highest truth leads "from man, not to man." In their own way, Melville, Thoreau, and Whitman each literalize this notion, carrying their readers into the middle of the ocean, the depths of the woods, away from all houses and rooms. Hawthorne too is alone when he discovers the *A*, but he is alone in "the deserted chamber of the Custom-House" (33). He even finds it wrapped in "faded red tape" (29). The customhouse is an ambiguous setting, but an unequivocally social one. By identifying his symbol with it, Hawthorne implicitly insists that his path as a seeker of truth leads to the idea of society that the other writers want to transcend.[4]

The most striking of all the differences is the place where Hawthorne locates himself as an artist. While he pointedly tells us in "The Custom-House" that he often sought the invigorating influence of nature by walking along the "sea-shore" and "into the country," and that he had a room of his own—"my study"—to write in, it is in neither of these places that he describes himself "striving to picture forth imaginary scenes, which, the next day, might flow out on the brightening page in many-hued description" (35). Instead he places himself in the "parlour," amid "the little domestic scenery of the well-known apartment," including "a work-basket" and a child's "doll" (35). With varying degrees of vehemence and scorn, Emerson, Thoreau, Melville, and Whitman would all have rejected this portrait of the artist as somehow inextricably a part of the genteel bourgeoisie. The "volume or two" that lie beside the "work-basket" on this parlor's "centre-table" would never have been *Moby-Dick* or *Leaves of Grass*, for both aspire to a place entirely outside the decorous confines of this "domestic" environment. According to Thoreau, anything written in or for the parlor would certainly degenerate into mere *"parlaver."* These men's repudiation of this milieu, of course, was largely based on their impatience with the terms of contemporary conventional literature: the explicit connection that successful publishers and popular authors were fond of making between the comforts of the hearthside and the pleasures of sentimental fiction or elegant verses. That Longfellow, in his "Dedication" to *The Seaside and the Fireside* (1850), could speak so smugly of

> The pleasant books, that silently among
> Our household treasures take familiar places,

was the kind of gesture that made Whitman, in "Song of Myself," "swear I will never mention love or death inside a house." By the time Hawthorne wrote *The Scarlet Letter*, it already seemed to many that the realms of immortal art and truth and of the Victorian parlor were irreconcilably at odds with each other. For Hawthorne, however, according to the emblems of "The Custom-House," the artist conceives his vision and defines himself right in the midst of the conventional culture; his "imaginative faculty" (35) acts in the parlor.

Yet if he introduces *The Scarlet Letter* by establishing the patterns of his relatedness to contemporary society, it is with none of the complacency of Longfellow's "Dedication." Hawthorne is instead fixing the indices of a problem that will not easily be resolved. He said he wrote "The Custom-House" to mitigate the unrelieved gloom of the novel it introduces; as a reckoning of the place of the artist in American society, however, the sketch is only slightly less bleak than Melville's "Bartleby, The Scrivener." The ghosts of his Puritan ancestors appear to disdain his ambitions as a "writer of story-books!" (10). The living men with whom he works as a customs surveyor—"My fellow-officers, and the merchants and sea-captains" (26)—are at least equally indifferent to his literary works, and to all art: "None of them, I presume, had ever read a page of my inditing, or would have cared a fig the more for me, if they had read them all; nor would it have mended the matter, in the least, had those same unprofitable pages been written with a pen like that of Burns or of Chaucer, each of whom was a Custom-House officer in his day . . ." (26). "Unprofitable" is Hawthorne's oblique reference to the reason for his being in the customhouse at all, the economic reality that he indicates still more obliquely by having the "grim beadle" of Boston remind Hester at the beginning of the novel that she must "'show your scarlet letter in the market-place!'" (54). As someone who had to accept a political appointment because he could not making a living by his "imaginative faculty," Hawthorne had very practical reasons to resent the need to publish his *Scarlet Letter* in the literary marketplace, and to be appalled by the philistine mentality that governs the customhouse.[5] He may find his originating symbol inside it, but no other officer is ever likely "to be summoned" from it "for apostolic errands" (7); nor can Hawthorne, with his own prophetic aims as a writer, find any possible source of support or appreciation among these men of business.

In the face of these innutritious circumstances, Hawthorne was tempted to assume the stance that many nineteenth-century writers wound up adopting: that to be great is to be misunderstood, because the true artist is immeasurably superior to the tainted pursuits, the sordid values of his culture. The conflict between the writer of genius and the unpoetic mass of readers is a frequent theme of his short fiction. It would take too long to examine his conflicted treatment of this subject in detail, but the one story to look at closely is "Ethan Brand." Almost the last tale he ever wrote, it was composed in 1848, just before he began *The Scarlet Letter*. It comes at the end of the twenty-five years he spent writing tales and sketches for magazines and annuals, the long period during which, Hawthorne said, he felt like "the obscurest man of letters in America," because his works brought him so little fame, or money, or mere response.[6] In his public statements about this stage of his career he modestly attributes the neglect to the inadequacies of his work, but in his own mind there was a growing fund of bitterness and hostility toward the public. As a kind of summary of his career before *The Scarlet Letter*, "Ethan Brand" pushes both issues—Hawthorne's misgivings about his own quest as an artist and his incipient contempt for his audience—to almost lurid extremes. Most analyses of this story focus on Brand himself: on the crime he commits when his pride of intellect usurps his sympathy and reverence for the truths of the human heart he sets out to explore. Although Hawthorne presents Brand as a type of Faustian scientist, it is easy enough to see how self-referential this quest is; what the tale moralizes about are the dangers of writing allegorical psychological romances, the potential sin of Hawthorne's own art.[7] But the tale chooses to *dramatize* a very different issue: the grotesque failure of American society as a potential audience.

For the tale presents Brand's story largely from the outside, in terms of the impression his figure and fate make on the conventional world. It begins and ends with Bartram, an "obtuse, middle-aged clown" who "trouble[s] himself with no thoughts save the very few that were requisite to his business."[8] Despite intimations of Brand's visionary greatness—indeed, probably because he fears what he might learn about himself from Brand's disturbing presence—Bartram conveniently dismisses the damned prophet as simply a "madman" (11:90). At the end he measures the tragedy of Brand's life and death in the basest but most recognizably American terms: Brand's suicide simply makes him "'half a bushel richer'" (11:102). Nor do the other people who flock from the village to see the return of Ethan Brand—which Hawthorne stages as a performance, stage-lit by the kiln door that Bartram opens, "flooding the spot with light, that the whole company might get a fair view of Ethan Brand, and he of them" (11:91)—prove any more adequate to the human, or moral, or aesthetic demands of the occasion. Hawthorne wrote the tale while still at the customhouse. The three old men who appear next to witness Brand's return, the stage agent, the lawyer, and the doctor, have a lot in common with the aged veterans whom Hawthorne describes in "The Custom-House." Their only appetites are crudely physical ones; they greet Brand with a bottle, "in which, as they averred, he would find something far better worth searching for, than the Unpardonable Sin" (11:92–93). This anticipates the description of the Weighers and Gaugers watching Hawthorne pace the floor of the customhouse; he's brooding on "Hester Prynne's story," but they assume his "sole object—and, indeed, the sole object for which a sane man could ever put himself into voluntary motion—was, to get an appetite for dinner" (34). By giving us Brand's reaction to the old men's loutishness, Hawthorne allows himself a more aggressive revenge on his associates than he permitted himself when speaking in the first person in "The Custom-House": "No mind, which has wrought itself, by intense and solitary meditation, into a high state of enthusiasm, can endure the kind of contact with low and vulgar modes of thought and feeling, to which Ethan Brand was now subjected" (11:93). Brand's next thought is to wonder "whether he had indeed found the Unpardonable Sin" (11:93) because there is so little to sympathize with or revere in these imbruted specimens of mankind.

Hawthorne hastens to reassert his moral, but then goes on to implicate more of society in this pattern of failure. "A number of the youth of the village, young men and girls, had hurried up the hill-side, impelled by curiosity to see Ethan Brand" (11:94). They turn out to be just as unworthy an audience. Seeing "nothing" in "his aspect" (11:94), they find "amusement" in the wretched "diorama" of an itinerant "showman," who passes off "a series of the most outrageous scratchings and daubings" as "specimens of the fine arts" (11:94–95). His "exhibition" of clichéd historical scenes and foreign scenery is surely Hawthorne's sarcastic jab, as an author who wanted to show people the truth of their own heart, at the conventional literature, the cheap modes of escape, that apparently delighted his contemporary audience. In an episode that anticipates what *Huckleberry Finn* points out about the kind of entertainment that goes over best in village America, Hawthorne winds up this part of the tale with the "exhibition" that makes the greatest impact on "public notice": the stupid "performance" of a dog frantically chasing his own tail (11:96). There can be no doubt about the lesson this "tail" teaches concerning the debased taste of the crowd. While they are utterly indifferent to Brand, the tragic hero, the visionary seer in their midst, they are captivated by the dog: "As may be expected, the exhibition was greeted with universal laughter, clapping of hands, and shouts of encore" (11:97). Brand sees "some remote analogy between his own case and that of this self-persuing cur" (11:97), but the incident evokes much more immediately the case of American artists and the cynicism about the standards of their democratic audience that so often threatened to leave them festering in contempt for the readers they hoped to reach.

That Hawthorne apparently planned "Ethan Brand" to be the full-length work of fiction he had been exhorting himself to write for a decade is a suggestive fact. We do not know how far he got with that intention, or when he abandoned it to publish the tale as "A Chapter from an Aborted Romance" instead. But the tale itself contains an explanation for his decision to abandon the romance: he could not convince himself that anyone would be more interested in the book he projected than the villagers are in Brand himself. The subject Hawthorne turned to for *The Scarlet Letter*, the full-length fiction he eventually finished after giving up on "Ethan Brand," is much better calculated to attract the public's attention. But the question "Ethan Brand" makes most urgent by emphasizing the community's reaction to the returning visionary is whether anyone in Hawthorne's potential audience is *worthy* of his art. By exposing the crudeness of the villagers' taste and the crassness of their values so unmercifully, Hawthorne as narrator comes close to committing the very sin of prideful intellect for which Brand as questor is damned. His haughty disdain for humankind at times can seem a legitimate response to the empty benightedness of the people around him. To be sure, Hawthorne himself resists this temptation. He keeps touching base with Bartram's son, little Joe, a cousin I believe of little Eva St. Clare. Joe, who can intuitively sympathize with Brand's "bleak and terrible loneliness," is the "tender spirit" who serves to reestablish "the magnetic chain of humanity" that Brand breaks, and in breaking damns himself (11:98, 99). But Joe is almost as much an outcast from this sordid society as Brand, and is an awfully slight figure with which to occupy the middle ground that Hawthorne depends on, not just as a moralist, but as an author: the ground between Brand's intellectual superiority and the mental squalor of the other characters' lives.

It is not surprising that before scholarship had settled the date of the tale's composition, Lewis Mumford assumed that Brand was based on Melville, whom Hawthorne met in 1850.[9] The Byronic mood of the story, its valorization of damned greatness, and its contempt for conventional minds fit easily into the patterns of Melville's career. What the story reveals to us, however, is that Hawthorne's own experience as a performing artist could bring him to the verge of such self-glorifying bitterness as well. The other major piece he wrote while working at the customhouse is "Main-street," which presents the writer as a "persecuted showman" whose imaginative powers are continually at the mercy of a critical, unsympathizing audience.[10] Although this piece strives for a comic rather than a tragic tone, it too is about the artist as an exile. And despite the differences in tone, there is a profound similarity between the way "Ethan Brand" ends with the seer's suicide and the way "Main-street" ends with the breakdown of the showman's performance. In both instances, the philistines get the last word: Bartram gloating over his extra dollar, the audience demanding its money back. In both cases Hawthorne leaves it to readers to supply the relationship between the causes and effects, but we have to say that one reason Brand dies, one reason the performance ends, is the failure of their respective audiences.

The imaginative death of the artist exiled among his own neighbors is the central concern of "The Custom-House" as well. Writing for publication, about himself, Hawthorne manages to control most of his bitterness toward the society that is so hostile to "his faculties and sensibilities" (40), although the modest pose he tries to maintain, belittling his own artistic gift and refusing to "make much moan" about its atrophy (38), wears increasingly thin as he keeps coming back to the blighting "antiliterary" atmosphere of the house of custom.[11] In his letters, however, he could occasionally unleash his rage. Writing from the customhouse to Longfellow in 1849, he flirted with the idea of using his pen to take revenge on those who "have violated the sanctity of the priesthood to which we both, in our different degrees, belong":

> If they will pay no reverence to the imaginative power when it causes herbs of grace and sweet-scented flowers to spring up along their pathway, then they should be taught what it can do in the way of producing nettles, skunk-cabbage, deadly night-shade, wolf's bane, dogwood. If they will not be grateful for its works of beauty and beneficence, then let them dread it as a pervasive and penetrating mischief, that can reach them at their firesides and in their bedchambers, follow them to far countries, and make their very graves refuse to hide them.[12]

Everyone these days is familiar with his diatribe against the "damned mob of scribbling women," but an earlier letter to his publisher strikes out still more viciously at the most popular American writers of his days: "*All* women, as authors, are feeble and tiresome. I wish they were forbidden to write, on pain of having their faces deeply scarified with an oyster-shell."[13] The violence in both these passages is clearly overcompensating for a sense of artistic impotency. If the American public will not appreciate what, in the letter to Longfellow, he calls the "sacredness" of the true artist's calling, let them be damned.

No account of Hawthorne's career can ignore these symptoms of his frustration. There was, however, nothing hypocritical or even sly about the place in the "parlour" that Hawthorne assigns himself as a writer. Deeper than his pride in the power of his "imaginative faculty" was his fear of it, and what always remained underneath his fits of impatience with his audience was his need to "open an intercourse with the world." The human situation he returns to most often in his fiction is that of the solitary heart, and solitude for him has none of the positive connotations with which Emerson invests it. Instead, and this is probably the most modern aspect of his work, Hawthorne is a brilliant analyst of alienation, of all the ways in which consciousness can find itself estranged from other people. And of all the isolatos in his works, the most dangerously situated are those who seek for buried truth in the recesses of the human heart—which of course was also Hawthorne's errand as a writer of "psychological romance."[14] When Young Goodman Brown arrives at the climax of a Black Mass in the midnight wilderness, Satan defines the demonic power that he shall possess in terms that cannot be distinguished from Hawthorne's definition of his own aesthetic quest: "'It shall be yours to penetrate, in every bosom, the deep mystery of sin, the fountain of all wicked arts.'"[15] It is by sitting up alone at midnight and "look[ing] into the heart of man" that Ethan Brand first summons forth the devil and then becomes "a fiend" himself (11:98, 99). Hawthorne's acute anxiety about "the sin of art" reappears in *The Scarlet Letter* in his representation of Chillingworth as psychoanalyst.[16] "'Were it only for the art's sake,'" Chillingworth thinks, "'I must search this matter to the bottom'" (138). Before Hawthorne as narrator explores "The Interior of a Heart" in chapter 11, he shows in chapter 10 how Chillingworth, by digging "into the poor clergyman's heart" (129), transforms himself into a fiend. Indeed, Chillingworth allows himself to become the vengeful necromancer that Hawthorne told Longfellow he was tempted, as a spurned romancer, to become; when we see how hideous Chillingworth makes himself in the process, we realize how determined Hawthorne was to exorcise any such desire in himself.

The fates of both Brand and Chillingworth as seekers who pursue the truths of the heart in self-righteous solitude are Hawthorne's admonitions to himself that, while his art looks inward for its theme, it must, in peril of the artist's sanity and soul, look outward, to the community, for its ultimate meaning and value. The worst thing about the life he lived in the customhouse is not (as one might expect) that it is too commercial, or conventional, or societal, nor that it is "anti-literary"; no, if his last words on this subject are to be taken as his final judgment, the worst is that "the very nature of his business" in the customhouse "is of such a sort that he does not share in the united effort of mankind" (38). This was also his deepest fear about the nature of the artist's solitary enterprise. The parlor in which he locates himself is a "deserted" one, and he sits there "late at night" (35); despite the "domestic scenery," he seems as much alone there with the "illusive guests" (35) and "strange things" (36) evoked by his imagination as Brand had been in front of his fiery kiln. This simple scene is perhaps more genuinely frightening than any of the bizarre, outré settings that Poe concocted for his arabesques: it is a "familiar room" but is "now invested with a quality of strangeness and remoteness" (35) and "haunted" by "the forms which fancy summons up" (36). Estranged amidst the furniture of his own life, alone with the powers of his imagination, Hawthorne's only way to keep hold on the world of "men and women" (36) is sympathy: the "heart and sensibilities of human tenderness" (36).

Sympathy. This is the basis on which Hawthorne explicitly chooses to establish "some true relation with his audience" (4). In the first paragraph of "The Custom-House" he steps around all the accumulated frustrations of his experience as a writer. He ignores all the actual circumstances that had alternately appalled, enraged, or discouraged him, to claim this ideal relationship with his reader: "The truth seems to be . . . that, when he casts his leaves forth upon the wind, the author addresses, not the many who will fling aside his volume, or never take it up, but the few who will understand him, better than most of his schoolmates and lifemates" (3).

By thus trying to humanize his relationship with his reader, Hawthorne rejects both the intellectual exile in which Brand exults and the philistine society, the "many," who remain indifferent or hostile to his vision. The ideal of understanding forms the author and his or her audience into a community more intimately bound together than even the minister and his congregation. The reader sits with Hawthorne in the otherwise "deserted" parlor. Attractive as this idea is, it is hardly a "truth" about authorship in general, and it certainly does not describe the uncertain conditions of writing and publishing in the middle of the American nineteenth century. Yet neither is it a strategic ploy, an insincere attempt to create the illusion of escaping from the impersonalities of the literary marketplace. Instead, it is Hawthorne's most earnest wish; it explains what he meant when he said he wrote and published his tales "to open an intercourse with the world." In a letter written three days after *The Scarlet Letter* was published, he developed his "theory" of publication as going public with more candor than he permitted himself in the opening paragraph of "The Custom-House." The letter is addressed to a man named Mansfield, who sought Hawthorne's professional and editorial advice about a long poem he had written. What Hawthorne here tells Mansfield about writing as confession and communion is what governs the aesthetic of *The Scarlet Letter*:

Your poem is addressed not to the world at large, but to a class of cognate minds—to those most capable of understanding you—to your truest and closest friends, wherever they may be scattered throughout the world, who will never know you save through this work, but will nevertheless know you better than most of those who are familiar with your face. To whom should you speak of matters near your heart, if not to these invisible friends? You need not dread being overheard, however loudly you may speak. Your voice—or, at least, your meaning—will reach only those who are privileged to hear and understand it, and what sense is there in caring one fig about the helter-skelter judgments of those who cannot understand you. It might be, that only one person in the whole world would understand, while all the rest would ridicule you; but it would be worth a life's labor to be understood by that one, while the ridicule of the others would not be worth a thought. I do not express what I mean, and cannot just now; but my theory is, that there is less indelicacy in speaking out your highest, deepest, tenderest emotions to the world at large, than to almost any individual. You may be mistaken in the individual; but you cannot be mistaken in thinking that, somewhere among your fellow-creatures, there is a heart that will receive yours into itself. And those who do not receive it, cannot, in fact, hear it; so that your delicacy is not infringed upon. This is my theory; and if I were a less sophisticated man, I suppose I should act upon it more perfectly than I ever yet have.[17]

The Scarlet Letter keeps revolving around the very situation Hawthorne here describes. It begins with the public-ation of the scarlet letter. Chapter 2 is about the anguish Hester feels at being forced to "show [her] scarlet letter in the market-place" (54). In chapter 3, however, when Chillingworth appears on the outskirts of the crowd before the scaffold, Hester discovers that it is safer to reveal one's innermost self to the world at large than to this partner of her private life: "Dreadful as it was, she was conscious of a shelter in the presence of these thousand witnesses. . . . She fled for refuge, as it were, to the public exposure" (63–64). The scarlet letter is "published" again in chapter 12, as the meteoric *A* that appears in the sky above the scaffold that Dimmesdale mounts to seek "a moment's peace" from his guilty secret, from "the constant introspection wherewith he tortured, but could not purify, himself" (146). It is interesting to note that he is fleeing from the "ugly nights" (146) he spends in "the remote dimness" (145) of his own room, which his "spectral thoughts had made so ghastly"; exactly like the writer depicted in the deserted parlor, he is haunted there by the "visions" that "flit before him" (145).[18] But though the letter is revealed on the "page" of the heav-

ens (155) and all the intimates of his life—Hester, Pearl, Chillingworth—
are present at this scene, the absence of a larger audience makes Dimmesdale's performance a mockery of confession in which he finds no true
communion or relief. The novel's dramatic climax is the third, penultimate "publication" of the scarlet letter, when at last Dimmesdale exposes
his heart "before the people" (257). Hawthorne's handling of this performance is full of ambivalences, which I will discuss later. But the novel
anticipates Dimmesdale's public confession in its account of the Election
Sermon he preaches just before ascending the scaffold. We never hear the
sermon itself. Instead, we stand outside the church with Hester and hear
him as Hawthorne had promised Mansfield the truest audience would
hear and understand the voice of the writer who speaks out his "highest,
deepest, tenderest emotions to the world":

> still, if the auditor listened intently, and for the purpose, he could detect the
> same cry of pain. What was it? The complaint of a human heart, sorrow-
> laden, perchance guilty, telling its secret, whether of guilt or sorrow, to the
> great heart of mankind; beseeching its sympathy or forgiveness, —at every
> moment, —in each accent, —and never in vain! (243–44)

In this deeply heartfelt passage, Hawthorne is describing the relation in
which, as "the speaker" of *The Scarlet Letter* (4), he hopes to stand with
his audience. He is describing the sympathetic role he counts on readers
to play as accomplices in his exploration of the human heart and its dark
secrets, guilts, and sorrows.

The quest for such sympathetic communion governs the narrative
strategies of the novel. For the rest of this chapter I will try to indicate the
means by which Hawthorne seeks to engage the reader, as accomplice, in
his exploration. There is nothing simple about these means. As he told
Mansfield, his sense of how to address the public was "sophisticated." In
the twenty-five years he spent writing and publishing short fiction, Hawthorne lost any naivete he might have had when his career began. He
knew well what kind of constraints—rhetorical, cultural, even commercial—affected the actual conditions of literary performance in his time.
Before any character in the novel has spoken, for instance, he has already
raised the issue—for any writer, the vital issue—of language: what kind of
words he can use. When he measures the distance between the Puritan
matrons outside the prison and their delicate Victorian American descendants and points out that the "boldness" of their "speech" would "startle
us at the present day" (51), he is also acknowledging the linguistic problem of telling the truth to a culture of euphemism.[19] "'The Scarlet Letter'
is rather a delicate subject to write upon," he told his publisher, but then
he added, to allay any fears Fields might have about the book's "prospects
with the public," "in the way in which I have treated it, it appears to me

there can be no objections on that score."[20] Once the novel was published, despite the tactful respect it shows for the decorums of contemporary culture, there were objections[21]—for as Hawthorne knew all along,
the book he was writing was one that would be ill-suited for a place on
the center table in the parlor he describes in "The Custom-House."
Three times in the novel itself he points out that the children of Puritan
Boston were "too young to comprehend" the issues with which the story
deals (81, 54, 85). He is thus indirectly asking his readers to set his novel
apart from the most popular fiction and poetry of his time, which was not
only often about children but also written for "home reading," which
meant that parents could and did share it with their children.[22] Although
the artist sits in the parlor, Hawthorne by no means intends for him or
her to sacrifice truth to polite manners, by no means disarms art of its
revelatory power. He "dream[s] strange things" there (36). He dreams
The Scarlet Letter, which in some respects has the same relation to the
daytime complacencies of the Victorian parlor as the family and neighbors that Goodman Brown sees at the Black Mass in the wilderness have
to their public lives in Salem village. Hawthorne knew that the adult and
tragic difficulties of his novel's theme set him in conflict with the predominant tastes and values of the available reading public. Nonetheless he was
committed to reaching that audience with his vision. He could be cynical
about this quest: he told Fields it would be a good idea to print the title
page "in red ink," as a way of catching the eye of "the great gull whom
we are endeavoring to circumvent."[23] But on the whole he sets out to
close the gap between his culture's assumptions and his vision, between
his readers' literary expectations and his deepest needs as an author, with
patience, craft, and respect.

Like Hawthorne, then, the novel begins with an audience that is there
before the story begins: the "throng" (47) of Puritans who, in the first
paragraphs of both the first and second chapters, are staring at "The
Prison Door" from which the story emerges with the concentrated attention and expectation of an audience in the theater waiting for the curtain.
Although at one crucial point near the end—in chapter 20, just after
Dimmesdale has thrown off the moral ties that linked him to his congregation—Hawthorne individualizes several of the men and women in this
throng, by and large the role played by the Puritan community in the
novel is to be the immediate audience to its "drama" (253). They play
that part very explicitly in the theatrical scaffold scenes that open and
close the story. But throughout the novel Hawthorne regularly gives
summary accounts of how the Puritans, as "spectators" (50), respond to
the book's main "actors" (253)—Hester, Dimmesdale, Chillingworth,
and Pearl—at different stages in the story. In this awareness of perfor-

mance one can see another similarity between *The Scarlet Letter* and *Walden, Moby-Dick*, and *Leaves of Grass*, all of which also begin by introducing an audience right into the text. Yet there is also a difference. Thoreau, Melville, and Whitman begin by encountering their contemporary reader directly, as "you." The Puritans are *an* audience, but not *Hawthorne's* audience, which is fortunate, because they are a terrible audience. As a symbolic event, the first publication of the scarlet letter—Hester's hour on the scaffold before the Puritans' "unrelenting" and "concentred" eyes (57)—is an entire failure, because this immediate audience sees the *A* only in terms of the "lurid" "terrors" "of the infernal pit" (68–69). Nor do their interpretive powers grow much during the course of the story. By chapter 13, the Puritans have come to take "Another View of Hester": because outwardly she conforms "to the external regulations of society" (164), they see her as "our Hester, —the town's own Hester" (162) and now interpret the *A* as "Able" (161). But the title of this chapter is another pun. It is the reader who must take another view of Hester. After elaborating the Puritans' misreading of her character, the chapter shows her as much more radically estranged from Boston than she had ever been earlier. "The scarlet letter had not done its office," Hawthorne pointedly insists (166); he is referring most directly to Hester's moral alienation,[24] but he could just as well be summing up the impact his drama has had on *its* contemporary audience.

Hawthorne's representation of his story as a performance makes it clear that he felt the same conflicted self-consciousness as an American author that distressed his friends Melville and Thoreau. Yet by casting the Puritans in the role of audience, he found a creative way to express his frustrations and anxieties without allowing them to increase the friction between his imagination and his own audience. He could work out his resentments at one remove from the public with which he hoped to communicate. Beginning *The Scarlet Letter* with an attack on this surrogate audience doubtless made it much easier to begin "The Custom-House" with the idea of his reader as "a kind and apprehensive . . . friend" (4). At the same time, by specifying the ways in which the Puritans fail, he could cue that reader how to respond properly. As in chapter 13, he repeatedly rehearses the judgments of Boston on the events of his story before offering his own analysis of them. From the start, we watch the Puritans watching the main characters; we interpret their interpretations of the events. From them we can learn how not to understand *The Scarlet Letter*.

The complaint that Hawthorne files most insistently against the Puritans, especially in the opening chapters, is their lack of sympathy for Hester as a sinner. Behind this, however, he also undertakes a subtle analysis of why they thrust her, as a scapegoat, outside the pale of their compassion. Their larger failure is to be honest with themselves and each other about the truths of their own nature. By means of the "sympathetic knowledge of the hidden sin in other hearts" that Hester's letter gives her (86), we see the people of Boston in much the same light that Goodman Brown sees Salem in the wilderness: as a brotherhood of shame and guilt. Like Brown, however, the Puritans reject this community: he exiles himself from society; they project their hidden sinfulness onto Hester and then, as a kind of repression, banish her and her *A* from their knowledge of themselves.[25] It is this unwillingness to "be true" (260) to their own unconscious selves that ultimately accounts for their inadequacies as "spectators." They see the world in the simplistic terms on which the repression of self-knowledge depends. They keep seeing the drama, to bring this issue back to Hawthorne's rhetorical concerns with Victorian America, in the black-and-white terms of moral melodrama. Either Chillingworth, for instance, has been brought to Boston to save Reverend Dimmesdale by "an absolute miracle," by the "providential hand" of "Heaven" (121), or he is "Satan's emissary," sent to "plot against" the "especial sanctity" of Reverend Dimmesdale's soul (128). In either case, their reading of Chillingworth is based upon their interpretation of Dimmesdale as "a miracle of holiness" (142), for their reading of his character is simply the obverse side of their repression of Hester. Onto the minister they project their image of the pure, angelic self, the self-gratulatory image that is fostered by their denial of the sinful self. Their misreading of Dimmesdale is as egregious as their inability to identify or sympathize with Hester, and it is treated even more explicitly as their failure as an audience. The minister achieves "a brilliant popularity in his sacred office" (141), but "the people knew not the power that moved them thus" (142). Hawthorne's discussions of Dimmesdale as a performer provide yet another instance of the way he keeps refracting his own preoccupations with audience onto the novel. But he raises the issue I am concerned with here most directly—indeed, most personally—in the last three sentences of chapter 22, just before he brings his tale to its dramatic climax: "The sainted minister in the church! The woman of the scarlet letter in the market-place! What imagination would have been irreverent enough to surmise that the same scorching stigma was on them both?" (247). The answer, of course, is Hawthorne's imagination.

This is not, however, a rhetorical question. It is a reminder of Hawthorne's rhetorical situation. For the moral simplifications of which Boston is guilty are far more characteristic of a Victorian-American audience than of a group of Calvinists. When Hawthorne mentions, for example, how the Puritans "etherealized" and "apotheosized" Dimmesdale (251) or how they expect at the end to see him "ascend . . . before their eyes . . . into the light of heaven" (252), he is evoking the patterns of popular contemporary literature.[26] It was Hawthorne's culture, not Hester's, that tended to flatten out the complexities of human nature into the sentimentalizations of melodrama: to represent the issue of slavery, say, in the terms made available by little Eva and Simon Legree (the unspotted angel and the sooty demon) or to divide "woman" into light and dark heroines—virginal mothers (or motherly virgins) and seductive temptresses. Hawthorne's work is by no means free of such tendencies, but a major source of the power of his best work is its dramatic complication of Victorian archetypes. He forces Brown in the woods, or Giovanni in Rappaccini's garden, or Robin in Major Molineux's Boston, or Hilda and Kenyon in Rome to confront the profound ambiguities of human experience—the dark in the light, and vice versa. Of the characterizations in *The Scarlet Letter*, Pearl's suffers most from the stylizations of contemporary convention. (Although Chillingworth's character as a "fiend" comes close, Hawthorne works hard to keep us from forgetting that Chillingworth is also a "mortal man, with once a human heart" [172]; his fiendishness is much more carefully and believably motivated than someone like Legree's.) And even in Pearl's case, it is more the diction with which the narrative recounts her behavior than that behavior itself which is stereotypical. She can be both tender and perverse, angelic and impish, vulnerable and despotic; she is probably, in fact, the most realistic representation of a child among the thousands of children who populate mid-nineteenth-century American literature.

Because twentieth-century culture, thanks particularly to the light Freud shed into the depths of the psyche, rejected these simplifications of human nature, modern readers tend to take for granted the very issue that Hawthorne was most acutely aware of as a writer of psychological romances. By burrowing into the depths of our common nature to see what was really there, he was, as far as the pieties of his culture and the conventions of genteel literature went, engaging in an "irreverent," indeed, a subversive act. How concerned he was is what we see when we realize that the Puritan spectators to his story are essentially a group of Victorian readers disguised by their historical costumes. What they lack—self-knowledge and sympathy—defines the "apostolic errand" of *The Scarlet Letter*. By "imagining" the same stigma over both Hester's and Dimmesdale's hearts, Hawthorne remarries the aspects of human nature that the idealizations of his culture had divorced, and thus seeks to introduce his genteel audience to the morally intricate truth about themselves.

It may seem strange to accuse mid-nineteenth-century readers, who by their own reports shed so many tears over the pages that they read, of lacking sympathy. Yet as Hawthorne knew, sentimentality for victimized innocence is not true sympathy but self-indulgence.[27] As Hawthorne also knew, the readers who were eager to suffer with Longfellow's Evangeline or Warner's Ellen were not therefore prepared to admit Hester Prynne, a convicted adulteress, into the circle of their sympathies. Of all the novel's elements, his development and use of Hester's characterization shows the most "sophistication" about appealing to the audience of his time. It is also probably the hardest thing about the novel for us, in our time, to recreate. For if the responses of his contemporary readers to Hester were preconditioned by the admonitory convention of the dark heroine, our own reaction is bound to be guided by the exemplary heroism of the feminist protagonist who has appeared in so many avatars since the end of the last century. For most of us, Hester is the novel's greatest achievement, and what the book leaves us with is the tragic waste of her extraordinary powers. For Hawthorne, on the other hand, and actually for Hester as well, the greatest moment in the novel is Dimmesdale's confession and the complex lesson it teaches: about knowing one's self and living up to one's responsibilities to other people. Hawthorne began with Hester for many reasons, but ultimately the novel is "about" Dimmesdale, the tragic hero who dies in its climactic scene. However, it is understandable that readers, particularly modern readers, cannot quite accompany the novel when it begins, as early as chapter 9, to shift its focus from Hester to Dimmesdale. Even at the end, though Dimmesdale's death is as Christ-like as Hawthorne could make it, we are likely to be less moved by it than by Hester's lost happiness. Hawthorne's inability to convince us about Dimmesdale's "triumphant" death (257) is surely a reflection of the fact that our culture has lost sight of the Christian scaffolding that Hawthorne's culture "saw" so clearly.[28] Our unresolved feelings surely point as well to Hawthorne's own misgivings about the price that Dimmesdale and Hester each paid, the price all of us must pay as adult members of a community of roles and responsibilities. One can read *The Scarlet Letter* as a stunning anticipation of *Civilization and Its Discontents.* One can also read it as the first novel to use a woman's sexuality as the basis for questioning the structures of society. It is both, and these are among the reasons it is a timeless book. But I'm trying here to read it as a novel published in 1850, which means one must consider Hawthorne's decision to begin with Hester in its contemporary context.

In the audience before the scaffold at the start, Hawthorne tells us, the women take "a peculiar interest" in the scene (50). That women are featured so prominently as the audience in chapter 2 reminds us of the sociological fact of life for an American novelist in 1850: that the reading public she or he addressed was predominantly feminine. By beginning with Hester, Hawthorne chooses the most direct means possible to secure that public's interest in his story. We could even say that in the first eight chapters he works Hester's femininity for all it's worth to him as a professional novelist, for these chapters locate Hester among the situations that popular fiction had already proven were the most attractive to the reading public. There is "Hester at Her Needle," struggling to make her way as a woman in the world.[29] There is "Pearl," which concentrates on Hester's struggle to rear her daughter. The most dramatic episode in the novel's first half comes in chapters 7 and 8, where Hester pleads "a mother's rights" (113) against the society that would separate her from her child. In this scene Hawthorne shows the same instinct for his audience's sensibilities as the one that prompted Stowe to iterate and reiterate the forced separation of mothers and children to dramatize the evil of slavery. In these chapters the surface of Hawthorne's novel is largely given up to the kind of concerns that preoccupy the best-selling fictions of the time.

But one has to talk about the narrative's depths very differently. If these chapters reveal Hawthorne's willingness to meet his audience's expectations and appetites halfway, he is also radically challenging them. Hester's needlework and her trials as a mother would be perfectly at home amid the workbasket and toys of the Victorian parlor where Hawthorne locates the artist, but Hester herself—with her black hair, black eyes, "rich, voluptuous, Oriental" nature (83), and a scarlet A on her breast—would never be permitted there. Hester, Hawthorne says in his first description of her appearance, is "lady-like," but then he adds, a bit slyly, "in the antique interpretation of the term" (53). The contemporary definition of "lady," as he does not go on to say, entirely excluded adulteresses. Given the program of conventional literature to segregate "ladies" from sin, especially from sexuality, he doubtless felt that his readers' preconditioned reaction to Hester would have been essentially the same as the Puritans'. There can be no doubt, at least, about the care with which he arranges the representation of Hester to *re*condition their response, to coerce their sympathy for "this poor victim of her own frailty, and man's hard law" (87). Before he lets his reader see Hester he depicts the "baby" "in her arms" (52), so that when Hester stands "fully revealed," it is first and foremost as "the mother of this child" (52). "Mother" was to Hawthorne's audience what "sainted minister" was to the Puritans he is ostensibly writing about, but by repeatedly referring to the fallen woman as "the mother" and even wondering what "a Papist" would have made of Hester's Madonnalike image on the scaffold (56), he is deliberately breaking down the boundary between the most sacred and the most despised cultural categories. The confrontation about Pearl that Hawthorne stages in "The Governor's Hall," between "the public, on the one side, and a lonely woman, backed by the sympathies of nature, on the other" (101), is brilliantly designed to divide the Puritans' attitude toward Hester and his readers' response: his audience can only take Hester's side in this encounter.

The Puritan women see Hester as an other: a "'brazen hussy'" (54).[30] But Hawthorne's narrative provides a different vocabulary for responding to her. As she moves in that opening scene through the throng of spectators to the scaffold of ignominy, the novel pointedly describes her emotions in terms of "our nature" and "our common nature" (55). Hawthorne's paramount concern in the first third of *The Scarlet Letter* is to stretch his readers' sympathies well beyond the limits defined by gentility. They have been subtly forced to include the figure of the dark heroine, the convicted sinner, inside their sense of what it means to be human, even inside their sense of what it means to be a mother. As a way of creating a middle ground between his audience's values and his own vision, between the parlor and the artist's haunted, irreverent imagination, his development of Hester is a remarkable performance. Although the Puritans banish her from their society, her presence in the novel's first half allows Hawthorne to create a community, a fellowship of sympathetic seekers into the dark truths of the human heart. (In the second half, on the other hand, having gone astray in the moral wilderness to which the Puritans' lack of sympathy condemned her, Hester herself becomes the greatest threat to such a community. As we will see, it is then up to Dimmesdale to reestablish the fellowship that Hester proudly spurns, first by rejecting her temptation in the wilderness, then by publishing his own guilt. I should anticipate the climax here on one point: what leads Dimmesdale to confess is what he learns from Hester in their encounter—not from what she says, but from what his response to her reveals about himself: "Another man had returned out of the forest; a wiser one; with a knowledge of hidden mysteries which the simplicity of the former never could have reached" [223]. In this sense, even in the second half of the novel Hester's role is still to lead others away from their simplifications toward the repressed truth about themselves.[31] It is Dimmesdale's role, however, to show them, including Hester, how to act upon that knowledge.)

The same goal of community underlies the novel's narrative style. When Hawthorne calls himself the "editor, or very little more" of *The Scarlet Letter* (4), he is making room for the reader to participate. Not only does he offer various legends and rumors without the sanction of his own author-ity, so that readers must choose whether to credit or discount them; the syntactic characteristic of his own voice is incessant qualification. Here is a typical example:

This *might be* pride, but was so like humility, that it produced all the softening influence of the latter quality on the public mind. The public is despotic in its temper; it is capable of denying common justice, when too strenuously demanded as a right; but quite as frequently it awards more than justice, when the appeal is made, as despots love to have it made, entirely to its generosity. Interpreting Hester Prynne's deportment as an appeal of this nature, society was inclined to show its former victim a more benign countenance than she cared to be favored with, *or, perchance*, than she deserved. (162)

Admittedly, I have not chosen this example at random. It is one of several passages that explicitly discuss the "public" as a judgmental and undependable audience, and Hawthorne's shift to the present tense shows (again) how alive he was to this issue as he was writing the novel.[32] It is also (again) an instance of using the Puritans' misinterpretations to guide his reader aright. At the same time, though, the phrases I have italicized show how much he leaves for that reader to decide. Despite the very doubts about them that the passage admits, he requires his audience to share the burden of interpreting the events of his story. Here is another example, which I did choose at random: "It might be, too, —doubtless it was so, although she hid the secret from herself, and grew pale whenever it struggled out of her heart, like a serpent from its hole, —it might be that . . ." (80). The allegorical emblem of the serpent works to impose *an* interpretation here, but the stuttering qualifications of his style—it might be, doubtless it was, it might be—work against that tendency and create a realm of ambiguity in which the reader's own interpretive powers are brought into play.[33]

This rhythm is apparent on a larger scale in the narrative's strategy of delay. The story begins in chapter 2 with the audience of Puritans waiting to witness . . . something. Hawthorne of course knows what it is, but the first three hundred words of the chapter offer different possibilities of what "might be" about to happen, none of which is right (49–50). This pattern of withholding closure, of requiring the reader to suspend judgment and keep a number of alternatives in mind, recurs throughout the novel. Hawthorne leaves open such trivial questions as whether Hester cut her hair or just confined it under her cap (163), and such crucial questions as "where was [Dimmesdale's] mind" as he marches forward to give the Election Sermon after having agreed to run away with Hester (238–39). The answer to the novel's first explicit question—who was Hester's lover?—is withheld from the reader till the middle, and from the Puritans till the very end. It is a characteristic of the Puritans' exegetical intolerance to leap to conclusions, but Hawthorne teaches his readers to defer judgment, to experience the ambiguities of his story.

We must be careful of the modern conclusions we might leap to here. The background against which his text creates ambiguities is not our twentieth-century loss of certainty, but the mid-nineteenth century's conventional assurances. The purpose of his representational strategies is to wean his readers from Victorian moral and psychological simplifications, not to suggest that the truth is indeterminate.[34] Before the story begins, and again some "years" after it is effectively over, he offers two definitive points of interpretive closure, two authoritative readings of the scarlet letter. The first is in "The Custom-House," where, after analytically considering various meanings for the *A* he has found, he places it against his own heart and "shudders" at its "burning heat" (31–32). He is not just alerting his genteel audience to the fact that his is (as he called it in a letter) "a h-ll-fired story";[35] he is also cuing those readers that the only way to interpret his "mystic symbol" correctly is to acknowledge their common sinfulness. It is only, as he reminded himself and his readers in "Ethan Brand," by "opening the chambers or the dungeons of our common nature by the key of holy sympathy" that one can solve the "riddles" of the heart.[36] The other exemplary interpretation comes in the novel's second-to-last paragraph, where we learn that after Hester has returned to Boston and resumed the *A* voluntarily, "the scarlet letter ceased to be a stigma which attracted the world's scorn and bitterness, and became a type of something to be sorrowed over, and looked upon with awe, yet with reverence too" (263). Those who read the letter in this way form a community based on kindness and apprehension, self-knowledge and sympathy, reverence and responsibility. It is this community that, thematically, Hawthorne seeks as a third term to mediate between the antinomian individualism Hester preaches in the wilderness and the repressive legalism of society. It is also this community that, rhetorically, Hawthorne seeks as a writer trying to open an intercourse with the world.

Whether such a community really emerges within the novel is another ambiguity. In "The Revelation of the Scarlet Letter," Hawthorne uses Dimmesdale to try to create it. By rejecting the fantasy of self-fulfillment with which Hester tempted him in the woods, Dimmesdale points both Hester and the Puritans back toward a sense of their common nature and its moral obligations. By mounting the scaffold voluntarily, he tries to reinvest the forms of law with the spirit that gives them their human meaning, their moral authority. By confessing his guilt, he also affirms his relatedness and accountability to others: to Hester as the partner of her sin, to Pearl as her father, to the people as their minister. He is finally living up to the responsibilities of those roles.

This public-ation of the letter is, like the opening scene, a performance, and as before Hawthorne describes the reaction of the immediate audience in great detail. In the Election Sermon Dimmesdale preached in the preceding chapter, he told the Puritans what they wanted to hear about their glorious destiny as an American people, and they responded with "an irrepressible outburst of . . . enthusiasm": "Never, from the soil of New England, had gone up such a shout! Never, on New England soil, had stood the man so honored by his mortal brethren as the preacher!" (250). Although Hawthorne tries not to show any cynicism, this reaction is a reminder that the surest way to reach an audience is to flatter their assumptions. When Dimmesdale mounts the scaffold, on the other hand, the truth he tells about himself challenges, indeed destroys, the whole structure of appearances by which the Puritans had defined reality. Their immediate response to this is understandably confused: "a tumult" (253), "appalled" (254), "horror-stricken" (255), and so on. After Dimmesdale's death brings the scene to an end, the chapter goes on to note the audience's final reaction: "The multitude, silent till then, broke out in a strange, deep voice of awe and wonder, which could not as yet find utterance" (257).

Was Dimmesdale's publication of the scarlet letter in the marketplace a success? The "Conclusion" begins with the re-views of the audience that had witnessed it (258). Their continuing confusion about what, if anything, was revealed in chapter 23 and what, in any case, it meant—what chapter 24 reveals is how much anxiety Hawthorne still felt about his own performance. He had been "irreverent" enough to "imagine" that "the same scorching stigma" emblematically belongs on every human breast, and that recognizing and confessing those "hidden mysteries" is the only real basis for either self-knowledge or true community. Yet in chapter 24 the only Puritans who interpret Dimmesdale's performance along those lines are the ones whose reading of the scaffold scene Hawthorne authoritatively dismisses, because they deny that "there was any mark whatever" on the minister's breast (259). For them, apparently, the truths of the human heart are comfortable truisms that have no revelatory power over their own lives; or rather, their orthodox theology has become a way to avoid the truth about themselves. Among the other witnesses, those who did at least see "a SCARLET LETTER" (258), it is hard to tell what they learned from the revelation. On the evidence of the community that gathers around Hester at the very end, one could conclude that Hawthorne felt hopeful that his "tale of human frailty and sorrow" (48) would bring people into a truer relationship with each other and with their own selves. But the grounds for prophetic pessimism are marked out just as clearly, and not only in the confusion that remains among the spectators. The most discouraging detail is the fate of Pearl. Not her private fate, for when Dimmesdale publicly acknowledges her as his daughter, she is freed to be "a woman" in "the world" (256). But if Dimmesdale's revelation taught the Puritans anything, it should have taught them to readmit Pearl into the circle of their sympathy. There is in fact "a very material change in the public estimation" of Pearl (261), but not because Dimmesdale kissed her on the scaffold. Hawthorne means *very material*: Boston sees Pearl with new eyes only after Chillingworth dies and bequeaths her "a very considerable amount of property." Once she becomes "the richest heiress of her day," the public smiles on "the demon offspring" (261).

That money succeeds when revelation fails in impressing the mind of the public brings us back to the conflicts of "The Custom-House": whether American society can give the insights and achievements of the artist any place among the commercial and domestic pursuits it cherishes. There is no doubt about Hawthorne's deepest anxiety. He did not want to be an artist estranged from his culture, alone in the haunted parlor. His novel repeatedly measures the horrors of such alienation in its accounts of all three main characters. Dimmesdale's "ugly nights" beset by "visions" in "the remote dimness of [his] chamber" (145–46) bring him to "the verge of lunacy" (166). Hester's and Chillingworth's lives also make vivid the perils of the artist's solitude. The "thoughts" that "visit" Hester "in her lonesome cottage" are described as "shadowy guests" (164), which again refigures the artist in "the deserted parlour" and his "illusive guests" (35). With no other company besides these thoughts, Hester's solitude is terrifying: she "wandered without a clew in the dark labyrinth of mind; . . . There was wild and ghastly scenery all around her, and a home and comfort nowhere" (166). And the "devil's office" that turns Chillingworth "into a devil" is yet another, more explicit refiguration of the Hawthornean artist's work: "This unhappy person had effected such a transformation by devoting himself, for seven years, to the constant analysis of a heart full of torture" (170).

Taken together, these accounts suggest the urgency behind Hawthorne's desire to open an intercourse with the world. To them one can add what he says in the text, just after Dimmesdale has revealed the sign that has been branded into his flesh, about how the letter has tormented him: "We have thrown all the light we could acquire upon the portent, and would gladly, now that it has done its office, erase its deep print out of our own brain; where long meditation has fixed it in very undesirable distinctness" (259). For Dimmesdale the only escape from private torment is public confession. Hawthorne, though he "keep[s] the inmost Me behind its veil" (4), is determined to divide the burden of his story with the reader. We are made his accomplices very explicitly at the end. The most dramatic instance of narrative withholding comes at the climax: Dimmesdale throws open his shirt, but Hawthorne will not tell us what he reveals: "It was revealed! But it were irreverent to describe that revelation" (255). This is followed by the book's most impressive instance of narrative ambiguity: Hawthorne gives us the several Puritan accounts of "what had been witnessed on the scaffold" (258), then gives our interpretive powers absolute freedom—"The reader may choose among these theories" (259). On the one hand, these are acts of faith in our ability to be the community of readers he posits at the start of "The Custom-House," the ones "who will understand him" (3). They also testify, however, to the earnestness of his desire for communicants to share his burdensome vision of the awful, sacred mysteries of the human heart. The scarlet letter is his "passport into regions" where Victorian-American readers "dare not tread" (199), into "the depths of our common nature." But as befits the first letter of the alphabet, its ultimate office, for the author as well as for his characters, is to communicate the repressed truth to the world at large, and thus to give his haunted vision a home and comfort somewhere: in his reader's "heart and mind" (3).

In his first major full-length fiction, therefore, Hawthorne worked very deliberately to interest and engage his contemporary audience. Yet he doubted the prospects for his scarlet letter's success in the marketplace. The day after he finished writing the book, he told his friend Horatio Bridge that he had read the conclusion to his wife the night before:

> It broke her heart and sent her to bed with a grievous headache—which I look upon as triumphant success! Judging from its effect on her and the publisher, I may calculate on what bowlers call a 'ten-strike.' Yet [he went on] I do not make any such calculation. Some portions of the book are powerfully written; but my writings do not, nor ever will, appeal to the broadest class of sympathies, and therefore will not attain a very wide popularity. Some like them very much; others care nothing for them, and see nothing in them.[37]

There is of course nothing elitist about this discrimination: Hawthorne is not referring to readers in a certain class, but to readers with a certain temperament. (I say "of course," but most mid-century attempts to distinguish between various reading publics are based primarily on class.) In this ability to distinguish between his particular audience and the whole reading public, Hawthorne was better off than Melville, who could only see "the public" as a mass arrayed against the genius. There is no false modesty in this letter, but although Hawthorne clearly feels he has written a great book, he can realistically recognize why it will not be widely popular. As he tells Bridge, it "lacks sunshine." As he told Fields, it is "too sombre."[38]

We can see how far apart Hawthorne's imagination and the popular mind were by noting the two variants of the Victorian happy ending with which his novel concludes. The best-selling fictions of his time all ended with reunited or reconstituted families. Hawthorne does his best to reward his readers with such a vision in the "Conclusion," where he even sounds like Dickens: "In fine, the gossips of that day believed, —and Mr. Surveyor Pue, who made investigations a century later, believed, —and one of his recent successors in office, moreover, faithfully believes, —that

Pearl was not only alive, but married, and happy, and mindful of her mother" (262). Against this conventional conception of bliss, however, should be set the tragedy of the previous chapter. When Hester, Pearl, and Chillingworth join Dimmesdale on the scaffold, that too is a family reunion. But that scene insists on the instinctual cost by which the "family" is maintained, for what Dimmesdale gives up to fulfill his responsibility to Pearl is the individual happiness, the erotic fulfillment, that he and Hester "'dreamed of in the forest'" (254). In *The Scarlet Letter* Hawthorne faced this fact of civilization more directly than almost any other nineteenth-century writer, and accepted it as the "higher truth" (203) of adult life, but knew how profoundly it set him at odds with the unexamined complacencies of his culture.

In fact, *The Scarlet Letter* will always be a disturbing book, for the tragedy it reenacts when the aroused expectations of the forest give way to the painful exactions of the scaffold is the tragedy of our own instinctual lives. That our culture is more familiar with this conflict, that as readers we are more receptive to the idea of tragedy than Americans were in 1850, have not made the novel any less somber. Hawthorne was right about its chances for "wide popularity." The last distinction to make between *The Scarlet Letter*, however, and *Moby-Dick*, *Walden*, and *Leaves of Grass* is that its greatness was immediately appreciated by its contemporary audience. Its sales were nothing like the astonishing numbers attained by Warner's, Stowe's, and Cummins's best-sellers, nor did Hawthorne expect them to be—although Melville, for instance, complained that Hawthorne's books were not "sold by the hundred-thousand."[39] Despite the adult and unconventional demands of its theme, however, *The Scarlet Letter* was the most successful of all Hawthorne's books "in the marketplace."[40] That the book's achievement was recognized at once is a tribute both to Hawthorne's intricately determined concern to reach an audience, and to his reading public's willingness, when maturely addressed, to entertain the haunted artist in their parlors.

Chapter VII

"AT THE WRITER'S CONTROL":
POE'S PSYCHOLOGY OF COMPOSITION

"Now THIS is the point. You fancy me mad. Madmen know nothing. But you should have seen *me*. You should have seen how wisely I proceeded—with what caution—with what foresight—with what dissimulation I went to work!"[1] This, of course, is from "The Tell-Tale Heart." Despite its title, and despite the way it goes into detail about how to conceal a *body*, the tale is from first to last a telling of and on a *mind*. Never mind that its narrator has been caught as a murderer, has presumably been judged and confined as a madman, and that a plea of insanity would seem in his best interest. He is writing to convince his judges that he is sane. He offers two kinds of evidence: how masterfully he set about killing the old man, and "how healthily—how calmly I can tell you the whole story" (792). The testimony of his style is conclusive enough. Its compulsive repetitions, its ejaculations of complaint or denial or triumph, even the Rorschach pattern of its punctuation marks all point to what the narrator keeps trying to hide beneath the floorboards. And these stylistic self-betrayals just compulsively reaffirm the testimony of the actions he describes. His refusal for eight nights to oil the squeaky hinge of his lantern, the chuckle that escapes him in the dark, the "loud yell" (795) with which he leaps on the old man (before his heartbeat can be heard by the neighbors!) indicate long before he confesses his crime to the unsuspecting police how inevitably he must keep betraying himself. Despite his protestations of control, each action, each sentence, just adds another bar to the cage he is really trapped in—his own diseased and tattletale mind. That, I think, is the "evil I" he really wants to destroy. In that sense there is a consistent madness, at least, in the method of his statement: if found sane, and guilty of the premeditation he insists upon, he will be executed. Only by that means will he ever be free of the true source of the "uncontrollable terror" (795) disclosed by the tale: the mind alone with itself.

That we can perceive this self-destructive pattern as even grotesquely comic is one measure of Poe's limits. He can render the details and much of the horror of madness with clinical precision, but cannot remotely express any of its human pathos. Yet despite this narrator's record of failure, the pattern itself defines the characteristic concern of Poe's fiction: the struggle of the conscious mind to master whatever threatens it with the uncontrollable, which can be variously located within the mind or in some aspect of the external world. At the extreme of its largests implications, control is also the central, informing preoccupation of Poe's uneasy career as an American writer. The narrator of "The Tell-Tale Heart" urges readers to pay particular attention to his manner of telling the tale. His story, of course, masters him. As a critic and theorist, however, Poe also insists that great art must demonstrate two related qualities: perfect control over its material, and perfect control over its reader. In an essay like "The Philosophy of Composition" he proceeds to display the caution, the foresight, the wisdom, and even the dissimulation with which *he* went to work.

Baudelaire would have it that the artistic act is essentially criminal, and that Edgar Allan Poe was the supreme artist. For his part, though, Poe conceived of the poet as the agent of psychological law and order. In his "analysis, or reconstruction" (*ER*, 14) of how he wrote "The Raven," he depicts himself as a kind of detective, tracking down a poem about a bird that flies out of the night precisely as C. Auguste Dupin, in "The Murders in the Rue Morgue," tracks down the orangutan that climbed into the window of an apartment in Paris. For the process of literary creation Poe claims the same sovereign rationality and absolute mastery that govern the transactions of Dupin's superior mind with reality: "It is my design to render it manifest that no one point in ["The Raven's"] composition is referrible either to accident or intuition—that the work proceeded, step by step, to its completion with the precision and rigid consequence of a mathematical problem" (*ER*, 14–15). Or, as Dupin puts it in a parallel passage, " 'You will say that I was puzzled; but, if you think so, you must have misunderstood the nature of the inductions. To use a sporting phrase, I had not been once "at fault." The scent had never for an instant been lost. There was no flaw in any link of the chain' " (553).

Like most of Poe's tales, "The Philosophy of Composition" is about the workings of a mind, in this case ostensibly Poe's own. If I quote only a few of the locutions that characterize the essay, we see at once how easily they could instead be part of Dupin's supremely logical, personally disengaged re-solutions:

> The initial consideration was . . . My next thought concerned . . . being thus determined, I betook myself to ordinary induction . . . I proceeded to think thus—*a posteriori* . . . These considerations inevitably led me to . . . In such a search it would have been absolutely impossible to overlook the . . . It was clear to me, however, that . . . Here, then, immediately arose the idea of . . . and this corroboration of my idea . . . From what I have already explained at some length, the answer, here also, is obvious . . .

I have, in fact, sneaked three quotations from Dupin into this sampling, as the best way to show how indistinguishable Poe's account of writing a poem is from Dupin's explanation of solving a murder.* Before Dupin goes near the window over Mme L'Espanaye's bed that solves the puzzle of the locked room, his mind has confidently predicted what he will find. Similarly, Poe claims that before he "first put pen to paper," his analytical "preconsiderations" had already determined each detail—length, subject, versification, and so on—of the poem (*ER*, 20). Not once is his rational control less than perfect.

"The Philosophy of Composition" will never fool many of its readers. To borrow James Russell Lowell's phrase for Poe, it is considerably more than "two fifths sheer fudge." But there can be no doubt that Poe wished it were true. It was written after the three Dupin stories, which may explain why he chose to write about creation in terms of a reconstruction, but the essay's insistence on consummate rationality can be found in all Poe's considerations of the realm of art and the process of imaginative creation. One of the most striking aspects of his literary theory is that, deeply indebted as he was to Coleridge's aesthetic formulas, he nonetheless rejected Coleridge's crucial doctrine that creation is "organic." Although Poe agreed, for instance, that "a poem is such, only inasmuch as it intensely excites, by elevating, the soul" (*ER*, 15), he defined the means either by which the poet writes or by which the poem acts on its reader as a mechanical one. "Wheels and pinions"—a metaphor that looks not to a growing field but to a working factory—can serve to describe the way a writer turns out a finished poem.[2] The vocabulary of mathematics or empirical science is entirely appropriate to the task of the aesthetician: "And now it appears evident, that since Poetry, in this new sense, *is* the practical result, expressed in language, of this Poetic Sentiment in certain individuals, the only proper method of testing the merits of a poem is by measuring its capabilities of exciting the Poetic Sentiment in others" (*ER*, 511). The "new sense" announced here, in Poe's 1836 review of Drake's and Halleck's poetry, is precisely the Romantics' program for poetry. His idiosyncratic emphasis on the practical, on method, on testing and measuring, however, already points toward his transformation of the aeolian harp into a type of steam engine that can "elevate" the reader's feelings in the same way a cogged railroad can be designed to carry coal up out of a mine. The Romantics' belief that a poem could visit its reader with the power and mystery of grace gives way to Poe's version of the poem, to cite Daniel Hoffman's comment on "The Philosophy of Composition," as "an intricate mechanism for the production of the effects of passion."[3]

* The fourth, seventh, and ninth of these ten phrases are from "The Murders in the Rue Morgue" (*ER*, 15–19; 552, 554).

His earliest major theoretical statement, the Drake-Halleck review is much less guarded, less stagy, less self-serving than "The Philosophy," which was written ten years later, when being the author of "The Raven" was part of a public mystique that Poe worked hard to promote and exploit. On the whole the review is based on the distinction between Imagination and Fancy that Poe had learned from Coleridge. Yet in its two most original passages, this essay betrays the need that lay behind Poe's lifelong engagement with his imagination: the need to see art as separate from and uncontaminated by the "chaos of human intelligence": "With the *passions* of mankind—although [Poesy] may modify them greatly— although it may exalt, or inflame, or purify, or control them—it would require little ingenuity to prove that it has no inevitable, and indeed no necessary co-existence." (*ER*, 511). The other passage indicates still more clearly that what propels Poe's proclaimed philosophy of composition was his obsessive desire to master the truest sources of the terrifying in his life as well as in his tales. Art was a way to govern the unruly forces of the mind. As the passage makes explicit, writing was his personal quest for psychological salvation: "If, indeed, there be any one circle of thought distinctly and palpably marked out from amid the jarring and tumultuous chaos of human intelligence, it is that evergreen and radiant Paradise which the true poet knows, and knows alone, as the limited realm of his authority—as the circumscribed Eden of his dreams" (*ER*, 509).

This is how the cavern of Poe's temperament echoed back the greatest hope of the Romantic movement, the idea, given its fullest elaboration in America by the Transcendentalists, that by means of their innate creative faculties men and women could "return to paradise." Thus spoke Emerson in *Nature*, which appeared only a few months after the Drake-Halleck review. But Poe's version of the Emersonian injunction to "build therefore your own world" is radically diminished; his implicit distinction between life and art makes Poe seem closer to the modernists than to the Romantics. The Imagination's authority is limited to the supremely fictive order it can achieve within the lines of a poem or the pages of a tale. Nor is there any prospect for social regeneration in such an order, for the poet knows it "alone." The circle of art is a private refuge from the anarchy of life: build therefore your own text.

Yet while Poe circumscribes the reach of the Imagination's authority, he does not impose any limits on that authority within its own world. Like Dupin, whose rationality makes the "wildest disorder" of the grisly scene at the Rue Morgue (537) entirely explicable and structured, the poet creates a perfect order out of "the jarring and tumultuous chaos" of the mind. It is this psychogenesis of composition that Poe reveals in "The Philosophy." There from the start he firmly denies that he writes "by a species of fine frenzy—an ecstatic intuition" (*ER*, 14); as I have noted, he insists that composition involves nothing short of a concentrated, sustained, conscious purpose, subordinated at every point to the faculties of rationality and analysis. This preoccupation with controlling the text can also be seen in an oft-cited passage from his review of Hawthorne's short stories. The omnipresence of design broods like a cerebral but also sterile dove over the process of creation:

> A skilful literary artist has constructed a tale. If wise, he has not fashioned his thoughts to accommodate his incidents; but having conceived, with deliberate care, a certain unique or single *effect* to be wrought out, he then invents such incidents—he then combines such events as may best aid him in establishing this preconceived effect. If his very initial sentence tend not to the outbringing of this effect, then he has failed in his first step. In the whole composition there should be no word written, of which the tendency, direct or indirect, is not to the one pre-established design. (*ER*, 572)

This is less a declaration of writers' prerogatives than a confession of their vulnerability. The possibilities of organic growth are denied here with a vengeance: all the writer's energies are devoted to preserving a preconceived status quo. The "construction," like the House of Usher, seems right on the verge of falling; it is kept up only by the writer's continuously exerted will, which must permit "no word"—not even one—to escape his or her conscious control.

How much havoc a single word can produce is, in fact, the subject of "The Raven." When that bird flies out of the midnight darkness he brings with him one word, *nevermore*, and in Poe's paraphrase of the poem's plot, that one word is the password that opens the door of the poem's narrator's mind to *its own* darkness:

> the lover, startled from his original *nonchalance* by the melancholy character of the word itself—by its frequent repetition . . . is at length excited to superstition, and wildly propounds queries of a far different character—queries whose solution he has passionately at heart—propounds them half in superstition and half in that species of depair which delights in self-torture . . . because he experiences a phrenzied pleasure in so modeling his questions as to receive from the *expected* "Nevermore" the most delicious because the most intolerable of sorrow. (*ER*, 19)

The poet, having already certified that *he* felt no "frenzy," would have us believe that he calmly settled on the word *nevermore* because of its sonorous distribution of consonants and vowels. His claim of absolute self-possession in "The Philosophy" is the exact opposite of what happens to the narrator of the poem whose composition he is explaining: he becomes a helpless victim to this word that has apparently chosen him. He wildly, passionately, despairingly tortures himself—because his mind is so constituted as to "delight in self-torture." This, of course, is the very kind of irrational passion that the Imagination has "no inevitable" connection with; this is what Poe looks to art "to control."

This narrator, like so many others in Poe's work, surrenders to "The Imp of the Perverse": the primitive, innate instinct to self-destruction that cannot be contained by the mind's rational powers. Meanwhile, however, Poe as writer superintends the pattern of the anarchy. He shapes the work of art as a scrupulously controlled irony of each narrator's self-destruction, and therefore measures his triumph over the mind's "tumultuous chaos" directly against their failure. Yet as Poe parenthetically admits in "The Philosophy," the terrors that beset his protagonists are summoned from the depths of his own psyche. First, he says, he chooses an effect, then "afterward look[s] about me (*or rather within*) for such combinations of event, or tone, as shall best aid me in the construction of the effect" (*ER*, 14; my emphasis). In this transaction with his own interior, the role of the imagination is necessarily deliberate—not intuitive; rational—not passionate; analytical—and not even, strictly speaking, creative. Art, and this is the implication of his aesthetic theories, is properly a re-construction: the imposition of order on aboriginal chaos. Out of the underworld of his nightmares he brings the "Eden of his dreams," and the dream, let me say once more, is of perfect control. No reader of "The Philosophy" is ever supposed to suspect that "the death of a beautiful woman" (*ER*, 19) was a subject Poe was stuck with, rather than one he was free to choose, that "The Raven's" real "pre-text" (see *ER*, 18) was his own mother's death, which he was helpless to prevent or understand. This is why in his literary criticism Poe usually focuses on style to the practical exclusion of content, for style is the measure of the writer's mastery of content, while content is like the uninvited orangutan or raven at the window—content is what the writer cannot avoid, cannot decide for himself, must try to master. The protagonists whom Poe situates amid the obsessive anxieties he found "within" himself may be overwhelmed; they need not triumph in the tales, as long as Poe can triumph in the writing of them.

> As [the novel] cannot be read at one sitting, it deprives itself, of course, of the immense force derivable from *totality*. Worldly interests intervening during the pauses of perusal, modify, annul, or counteract . . . the impressions of the book. But simple cessation in reading would, of itself, be sufficient to destroy the true unity. In the brief tale, however, the author is enabled to carry out the fulness of his intention. . . . During the hour of perusal, the soul of the reader is at the writer's control. (*ER*, 572)

There is a certain amount of fudge in this passage too. Doubtless Poe would have written novels (he did once, in *A. Gordon Pym*, and tried a second time in the unfinished "Journal of Julius Rodman") if he could have been more popularly successful with the form. Much of his insistence on the preeminence of "the brief tale" is probably a compensation for the failure of his longer ones. Yet the theoretical consolation he finds is telling. What larger circumstances force upon him is converted into a putative source of power. This passage explicitly presents the writer in competition with life, and what he or she is competing for—the attention of the reader—reveals the full shape of Poe's literary program for triumphing over circumstance. No word can be permitted to escape the writer's control, and no reader.

The idea of achieving a "unity of effect," Poe's usual phrase for the "totality" he speaks of here, is probably his most original contribution to aesthetic theory. Innumerable teachers have passed it on to students hoping to learn how to write a short story. In his early references to it, Poe credits the idea to A. W. Schlegel, though the concept of "unity of interest" Schlegel himself borrowed from De la Motte, and uses to describe in general terms the spectator's involvement in a drama.[4] By substituting "effect" for "interest," however, Poe makes the idea very much his own. That change shifts the emphasis from the reader and how he or she feels about a work, to the writer and how he or she is forcing the reader to feel.

Along with Schlegel and the other theorists of Romanticism, Poe moves the definition of a successful work of art into the subjective realm. "Unity" is not a formal concept (dependent on such external qualities as time and place and action), but a psychological one, with its source in the mind of the responding audience. Yet it is not too much to say that Poe's emphasis effectively dehumanizes the relationship between the work of art and the soul of the reader that the Romantics staked so much on. To a contemporary writer like Emerson, elevating the soul by exciting it was a religious experience; the aesthetic of his lectures and essays looks back to the kind of Protestant revivalist sermon Jonathan Edwards preached in the Great Awakening. To Poe, however, "elevating" the soul was a purely secular, rhetorical display of his own manipulatory skills; from his aesthetic, for example, Hitchcock's films or even television commercials are lineally descended. The writer Poe describes in his theoretical statements is not trying to liberate readers but rather to coerce, even to oppress them. In explaining the mechanism that drives the plot of "The Raven," for instance, Poe admits his desire to project the breakdown of his narrator's rationality onto his audience: "This revolution of thought, or fancy, on the lover's part, is intended to induce a similar one on the part of the reader" (ER, 23). After what had happened in America and France at the end of the eighteenth century, "revolution" became one of the most significant words in nineteenth-century aesthetics. But this is a "revolution" with only one social purpose: to prove Poe's power over his audience. That's how radically antidemocratic Poe's aesthetic is: not only does the writer "alone" know the "evergreen Paradise" of art—he or she attains it by regarding readers as subjects.

The consequence of Poe's fixation on "effect" is that the sensibility of his reader is the ultimate subject of his art, the "material" on which it strives to work. In his helpful study of *The Histrionic Mr. Poe*, N. Bryllion Fagin points out the pervasive theatricality of Poe's work, noting, for example, how the tale that can be read at a single sitting resembles the experience of attending a play.[5] Besides the machine, the theater is the chief source of Poe's analogies for the workings of the Imagination: "wheels and pinions" in that passage from "The Philosophy" are followed by "the tackle for scene-shifting—the step-ladders and demon-traps—the cock's feathers, the red paint and the black patches" of the stage, and Poe regularly refers to a writer as a "literary *histrio*" (*ER*, 14). Since their plots typically follow the workings of *a* mind, Poe's tales do not really lend themselves to dramatic presentation, despite Hollywood's many attempts to do so. But if their conflict is the unfilmable drama of consciousness struggling with reality, the method of portraying that conflict is as theatrical as Poe can make it. That is because the larger drama in which each tale comprises a scene involves Poe's determination to dominate the reading public. His stories begin with the studied effect of a curtain going up, and end at the most effective moment for the curtain to drop back down: "'Here then, at least,' I shrieked aloud, 'can I never—can I never be mistaken—these are the full, and the black, and the wild eyes—of my lost love—of the lady—of the LADY LIGEIA!'" (330). This shriek, these stutterings, and especially the signboard capitals locate the place where Poe performs for his audience: right at the front of the stage, writing with the persistence of a salesman trying to close the deal, and characteristically on the brink of overreaching his mark. But what happened next? This is the question that any reader of "Ligeia" who cares about its narrator as a fellow human being or who shares the tale's apparent interest in willing a victory over death must ask. Poe called "Ligeia" his favorite story, but by ending it on this shrilly melodramatic note, he sacrifices its emotional and thematic content for the sake of producing a trite effect.

Poe never wrote anything, not even a letter home or a note to a fiancée, that does not betray his sense of performing for an audience, just as his various literary hoaxes explicitly attempt to manipulate one. But we need go no further than "A Descent into the Maelstrom" for a complete paradigm of the dynamic that governed his relationship with his readers. Halfway down the dizzying slope of the whirl that has caught him, the Norwegian fisherman who tells the tale within this tale also struggles with his own psyche. By not yielding to his perverse "desire" to go down, by searching for an empirical way to order the tumult, the rational mind keeps itself from being sucked into the abyss. This is sufficiently analogous to what Poe himself did whenever, "looking within himself" for a story, he sought to impose an analytical will and an artistic order on the chaos he found there. To tell his tale, however, the fisherman must first take his "audience," the story's unnamed narrator, to the dizzying top of the huge cliff that overlooks the maelstrom. As one would have guessed, that narrator is afraid of heights. The fisherman turns out to be as anxious to produce an effect as Poe ever was, because the process of mastering circumstance is complete only when his fear has been displaced onto an audience. As Poe himself said about the sequence of composition, "I prefer *commencing* with the consideration of an effect" (*ER*, 13; my emphasis). Concentrating from first to last on manipulating someone else's mind serves both the fisherman and Poe as a prophylactic against the terror they might otherwise be naked to when they look, respectively, back into the maelstrom or within the self. Thus Poe's aesthetic is properly a psychology of composition. Throughout his career, he wrote for the same reason that drove the narrator of "The Tell-Tale Heart" from his own bed to the old man's bedroom. Like Poe, this narrator needs an audience on whom to project "the terrors that distracted me" (794). This, by the way, explains why that narrator chuckles aloud after spending an hour soundlessly entering the old man's room; until he wakes the old man up, he is alone with his dread. Like this narrator, Poe sought to assert control over his own mind by manipulating ours.

Even Dupin shares this dependency on an audience. At the end of his reconstruction in "The Rue Morgue," he turns to the narrator to ask the question that underlies all that Poe wrote: "What impression have I made upon your fancy?" And if Dupin is a wish-fulfillment figure for Poe himself, the narrator here functions as a perfect audience: "I felt a creeping of the flesh as Dupin asked me this question" (558). It is no coincidence that the first conversation between Dupin and the narrator concerns an inept actor named Chantilly who has embarrassed himself by performing for a wholly unappreciative audience; this is the fear on the other side of the wish that Dupin fulfills. In "The Purloined Letter" the part of audience is played by both the narrator and the prefect of police. When Dupin produces the missing letter, their response indicates how little subtlety there was in Poe's conception of producing an effect:[6] "I was astounded. The Prefect appeared absolutely thunder-stricken. For some minutes he remained speechless and motionless, looking incredulously at my friend with open mouth, and eyes that seemed starting from their sockets . . ." (983). Although it occurs in the middle, this visceral triumph produced by means of a piece of writing is the tale's dramatic climax. It anticipates the ending, which itself anticipates the same kind of triumph. The last thing Dupin tells the narrator is how, having converted his antagonist, the Minister D——, into the duped spectator of a hoax he stages, he left a substitute letter behind. Dupin does not get the direct satisfaction of seeing the look on the minister's face when he opens that letter, any more than Poe could "watch the countenances of his audience" (12:126) once he had committed his tales to print. But in this story we see Poe savoring a sense of certainty about the control that he and Dupin have both achieved over their prospective "readers."

Poe's greatest innovation upon the forms of fiction in the Dupin stories is not the "detective" plot, for, as others have noted, the device of moving a narrative forward by retracing and unfolding an event that has already occurred is at least as old as *Oedipus Rex*. Rather, what is new about these tales is that in them the first-person narrator is neither a surrogate for the author nor a true character in the story, but instead—simply, purely—the writer's surrogate for his reader. His only role is to exist as the awed, appreciative audience to Dupin's mental prowess. Structurally, in other words, these tales are less about detection than they are about display. In much of his work Poe enacts the same drama, playing Dupin to our anonymous admiration. To show off his intellect, he exposed "Maelzel's Chess-Player," predicted the plot of *Barnaby Rudge*, advertised his ability to decode any cryptograph people might send him (thus giving his readers one chance to write their own role in this drama), competed with the New York police to solve the murder of Mary Rogers, and (as the cosmic culmination of his impulse to prove his superiority to any puzzle, to *any* mind) claimed in *Eureka* to have figured out "the Universe" as "a plot of God" (16:292). What should be noted about Poe's need to re-solve the mysterious into the explicable is that it was only half-expressed in the act of ratiocination. His final satisfaction lay in compelling the rest of the world to admire his performance. According to the second sentence of "The Rue Morgue," "We appreciate them [the mind's analytical powers] only in their effects" (527–28). This means that Dupin is as dependent on his narrator as the narrator is on him.[7] Without someone to register those "effects," his analytical powers have no meaning.

We can see this bond still more plainly in "The Gold-Bug," which also makes explicit the implication of "The Purloined Letter," where Dupin's audience includes his rival (the prefect) and his antagonist (the minister): the implication, that is, that the relationship between author and audience is at bottom an adversary one. Legrand, the tale's protagonist, is another version of Dupin. His powers of observation and deduction enable him to track down Captain Kidd's buried treasure, worth more than one and a half million dollars. But there are no mirrors in the chest he digs up, and more than money he seems to treasure the stunned, adulatory look he can provoke in the eyes of this tale's anonymous narrator. Everyone remembers that the story's action begins when Legrand sketches on a piece of paper he finds in his pocket the outline of the rare beetle he had caught, then hands the drawing to the narrator sitting by the hearth. The paper turns out to be parchment, the heat of the fire brings out the figure of a death's-head that had been drawn in invisible ink, and so on. Once he sees that skull, Legrand begins thinking his way toward the treasure, though first he must solve the puzzle behind which Kidd concealed it. Here again we can see how rationality vanquishes the terrible. In Legrand's presence a death's-head, even one that appears so mysteriously, is no reminder of mortality, but an invitation to triumph— which is what Dupin makes of the carnage in the L'Espanayes' apartment, the fisherman of the whirl, or Poe (in "The Philosophy") of the death of a beautiful woman. Yet why would Legrand, after breaking Kidd's code and unraveling Kidd's cryptic directions, invite the narrator along on the actual quest for the loot? What is the logic behind sharing a fortune with a casual acquaintance he doesn't even seem to like, and whose help he doesn't need?

Well, perhaps the story really begins when the narrator, looking at the parchment and seeing only the death's-head, which bears little resemblance to the bug Legrand has been describing, turns to him and says, "Legrand, I fear you are no artist" (809). Given Poe's compulsion to impress an audience with the work he delivers into their hands, this may be as dreadful a moment as any in his fiction. Taking the comment very personally, Legrand determines, first, to make the narrator suffer in the role of unappreciative audience in which he has cast himself, and second, to force him to recant, to concede Legrand's mastery. In the story's second half, Legrand explains how he read the riddle of the parchment, and the pattern there is the familiar one of Dupin's reconstructions: the narrator's commonplace intellect limping along behind the analyst's feats of brilliance. But the first half, until they dig the second hole and strike the chest, is a comedy of manipulation. By affecting a set of eccentricities, Legrand forces his acquaintance to conclude he is crazy; the narrator is made to feel more and more alarmed for his "poor friend" (819, 822) and more and more superior to him—right up to the instant when, by springing his golden effect, Legrand completes his contrived victory over him.

Poe invented the tale's mischievous epigraph, another Kidd-ing code:

> What ho! what ho! this fellow is dancing mad!
> He hath been bitten by the Tarantula.
> *All in the Wrong.*   (806)

The title he cites (a real play, by Arthur Murphy; Poe's wit here is worthy of Nabokov) is meant to label his readers, for throughout the first half Poe plays with them exactly as Legrand diddles the narrator. For Poe this struggle for appreciation between genius and mediocrity, between the superior artist and the audience, is not entirely comic. Legrand just hints at its darker side at the very end:

> "But your grandiloquence [the narrator protests], and your conduct in swinging the beetle—how excessively odd! I was sure you were mad. . . ."
>
> "Why, to be frank [replies Legrand], I felt somewhat annoyed by your evident suspicions touching my sanity, and so resolved *to punish you* quietly, in my own way, by a little bit of sober mystification." (843–44; my emphasis)

Yet this is not quite frank enough. Legrand had deliberately prompted the questions about his sanity. The only motive the story ever gives for his conduct is his resentment of the narrator's "sneer at my graphic powers . . . for I am considered a good artist" (828). With considerable aptness, Nathaniel Hawthorne saw art itself as a kind of treasure hunt. When we read Hawthorne, we feel we are invited to share the quest for insight into the truths of our mutually human hearts. In the chilly economics of Poe's tales, however, the one way for an artist to establish his or her "powers" is by dominating the audience. Like Legrand, Poe invites readers along solely to triumph over them. When we realize how much Legrand pays for this privilege, however, we may wonder who is the real victim of his hoax. There are still reasons to suspect his sanity.

"The Gold-Bug" is usually treated as one of Poe's most negligible works.[8] The same drama, however, also informs and organizes his greatest tale, "The Fall of the House of Usher." This story too takes place within the realm of the human mind: "the monarch Thought's dominion" (406) that is Poe's characteristic setting and concern. Yet in most of his arabesques, his customary practice is to work for a consistent and immediate effect, to initiate us abruptly, with his first sentence, into the nightmarish, half-lit, sensational reality of his stories, to detach us at once from our hold on conventional time and space. "The House of Usher" manipulates us in more complex ways. This time Poe creates his effect dramatically as well as theatrically, and finally springs it not as a surprise ("the LADY LIGEIA") but as a revelation, a thematically genuine recognition scene. The effect depends upon the reader's response to the tale's narrator, and to Roderick Usher. The question is which should be our guide, or "usher," through the intricacies of the mind—though we cannot appreciate the pun until the end.

From the start, the narrator is probably right to assume the reader shares his conventional certainties, not Usher's wild ideas. "Such opinions need no comment, and I will make none" (408): this kind of sentence takes our assent for granted. Similarly, the adjectives with which he keeps trying to diagnose Usher's condition—"hypochondriac," "morbid," "fervid," and so on—are offered as self-evidently appropriate. We are invited to identify with the narrator's reasonable point of view and are sympathetic to and probably grateful for his attempts to impose a logical order on Usher's weird world. His own growing dread he labels "my superstition—for why should I not so term it?" (399). Like a debased Dupin, he persistently seeks to analyse, explain, and therefore control whatever happens, from the first afternoon when the mere sight of the house completely unnerves him ("beyond doubt," he reasons, "there *are* combinations of very simple natural objects which have the power of thus affecting us" [398]), to the last night, when the anarchic storm outside exposes how desperate is his need for an explicable reality ("These appearances which bewilder you," he lectures Usher, "are merely electrical phenomena not uncommon" [413]).

The narrator soon realizes that Usher's disease is "irredeemable" (401), yet even after Usher has begun instead to lead "the way" into his "phantasmagoric conceptions" (405), we are still likely to endorse the narrator's reassuring labels: "At times, again, I was obliged to resolve all into the mere inexplicable vagaries of madness. . . . It was no wonder that his condition terrified—that it infected me. I felt creeping upon me, by slow yet certain degrees, the wild influence of his own fantastic yet impressive superstitions" (411). The irrational has apparently started to contaminate the rational; the narrator still thinks he knows, however, which is which: who is sane and who is mad. And we can share his assumption right up till the tale's final night, when Madeline Usher walks away from her tomb to keep her "Mad Trist" with her brother.

Madeline's movement through the house is a literal return of the repressed that demonstrates how brilliantly Poe complicated and reinvigorated the clichés of Gothic fiction. Standing the formulas that Mrs. Radcliffe established on their head, he has brought a man into a mysterious house; now it is midnight, and the strange noises in the house are those of a virginal maiden making her forbidden way to this man's bedroom. By these sexual reversals, Poe strips the scene of its moral and emotional complacencies: conventionally, of course, the young women who have lain awake in so many hundreds of Gothic beds are never allowed to hope that the door will open; the locus of desire is displaced outside their innocence, outside the walls of their room, onto the Gothic villain who transforms their sexuality into a self-gratulatory and self-protective desire for them. The Gothic heroine's virginity may be threatened, but never her innocence. When Madeline heads for the narrator's bedroom, on the other hand, his body is safe; it is his mind, his psychological innocence, that is at risk.

By this last night the narrator has "fallen" into what he calls a "pitiable condition" (412), yet he nonetheless "struggle[s]" with all the resources of his intellect "to reason off the nervousness which had dominion over me" (411). By calling his anxiety "utterly causeless" (411), by explaining the storm empirically, by referring Usher's case to "the history of mental disorder" (413), by sitting down to read his distraught friend a book—in the midst of this whelming chaos he tries to hold on to the conventional categories he brought with him into the house. To this point the tale has worked by steadily but gradually eroding the "sane" perspective represented by the narrator, while Poe does a marvellous job of tempting us to keep identifying with that perspective. Certainly Usher, who speaks "in a low, hurried, and gibbering murmur" (416), seems crazier than ever. But then Poe springs his recognition scene: "'Madman!' here [Usher] sprang furiously to his feet, and shrieked out his syllables, as if in the effort he were giving up his soul—'*Madman! I tell you that she now stands without the door!*'" (416). This italicized shrieking may suggest just another histrionic effect, especially after the door does indeed open and the Lady Madeline comes in looking like a Grand Guignol Ophelia wearing blood instead of flowers, or after the house itself falls down like a stage set being struck and the waters of the tarn "close over" it like a curtain (417). The scene, however, is a true reversal. Why does Usher, of all people, call the narrator a "madman"? Because if the test of sanity is being in touch with reality, then Usher is right: the narrator is mad, and has been so since the beginning of the tale.

In this work Poe thematically subverts his theatricalities, including the figurative curtain that opens in the first paragraph. Seeing Usher's house for the first time, the narrator admits to "an utter depression of soul which I can compare to no earthly sensation more properly than to the afterdream of the reveller upon opium—the bitter lapse into every-day life—the hideous dropping off of the veil" (397). All the banalities in this passage work beautifully against their conventional significance: Usher's realm is not an opium dream, but everyday life. Like Hawthorne's "Young Goodman Brown," "The Fall of the House of Usher" depicts an initiation into the true nature of humankind, the truth that darkness illuminates. Just as Brown encounters all the people closest to him at the satanic service in the depth of the woods, so Poe's narrator reveals that the cracked, "hideous" world of Usher's house is uncanny precisely because it is homely: "while I hesitated not to acknowledge how familiar was all this," he remarks as he is first being led through the house, "I still wondered to find how unfamiliar were the fancies which ordinary images were stirring up" (400–1). From the start the narrator calls Usher "a bounden slave" (403) to his irrational terrors, his "disordered" fancies. It turns out, though, that it is the narrator who is enslaved, by his illusory faith in reason. His belief in the rationality of the human mind is itself mad, but to sustain this illusion he is forced to repudiate Usher's superior insight by labeling *it* madness. My favorite line in the story is a very inno-cent-looking one that comes right at the start, the narrator's reference to his attempt to disarm his reaction to the house: "There was an iciness, a sinking, a sickening of the heart—an unredeemed dreariness of thought which no goading of the imagination could torture into aught of the sub-lime" (397). To be sure, the violence, the grotesqueness here is merely epistemological; he goads his own mind and tortures experience itself to make it fit some preconceived, safe category like "the sublime." But the desperate need to deny reality indicated by this failed act of torture di-rectly anticipates the more recognizable violence of the attempt to repress Madeline, and it establishes the narrator's reactions as the true subject of the tale. Looking at Usher's face, which is the double of the house's fa-cade, he refuses to see any image of his own: "I could not, even with effort, connect its Arabesque expression with any idea of simple human-ity" (402). But the tarn into which the house dissolves at the end is, as we learned in the first paragraph, a mirror: what the tale leaves us to stare at is ourselves.

"The Fall of the House of Usher" stands at the opposite extreme from the world of Dupin and Legrand. Here the reasoning mind betrays its vulnerability to experience; here the irrational conquers. Far from fulfill-ing a wish, this tale explores Poe's most primal dread. Yet we can note the prophylactic structure by which Poe sought, as always, to control his ma-terial. If Usher stands for himself (as indeed the poem he composes is one that Poe had already published in his own name), and stands for himself at the mercy of his obsessions (as that poem is composed, not with the analytical calm boasted about in "The Philosophy," but in a frenzy of fear), Usher can nonetheless triumph over Poe's audience. That audi-ence, as I have suggested, is whom the narrator stands for, as indeed he winds up, on that final night, reading a story Poe had written. Usher can-not save himself from himself, but he does live long enough to pull off his grim hoax. "Madman!": with that last shriek he not only gives up his soul; he pulls the rug out from under the narrator and his assumptions and thus gets the last laugh on the reader who has been duped into iden-tifying with them. At the very end, Usher wears "a sickly smile" (416).

I have sometimes amused myself by endeavoring to fancy what would be the fate of any individual gifted, or rather accursed, with an intellect *very* far superior to that of his race. Of course, he would be conscious of his superi-ority; nor could he (if otherwise constituted as man is) help manifesting his consciousness. Thus he would make himself enemies at all points. And since his opinions and speculations would widely differ from those of *all* man-kind—that he would be considered a madman, is evident. How horribly painful such a condition! Hell could invent no greater torture than that of being charged with abnormal weakness on account of being abnormally strong.[9]

This is one of the "marginalia" that Poe published in the *Southern Literary Messenger* for June 1849, just a few months before his death. By that late date in his uneven career he had made a lot of enemies, been charged with lunacy, been publicly pitied and privately rebuked again and again for his weaknesses. This "fancy," which draws on the same emotional need as the fairy tale motif of the disguised or enchanted prince, is Poe's transparent attempt to compensate for the pattern of his frustrations with the American public. That pattern was laid down for Poe long before he became a writer. His parents were actors. To the Victorian descendants of the Puritans, acting was among the least reputable of all professions. Poe was not allowed to forget this, although when he grew up he frequently protested that acting "embraces all that can elevate and ennoble" (12:185). Elevate and ennoble—these two words point to Poe's unceasing concern with superiority. Yet by the time his foster father, John Allan, had "taught me to aspire to eminence in public life"[10] and then driven him into exile from the ranks of the Virginia gentry, the pattern of his frustrations was complete.[11] Loved by two mothers who died, abandoned or rejected by two fathers, classless and chronically broke, Poe came to see himself as an aristocrat manqué, a vastly superior man to whom circumstances had denied his proper rank. His double need was to nurse his sense of nobility and to force "the world" that he vowed to take as his "theatre" after leaving Richmond to applaud that preeminence (*L*, 1:12). When he became a man of letters, it was in large part to establish title to his place at the top of what he called "the sole unquestionable aristocracy—that of intellect" (*L*, 2:410).

This ambition, which frustration only reanimated, underlies the tales we have been looking at, somewhat equivocally in the case of Usher but as pure fantasy in the Dupin and Legrand stories. Like Usher, both of these men are "regarded as madmen" (532). Both are fallen aristocrats: "This young gentleman was of an excellent—indeed of an illustrious family, but, by a variety of untoward events, had been reduced to . . . poverty" (531); "He was of an ancient Huguenot family, and had once been wealthy; but a series of misfortunes had reduced him to want" (806). Both have withdrawn from the world, in Legrand's case explicitly to "avoid the mortification" of being unable to command his rightful place in society (806). Poe will not allow us to pity either man in exile, for each is presented as self-sufficient, as intellectually immune to his social and economic reverses. The events of their tales, however, betray the hollowness of that pose. They not only wind up triumphing over the larger world and their impoverishment, forcing fate itself to own them as a master; in the meantime they eagerly play to whatever public their reduced environment affords. The two narrators who tell their stories assume the role of friend, but are cast by Dupin and Legrand into the necessary role of admiring audience, so that their feelings become the material for the superior men to fashion into preconceived, self-adulatory effects. We could accuse them of heartlessness, a term that would also fit Poe's all-too-calculated psychology of composition. But that would miss the point. It is easy enough to grow impatient with Poe's overwriting, and with the blatancy of his design to manipulate us. Yet we can remember what Poe himself was determined to prove about Maelzel's Chess-Player—that there was a *man* inside the machine. His statements about his own art desperately seek to prove the opposite, that no human needs are concealed within its workings. But it is precisely in that claim that we can discover Poe crouched most uncomfortably, most poignantly. He, Dupin, and Legrand are all too needy. Because each man's sense of identity is tied to impressing an audience, and his sense of control to manipulating it, sharing is out of the question. Other people become another adversary circumstance—indeed, the most crucial circumstance—for the superior mind to defeat.

And this describes the program of Poe's career as a "literary *histrio*." The French symbolists prized his defense of *art pour l'art*, his assertions that "there exists no work more intrinsically noble, than this very poem *written solely for the poem's sake*" (*ER*, 295). Yet since Poe's own intrinsic nobility was exactly what he needed to prove, all his work was written for the sake of the effect it could produce on the public mind. He is much more candid about his motivation when, in a review of Hawthorne, he refers to writing poetry as an occasion for "the best display" of genius; next in this ranking comes the brief prose tale as "the fairest opportunity of display" (*ER*, 584–85). The consequence of this emphasis on "display" is that his readers' reaction becomes the final arbiter of his achievement. Thus the effect of his needs was to bind him tightly to an audience he despised. As Poe himself wrote in the *Marginalia*: "Genius of the highest order lives in a state of perpetual vacillation between ambition and *the scorn of it*."[12] For like any émigré, he hated democracy, yet also needed popularity as much as any politician. "To be appreciated," he knew, "you must be *read*" (*L*, 1:58). "The uneducated," "those who read little," "the obtuse in intellect": "these three classes," he said, "constitute the mass" (*ER*, 177). Throughout his career he dreamed of presiding over a magazine that would be addressed exclusively to the most refined sensibilities in America. But he never realized this fantasy "to lead & to control" the republican equivalent to an aristocracy (*L*, 2:410), and so he had to take his audience as he found it, as it had been created for him by the existing magazines and journals.[13]

In *Poe and the British Magazine Tradition*, Michael Allen documents Poe's contradictory pronouncements on the taste and judgment of the reading public. Typically, whenever he had scored a "hit" (and we have to remember that "The Gold-Bug" and "The Raven" may have been the most widely read tale and poem published in America in the 1840s), Poe confidently endorsed the soundness of "the vast heart of the world at large" (15:247). Whenever his career seemed to stall (and none of his books, not even the collections of tales, sold well), he could insist that "the popularity of a book is *prima facie* evidence . . . of the book's demerit" (*ER*, 311–12). But actually Poe was split between his scorn for and his dependence on his audience every time he sat down to write, just as these two statements were published less than three months apart. Allen, for example, cites the testimony of a woman who visited Poe in 1846. During one visit he told her, "Fame forms no motive power with me. What can I care for the judgment of a multitude, every individual of which I despise?" On her next visit, however, he said: "I love fame—I dote on it—I idolise it—I would drink to the very dregs the glorious intoxication. . . . No man lives, unless he is famous! How bitterly I belied my nature, and my aspirations, when I said I did not desire fame, and that I despised it."[14] Neither comment belies his nature, but only together do they express it, and the bitterness left behind by his own aspirations. He loved popularity, and despised it. He delighted in success ("'The Raven' has had a great 'run' . . . but I wrote it for the express purpose of running" [*L*, 1:287]) and also felt disgust at the mere prospect of succeeding ("As for the mob [and 'Ligeia'] . . . I should be grieved if I thought they comprehended me here" [*L*, 1:118]). Within a single essay he can pose alternately as the fearless iconoclast, the lone unappreciated voice of literary truth (*ER*, 741), and as the adroit magazinist who built up the subscription list of every periodical he edited (*ER*, 742). Even Dupin can speak of "the popular opinion" respectfully in one tale, comparing it to the insight of "the man of genius" (757), and with pure contempt in the next.

In "The Philosophy of Composition" there is one question that Poe conspicuously refused to submit to analysis: "Let us dismiss, as irrelevant to the poem, *per se*, the circumstance—or say the necessity—which, in the first place, gave rise to the intention of composing *a* poem that should suit at once the popular and the critical taste" (*ER*, 15). This failure of self-analysis is exactly what dooms so many of his self-tormented narrators, and the conflict that Poe dismisses here is precisely the one that dominated his career. Poe could live without being famous, but could not so sustain the belief in his inherent nobility on which his sense of self depended. He said when leaving the army, "I have thrown myself on the world, like the Norman conqueror on the shores of Britain" (*L*, 1:10). The exaggeration of this is Poe's invariable style; he is posing for effect. But the attitude it displays is equally typical. Writers seek contemporary fame by suiting the popular taste, as Poe sought to do throughout his career. As David S. Reynolds has put it, "of all our major writers, Poe was the most obviously engaged in popular culture."[15] One reason he wrote so many "bugaboo tales" was his conviction that "these things are invariably sought after with avidity" (*L*, 1:58). Nearly all his pieces approximate popular forms. The three genres he excelled at and helped create— Gothic tales, detective stories, science fiction—remain the most salable modes of literature. Seen from a sufficient distance, the contents of his collected work suggest nothing so much as the contents of a Sunday newspaper: cryptograms, book reviews, personalities, interior decoration, landscape gardening, crime, popularized science and theology, humorous sketches, even fake news stories. Because the mind of his reader was the point around which all his writing revolved, Poe's concerns take us closer to the appetites of the nineteenth century American reading public than those of any other writer, even, say, Longfellow.

Yet the figure we reckon with when we read Poe is radically different. He has come down to us—he comes down to us in the style of his own work, in the stilted tautness of his prose—as an exile in the midst of Victorian America, aloof, deracinated, culturally impoverished, the victim of a hostile, philistine public. And this is accurate too, though we have to add that the hostility (like the setting of his tales) was mainly within Poe's mind.[16] He became a writer after resigning from the army, but nonetheless, like that Norman conqueror in Britain, saw the American public as the populace he had to contend with and defeat. Despite his appropriation of popular forms, wholly absent from Poe's work is any "instinctive sympathy and identification with [his] audience," as Michael Allen notes.[17] Since art offered the one means to master his obsessions and frustrations, he had to conceive of writing for others as something between an act of noblesse oblige and an invasion of enemy territory, and so evolved his aesthetic of absolute control and calculated effect, his psychology of composition. Yet he could not help thinking at the same time that the artist does "grievous wrong to his own genius—in appealing to the popular judgment *at all*" (*ER*, 313). This deep, inescapable ambivalence explains why, in a satire like "How to Write a Blackwood Article," Poe could expose and disparage the very tricks by which he sought to impress the reading public.

There was a self-destructive doubleness about his need to be, as he put it, "appreciated." It meant that he had to appeal to his audience, but, given his belief in his superiority and his compulsion to control, the most intolerable thought of all was that he was in any way at that audience's mercy. By commencing with the consideration of an effect, however, he necessarily, doctrinally gave his readers final control over his accomplishment. We might even say that Poe, caught inside this circle, resembles the distraught narrator of "The Tell-Tale Heart."[18] When the police arrive at the end of that tale, the narrator thinks of them as an audience he can manipulate, arranging chairs and having them sit down so he can "perfect" his "triumph" by a consummate display of his control (796). For a while he delights in his superiority, in his masterful production of an effect. Quickly, however, he realizes that he has betrayed and trapped himself; by needing to perform in the first place, he has delivered himself into his audience's power. Poe was finally at the mercy of this ambivalence. Succeeding with his audience, even on his own manipulative terms, simultaneously threatened the very notion of vast superiority that success was intended to prove. No wonder his work speaks so eloquently of alienation. Perhaps his dissociated consciousness—the quality of his fiction that seems most strikingly modern—reflects most his plight as an aristocratic claimant in the republic of letters, a nineteenth-century writer caught between his contempt and his need for the mass audience.

Chapter VIII

"YOU MUST HAVE PLENTY OF SEA-ROOM TO TELL THE TRUTH IN": MELVILLE'S *MOBY-DICK*

THE FIRST WORD of *Moby-Dick* is easily overlooked, but if Melville had prefaced the novel with a grammarian in addition to the etymologist and the sub-sub-librarian, he might have pointed out that its familiar opening sentence really says: "[You] call me Ishmael." From the start, Melville betrays his awareness of his reader, and this short sentence is the signature of his largest anxieties as a performing artist.[1] "Call me Ishmael" simultaneously includes and excludes, invites and repels us. It shows Melville's desire to enter into a personal relationship with his audience while reserving his right to his own estranged identity. By beginning with the folksy "call me," he gestures toward an unprecedented colloquial intimacy between an American novel and its readers. By calling himself *Ishmael*, he pulls away the hand he has just extended, abruptly putting a wilderness between himself and us.

The long novel that follows is still more conflicted than this opening gambit. It was Melville's most sustained, self-conscious attempt to be a great American writer. Many of its motivations are deeply patriotic; the tide that carries the book out to sea is Melville's faith in "the coming of the literary Shiloh of America."[2] At the same time, Melville's contemptuous doubt about contemporary American culture is the lee shore on which his ambition finally wrecks. Most of the novel goes after its reader as directly as that first sentence does, as persistently as Ahab hunts the whale. Yet Melville's intentions are much less consistent than Ahab's. Not until he has exhausted his own hopes in the effort to communicate with the book's reader does he surrender to Ahab's rage. Like Ahab's, this is a deliberately self-destructive choice. Although he had begun *Moby-Dick* acutely aware of his desire to make others want to read it, by the time he finished he boasted that almost no one would dare to. The various quests that Melville undertakes in the novel—for truth, for literary greatness, for self-expression—all ultimately depend upon the reader. The anguished paradox of his career was that he felt, as Ahab puts it at the very end of *his* quest, that his "topmost greatness" had to lie in his "topmost grief."[3]

In his first five years as a professional writer, Melville published five books. While the foreground to *Moby-Dick*, his sixth, was not long, from the standpoint of his relation to his audience it had been almost melo-dramatically eventful. Few American literary careers ever began more aus-piciously. Most reviewers responded very favorably to *Typee* (1846), though it did arouse two controversies. The first, a protest from Christian periodicals about the book's irreverence toward South Sea missionaries, Melville reacted to by expurgating his text for a second edition. The other, some reviewers' misgivings about the book's truthfulness, prompted him to add the deposition of his friend Toby in the form of a "sequel" to that edition. Neither objection, however, interfered with the healthy sales of *Typee*. *Omoo*, which followed a year later, also delighted the public. Melville wrote both these books from the outside in: he was clearly less interested in expressing himself than in establishing a career as a writer. By shrewdly exploiting the most romantic or adventurous epi-sodes from his career as a sailor, he shows how keenly he could measure the appetites and expectations of the audience of his time. As indicated by his dutiful revisions of *Typee*, his main intention was to gain a "wide & permanent popularity."[4] Yet Melville was soon profoundly at odds with his public image, and even with his private desire for popularity. "It is my earnest desire," he told his father-in-law in 1849, "to write those sorts of books which are said to 'fail.'"[5] Writing to Hawthorne in 1851, he com-plained that "what 'reputation' H.M. has is horrible"—and he is referring to the very successes that had so recently delighted him.[6]

As Melville's first attempt to establish a relationship with the American reading public, *Typee* is very instructive. In its six opening paragraphs there are five rhetorical apostrophes: to the "reader," to "ye state-room sailors," to a rooster, to a fellow sailor, to the ship. Like the first sentence of *Moby-Dick*, this pattern illustrates how invariably Melville's prose was summoned into existence and defined by the act of addressing someone. This is, of course, implicitly true of almost all writing—if it weren't for you, I would not be in the midst of this sentence—but Melville's syntactic habits, which find their great achievement in the homiletic prose of *Moby-Dick*, reveal explicitly how dependent he was on the felt presence of an audience while he wrote. What is also revealed at the start of *Typee* is how uncomfortable he was with the demands of such a performance. He seems as uneasy with the readers he is addressing as Tommo feels among the cannibals. Their situations are, in fact, analogous: both Tommo's life and Melville's book are at the mercy of the communities they enter. It is this dependency that makes Tommo's stay in "paradise" so anxious: re-peatedly he acknowledges the islanders' "friendly reception," their "smil-ing appearances," but remains suspicious and estranged from them, both unable and unwilling to surrender his alienated identity to their commu-nity.[7] Their friendly reception seems to him the deceptive prologue to "some horrible catastrophe" (*T*, 76).

Within a few years Melville would make Tommo's prophecies fulfill themselves, but it is not yet time to elaborate on how these forebodings anticipate the tragic shape of Melville's career. All that needs to be noted here is just how uneasy Melville is with his governing intention in *Typee*: to secure an equally "friendly reception" for his book. William Charvat, for instance, points out that Melville's "conflict with his readers" began "in the first paragraph of his first book," where Melville initially asks his "reader" to pity him as a luckless seaman, but then turns immediately on that reader to deride him as a mere "state-room sailor" (*T*, 2).[8] Throughout *Typee* the narrator's behavior alternates between these two poles, between deference to and disdain for the reader's position. Also in the first chapter, for example, the narrative looks ahead to its arrival at the Marquesas with an enticing advertisement of the "outlandish things" to be found there:

> Naked houris—cannibal banquets—groves of cocoanut—coral reefs—ta-tooed chiefs—and bamboo temples; sunny valleys planted with bread-fruit trees—carved canoes dancing on the flashing blue waters—savage wood-lands guarded by horrible idols—*heathenish rites and human sacrifices*. (*T*, 5)

The italics are Melville's. They underscore his determination to whet the white reader's curiosity. Already his instincts about the appetites of his audience are very keen; like "Jack," the "showman of the island" he mentions later, "he knows just the sort of information wanted" (*T*, 170). On *Typee*'s very next page, however, he displays a similarly keen sense of how to offend that audience; in an anecdote that, he says, he "cannot avoid relating," he attacks one of *its* most cherished idols. He recounts the fate of "the first white woman" to visit the Marquesas. While his diction envelops her with the nimbus of Victorian ideality—"mute admiration," "divinity," "charming," "sacred veil," "good breeding," "decorum"— this "gentle dame" is stripped naked and "showered" with "contumely . . . by the savages" (*T*, 6–7). This anecdote, which Melville deleted in the revised edition, seems as calculated to repel at least the majority of his contemporary readers as the preceding catalogue was to attract them.

By and large, even in the unrevised text, *Typee* lives up to its promise to amuse and entertain. It is entirely apt that Washington Irving served as the book's literary godfather, helping to secure its publication. Tommo encourages his readers to patronize the South Sea islanders as enjoyable, titillating, quaintly childlike, or mock-romantic caricatures. Kory-Kory is his "tried servitor and faithful valet" (*T*, 82–83), Fayaway a "river-nymph" (*T*, 131), the tribe's young men are "roystering blades" (*T*, 85); one of Tommo's running jokes is that the Typee language is "unintelligible and stunning gibberish" that more than once gives him a headache (*T*, 103). The book's tone, diction, and metaphors all privilege the white reader's larger, worldly perspective. Yet if the general effect of *Typee* is to meet and flatter its audience's expectations, even to give them a peep at the unlikely leftovers of a cannibal feast, as the book proceeds Melville grows increasingly aggressive. The most significant rebellion is not his exposé of the missionaries but his broader use of the Typees to challenge, more and more explicitly, his audience's assumptions about their own Christian culture. From being a romantic adventure among savages *Typee* moves toward becoming a Romantic indictment of civilization. Rousseau had already laid down the line that Melville is feeling his way along, but if he discovered a truth that he wanted to tell in his first book, it emerges here—and has its source in his own disaffection from the complacent bourgeois point of view that the rest of the book validates. Yet Melville was willing to be turned back from taking an adversary stance toward his audience's values. Satisfying their expectations mattered more than any truth he might want to tell them. When his American publisher expressed alarm over the reviews in the Christian press, Melville not only deleted his critiques of the missionaries but also "expurgated" almost all indications of his hostility to the cultural status quo.[9] In his preface to the revised edition he dismisses all the passages he removed as "irrelevant" (*T*, 361), and even urged his English publisher to adopt this revised text.[10]

Thus the success of his first book left Melville with a lot to be grateful for, but still more, he soon decided, to resent. Unfortunately, he found it easier to let the resentments fester than to examine his own contradictory desires. The issue of truthfulness is a case in point. There is no question that he embellished and fictionalized his experiences among the Typees, chiefly for the sake of a more entertaining story;[11] nevertheless he reacted bitterly to the doubts some reviewers raised about *Typee*'s veracity.[12] Melville insisted on making this issue a source of antagonism in the preface to his third book, *Mardi* (1849). There he boasts that, since readers of his first two books had refused to believe him, turning facts into fiction, this third book was written "to see whether the fiction might not possibly be received for a verity."[13] As an openly contemptuous attempt to work off an illogical grudge, *Mardi*'s preface invites animosity. Many of the novel's reviewers were quick to sense this challenge, and to respond in kind. "We think," wrote one, "he need be under no apprehension that the present volumes will be received as gospel—they certainly lack all show of truth or naturalness."[14]

By Melville's own account, it was the reception of his first two books that prompted him to write *Mardi*. Its first one hundred pages begin where *Typee* and *Omoo* left off, but then driven, as he puts it in the novel, by "a blast resistless" (*M*, 459), Melville sought to outgrow their modest limits. Impatient with meeting his readers' expectations and with merely entertaining them, he indulges in a confusing variety of generic modes (adventure narrative, romance, allegory, satire, philosophic dialogue) and in a windy host of digressions offered as metaphysical-psychological-political speculations. He wrote *Mardi* under a palpably intense excitement with the possibilities of self-expression, as though he were compensating, with a vengeance, for the previous way he had allowed his desire for public acceptance to govern his literary purpose, as though his pages had suddenly become a kind of promised land for creative opportunity. He rediscovers the world and fills it with the infatuated sound of his own voice. His prose is still defined by the rhetorical mode of address, but in this talkiest of novels he satisfies that need by having his characters address each other.

In *Mardi* Melville leaves his reader behind as decisively as the novel's protagonist shoves off from his ship. Yet he could not finally ignore the public that would, when it was published, pass judgment on his work—as he himself realized as he neared the end of his manuscript. Chapter 169 is an unmediated plea for his readers' sympathy: "ill-provided, young, and bowed to the brunt of things before my prime," he compares himself, as an imaginative voyager, to Columbus, who also "ploughed his own path mid jeers" (*M*, 556–57); in his case, Melville concedes, "the verdict [may] be [that] the golden haven was not gained" (*M*, 557). Self-aggrandizement, however, competes with self-pity in this passage: it is, he winds up announcing, "better to sink in boundless depths than float on vulgar shoals; and give me, ye gods, an utter wreck, if wreck I do" (*M*, 557). The way this passage turns away from the "reader" (*M*, 556) to address instead the "gods" is absolutely characteristic of Melville. Apparently he cannot decide what course he wants to steer—toward others who would receive him sympathetically, or out into the solitary depths—or whether success or failure is the consummation for which to wish.

Mardi was a failure, the first of the "catastrophes" that punctuate Melville's career. He seems to have sought to fail. As William Charvat has noted, Melville started the quarrel with his audience that so drastically affected his fate as a novelist: "It is sometimes wrongly stated that it was the critical attack on *Mardi* that caused Melville's increasing hostility to the public. The reverse is true, for the hostility is in the book and antecedent to its failure."[15] In chapter 180, Babbalanja's self-gratulatory defense of Lombardo, the Mardian poet whose genius could exact only scorn from his thick-headed compatriots, one can see Melville preparing himself, with perverse eagerness, for literary martyrdom. Contemporary readers were more baffled than annoyed by the book's quirky affronts to their expectations. "Professional critics," whom Melville calls "Asses! rather mules!—so emasculated, from vanity, they can not father a true thought" (*M*, 599), were generally harsher in their condemnation of the book. But although he himself had provoked it, Melville was seriously wounded—"stabbed" is how he put it[16]—by *Mardi*'s unfavorable reception. Somehow he had expected that it would be liked.

To court his audience's approval, to revolt against their assumptions— these two impulses define the pattern of conflict that Melville imposed on his career. In his own mind, his audience loomed between him and the imaginative worlds he hoped to create. By the time he finished *Mardi* he had come to see the space in which a novel happens not as something he and his readers could share (as, for instance, in Hawthorne's fiction, or Dickens's), nor as something he could presume his own artistic right to (as in Flaubert's fiction), but rather as a realm that could either be basely surrendered or aggressively fought for. After *Mardi* he wrote *Redburn* (1849) and *White-Jacket* (1850) specifically to resuscitate his image as a popular writer, to win back the readership he had lost. Both were well received. Yet because he felt he had betrayed himself by satisfying his readers, he bitterly dismissed both as "two *jobs*,"[17] as "trash."[18] As he told Hawthorne, he could write either his own way, or the way his audience expected him to, but could conceive of no middle ground, and so "all my books are botches."[19] We can only wonder how Hawthorne might have replied to this despair at the American writer's prospects. Certainly he was tempted at moments to agree. But from Hawthorne's work Melville could have learned, had he been willing to learn, that these absolutes— his way or theirs—were too starkly conceived. Beyond question, the nature of Melville's audience made any quest for a middle ground difficult, but it was Melville who made his failure to find it inevitable.

Although four of his first five books had sold well, increasingly Melville came to value only the one that had failed. He blamed his frustration on the inadequacies of his culture, an assumption that still underlies most analyses of his career.[20] It is not hard to find reasons to disparage Victorian America. Does anyone, however, seriously want to argue that *Mardi* is not a confusing, self-indulgent, practically unreadable book? The aboriginal source of the friction between Melville and his contemporary audience lay in his own divisive uncertainty about the response he wanted from them. By turns he was an unwilling supplicant for public favor and an uncommitted rebel against it: unwilling, because he was invariably ashamed of his successes; uncommitted, because no matter how vehemently he subverted the beliefs and expectations of his readers, he nonetheless wanted their support. After proving he could please them, what he revolted against were his own concessions to them. Characteristically, he does not say he wants to write great books—books, that is, that master their own material. Instead, he wants to write "books which are said to 'fail'"—books that refuse to allow an audience to master them but that still depend upon that audience's reaction. It was public response that determined the worth his works had in his own eyes. Indeed, his very sense of himself was inseparably, dyadically bound up with the reactions he provoked from the public. About to land in England in 1849, carrying the proof sheets of *White-Jacket*, looking back on the ten years since his last trip to England and especially the four years during which he had been a published writer, he defines his identity entirely in terms of his vexation with his popular reputation: "*then* a sailor, *now* H.M. author of 'Pedee' 'Hullabaloo' & 'Pog-Dog.'"[21] To Hawthorne he proclaimed that "all Fame is patronage. Let me be infamous: there is no patronage in *that*."[22] Even this desire, though, leaves him at the mercy of public opinion.

There was no genteel conspiracy to thwart Melville's talent. On the whole, readers of his first five books simply responded in the ways he had predetermined that they should. The part his audience played in his career was decided mainly by his own conflicted narcissism. The best place to study this conflict is in *Pierre*, the novel that followed *Moby-Dick*. As Hershel Parker has suggested, in Melville's account of Pierre Glendenning as a "Juvenile Author" trying to write a "Mature Book" we have "a psychological analysis of his own literary career."[23] Pierre seeks to become a professional novelist in the middle of the book, after he has been exiled from home and his mother's love: his ambition "to give the world a book, which the world should hail with surprise and delight," is an appeal for imaginative adoption.[24] Yet he winds up impaling his manuscript with a knife and spitting on it, to get "the start of the wise world's worst abuse of it!" (*P*, 357). It is significant that the public never even sees Pierre's novel: without leaving his writing desk, his hope of pleasing "the world" gives way to an exultant, suicidal rage at "the world the gods had chained for a ball to drag at his o'er-freighted feet" (*P*, 347). And what is most telling about Melville's account is his association of Pierre as a writer with a very young child engaged in the process of establishing his autonomy: "So now in him you behold the baby toddler I spoke of; forced now to stand and toddle alone" (*P*, 305).

Melville's favorite figure for himself as author was, as in *Mardi*, the voyaging sailor at the tiller, but I think this homelier image takes us closer to the emotional economics of his career. He regularly equated popular success, for example, with infancy: *Redburn* he called "a little nursery tale of mine," and *Typee*, he predicted, would be fed to babies "with their gingerbread."[25] His attitude toward his readers suggests precisely the unstable, testing narcissism of a "baby toddler," whose only means of defining his ego, of discovering the self, is by the reactions he can provoke from his parents. Melville's constant awareness of the public he addresses, his internalized overvaluation of their responses, his illogical resentments and contradictory needs, his impulse alternately to insist on his independence and to reaffirm his attachment—the pattern here is that of the unindividuated self, whose gestures are all dramatic ones, who cannot distinguish between a private desire and a public performance.

My own belief is that with *Pierre* we also get to the source of Melville's anxiety-ridden ambivalence toward his audience, the reason he both wanted and rebelled against their acceptance. Although no one else has yet read a word of his novel, and although he is still "an eager contender for renown" (*P*, 339), "Pierre at His Book" passes through a devastating reversal in his expectations from the public: "In that lonely little closet of his, Pierre foretasted all that this world hath either of praise or disparise; and thus foretasting both goblets, anticipatingly hurled them both in its teeth. All panegyric, all denunciation, all criticism of any sort, would come too late for Pierre" (*P*, 339). The novel's explanation for this mood is that Pierre has become disillusioned with literature itself: "Like knavish cards, the leaves of all great books were covertly packed. He was but packing one set the more; and that a very poor jaded set and pack indeed" (*P*, 339).[26] Yet while such a discovery could account for an indifference to public opinion, or even a cynical contempt for it, it can hardly explain Pierre's tantrum against the audience that, except in his own anticipations, has yet to let him down. On this point, however, the narrative can help us in ways that its narrator cannot. What would come too late for Pierre as an author had already been visited upon him in his role as Mary Glendenning's son. This reversal of his literary hopes is a psychological reenactment of the drama of his relationship with his mother.

In the novel's first half Pierre is harshly forced out of the seamless paradise he thought he shared with Mrs. Glendenning by his shattering realization that she only loves him for the servile way he lives up to her expectations: "to her mirrored image, not to me, she offers up her offerings of kisses" (*P*, 90). Sensing that he cannot be true to both himself and those expectations, he correctly foresees his coming exile from all maternal compassion:

> Then he staggered back upon himself, and only found support in himself. . . . Yet was this feeling entirely lonesome, and orphan-like. Fain, then, for one moment, would he have recalled the thousand sweet illusions of Life; tho' purchased at the price of Life's Truth; so that once more he might not feel himself driven out an infant Ishmael into the desert, with no maternal Hagar to accompany and comfort him. (*P*, 89)

Precisely this feeling of abandonment recurs, in the novel's second half, when Pierre decides that his faith in the reading public is equally delusive. When he thought of telling his mother the truth he has learned from Isabel, the truth that would affront her assumptions, he gave up in despair: "he knew his mother well enough to be very certain that, though he should unroll a magician's parchment before her now, she would verbally express no interest" (*P*, 129–30). The "magician's parchment" becomes the book that Pierre hopes to offer to the world, but with the obsessive certainty of a psyche that cannot forget where it has been wounded, he yields his hopes to the conviction that the world, like his mother, will disown him rather than accept the truth he has to tell:

> Who shall tell all the thoughts and feelings of Pierre in that desolate and shivering room, when at last the idea obtruded, that the wiser and the profounder he should grow, the more and the more he lessened the chances for bread; that could he now hurl his deep book out of the window, and fall on some shallow nothing of a novel, composable in a month at the longest, then could he reasonably hope for both appreciation and cash. . . . So now in him you behold the baby toddler I spoke of; forced now to stand and toddle alone. (*P*, 305)

Note the exact progression of Melville's metaphors: the unloved infant Ishmael becomes the abandoned toddler who "still clamors for the support of its mother the world" (*P*, 296). In the plot of *Pierre* Melville himself suggests that it was his own earliest experiences with another person that shaped the conflicted drama of his career. A central thematic concern of his work, certainly, is dependency and distrust: from Tommo's apprehensions among the Typees, who literally treat him as an infant (carrying, bathing, feeding him by hand, and so on), to the pages of *The Confidence-Man*, which the reader enters as a kind of newborn to be betrayed again and again by both the narrative and the narrator. One of the most terrific truths of *Moby-Dick* distills this preoccupation into a fierce epigram: "Though in many of its aspects this visible world seems formed in love, the invisible spheres were formed in fright" (169). Behind both this need for love and this terror of being betrayed and consumed by it stands the figure of the mother, established once and for all in Melville's work in the character of Mary Glendenning, who smiles at her son with very sharp teeth. I am suggesting that Melville, like Pierre, carried the unresolved terms of this relationship into the relationship he sought with the American reading public. Onto his readers he projected the hopes and fears of his unconscious life. Both the need to court his audience's approval and his angry rejection of that need can be seen as the quest of a scarred disbeliever, longing to find in readers' appreciation a source of maternal consolation and support at the same time that he cannot trust even their "friendly reception." Unable to stand alone, he despised his dependence on the public's approval, and impatiently struck out against his own desires. As he says of Pierre and his literary hopes, "there was nothing he more spurned, than his own aspirations" (*P*, 339).

"Let America then prize and cherish her writers"—so he pleads in "Hawthorne and His Mosses," where he explicitly develops the relationship between the American writer and the American audience in terms of the analogue to infant and mother. Native writers he calls America's "own children"; "while she has kith and kin of her own," he adds, "to take to her bosom, let her not lavish her embraces upon the household of an alien" (*PT*, 247). Written in 1850, this essay is Melville's fullest statement of the irreconcilable ambivalences I am trying to explore. The role he conceives for the American author, that of his audience's child, brings with it all of his anxieties and resentments. On the one hand, he entreats this maternal public's nurturing sympathy; on the other, he sharply refuses to be parented: "As for patronage, it is the American author who now patronizes his country, and not his country him" (*PT*, 247). On the one hand, he commends Nathaniel Hawthorne to his country's readers with the thought that popular acceptance would encourage him to even greater work: "so shall he feel those grateful impulses in him, that may possibly prompt him to the full flower of some still greater achievement in your eyes" (*PT*, 249). But on the other, he angrily dismisses popularity as crippling proof of artistic unworthiness:

> Besides, at the bottom of their natures, men like Hawthorne, in many things, deem the plaudits of the public such strong presumptive evidence of mediocrity in the object of them, that it would in some degree render them doubtful of their own powers, did they hear much and vociferous braying concerning them in the public pastures. (*PT*, 251)

The true subject of the essay is "genius and the masses." This was a topic no writer of the time, particularly no American writer, could escape. But despite its considerable value as a cultural document, the essay sounds most resonantly the fatal dividedness of Melville's relationship to American culture. In principle he is committed to democracy, to carrying "republican progressiveness into Literature" (*PT*, 245). But although the essay's last line proclaims that Hawthorne's books "should be sold by the hundred-thousand; and read by the million" (*PT*, 253), he began by characterizing the greatness of the great writer in a way that no reading public could bear, much less "prize and cherish." His use of Shakespeare to define genius opens an unbridgeable gap between art and the masses. It is not enough to say, as Melville says, that "few men have time, or patience, or palate, for the spiritual truth as it is in that great genius" (*PT*, 245). To this must be added his belief that the certificate of genius is the apprehension of a radically unsocial, profoundly dark reality, a knowledge that must make the genius a castaway from the common continent of men and women: "Through the mouths of the dark characters of Hamlet, Timon, Lear and Iago, [Shakespeare] craftily says, or sometimes insinuates the things, which we feel to be so terrifically true, that it were all but madness for any good man, in his own proper character, to utter, or even hint of them" (*PT*, 244).

"Hawthorne and His Mosses" is a powerfully spirited piece of prose. It shows every sign of being poured out at white heat, in the fullness of Melville's newfound enthusiasm for Hawthorne and with the emotions that had accumulated behind his first five years as a writer. Its vigorous pronouncements, however—about truth, about America, about genius, about public support—cancel each other out. Its assumptions about audience contradict its assumptions about great writing—indeed, contradict each other. The artist whom the essay describes is caught in an impossible bind, simultaneously reaching for and rejecting the succor of an audience that, whatever its response—whether it ignores him, condemns him, or reads him by the million—can only fail him. The essay implores the American public to help the American writer shape a space in which to create: "You must have plenty of sea-room to tell the Truth in" (*PT*, 246). But among Melville's own violently mixed feelings, that space never emerges.

I have finally arrived at *Moby-Dick*. Melville wrote "Hawthorne and His Mosses" in the summer of 1850, at which time he was "half way" done with a book about a "whaling voyage" that he expected to complete "in the latter part of the coming autumn."[27] As a man with a living to make from his pen, and as the head of the new household he was organizing in the Berkshires, he had every reason to finish quickly. He did not, however, finish until the next summer, and the great book he wound up writing is radically different from the one he began. As everyone knows, *Moby-Dick* is a complex masterpiece. I think many of its complexities, and much of its power, can be traced to and explained by the psychic drama of its performance. Melville reshaped his book about whaling more than once in the course of its composition. One thing remained constant through every stage: his acute awareness of the American audience he was writing for.

Even the issue of the "drama" in *Moby-Dick*, however, is complex. To understand the kind of dramatic performance the book ultimately enacts, it may help to note briefly the more recognizable drama Melville considered writing. "Hawthorne and His Mosses" registers the two most immediate influences on Melville as he was in the process of writing his sixth book: his reading in Shakespeare and his engagement with Hawthorne. Bringing them together in the pages of his essay reinvigorated his own instinct for greatness as an American author.[28] What this larger ambition initially led to can be seen most clearly in chapters 24–40 of *Moby-Dick*, where Melville elaborates the advocate's role he rehearsed in the essay. There he had said that the American writer had to believe, as a matter of republican principle, in Shakespeare's "approachability" (*PT*, 245). To prove this, he decided to transform his book about whaling into the democratic equivalent of a Shakespearian tragedy. Ishmael calls himself a "tragic dramatist" in chapter 33 (148) and insists that Ahab, "in all his Nantucket grimness and shagginess" (148), is nonetheless "a mighty pageant creature, formed for noble tragedies" (73). The muse he invokes in chapter 26 is the "just spirit of Equality," which justifies his determination to give his characters, although "meanest mariners," "high qualities" and "tragic graces" (117). By claiming that whaling has "aesthetically noble associations connected with it" (111), by repeatedly applying such words as "noble" and "regal" and "kingly" to the men on board the *Pequod*, by having Ahab speak in a quasi-Elizabethan idiom, Melville declares his intention to put the American here and now on an equal footing with the aristocratic assumptions of Old World tragedy. Chapters 36–40, by incorporating stage directions, dramatic soliloquies, and staged dialogues into the text, formalize this intention.

Echoes of this design, and of Shakespeare's tragedies, persist throughout the rest of *Moby-Dick*, but after chapter 40 it soon becomes apparent that Melville has just carefully prepared his reader for a drama he has changed his mind about writing. "The Town Ho's Story" (chapter 54) may be a vestigial remnant of the plot he had considered using, for in it the important relationships and events are legitimately dramatic ones. No part of *Moby-Dick*'s real power, however, can be attributed to any conflict between its characters. Ahab is like Lear without his daughters: a tragic hero with no human antagonist. His "drama" amounts to nothing less than the unmediated, unpopulated struggle with the whole of life, for even his hunt for the whale is emblematic of this largest antagonism. Instead of serving Melville as a stage on which to mount a conflict among human presences like Ahab and Starbuck, Ishmael and Bulkington, the *Pequod* becomes a prop on a much vaster stage, defined by the scale of the limitless ocean that itself stands for the unfathomed truths of existence that Ahab voyages to confront.

In thus excluding Shakespeare's human foreground, in reducing the dramatic complexities of conventional tragedy to this two-term opposition—of Me and Not-Me, will and reality—Melville's novel does carry out a revision characteristic of other American literature at this period. As dramas of the solitary mind's relationship to existence, Emerson's essays, Poe's tales, and Whitman's poetry take place on equally empty stages. Yet while Ahab's "quenchless feud" (179) with life provides the book with its narrative occasion, not even this "drama" is its most central one. That is equally unconventional, except in the context I have been trying throughout this study to explore: the conflict between the solitary author and the mass audience that I would call even more representative of the period. Looked at as a performance, all of *Moby-Dick* remains extremely dramatic. Its heroic protagonist is Melville himself, whose intensities, ambitions, and anxieties make him worthy in every way of the role.

The part of his dramatic antagonist is played by his reader; though "we" have essentially a nonspeaking role, our presence is felt in virtually every line of the text.[29] As a performance, *Moby-Dick* is a tragedy in four parts, though it is not until the last part that it becomes inevitably tragic.

It began as a kind of comedy. Because the manuscripts of *Moby-Dick* have been lost, we have to speculate about the book Melville thought he had "half way" completed in the spring of 1850. All the evidence, however, agrees with the distinction Howard Vincent makes: that the "great *Moby-Dick*" was mainly written after the Hawthorne essay, between November 1850 and August 1851, while the book he worked on before moving to Pittsfield was "modest" in its ambitions.[30] The record contains two comments by Melville about his original project. The first is from a letter in May to Dana: "It will be a strange sort of book, tho', I fear; blubber is blubber you know; tho' you may get oil out of it, the poetry runs as hard as sap from a frozen maple tree; —& to cook the thing up, one must throw in a little fancy."[31] Whaling was the only part of Melville's experience as a sailor that he had not yet drawn on as a writer. These remarks suggest that he had neglected it because whaling seemed unlikely to produce the kind of adventurous, exotic story that Melville was expected to write. His one other comment is in a letter written in June to his English publisher, pitching the manuscript to him along those lines: "The book is a romance of adventure, founded upon certain wild legends in the Southern Sperm Whale Fisheries, and illustrated by the author's own personal experience, of two years & more, as a harpooneer."[32] Both descriptions indicate a book in the mode of his popularly successful ones: a first-person narrative that would explore the anthropology of whaling while probably (as suggested by "fancy," "romance," and "legends") using the idea of a ferocious white whale as *Typee* uses cannibalism or *Mardi* uses Hautia, to give the larger story some element of melodramatic suspense. What this adds up to is another "job" like *Redburn* or *White-Jacket*: a work organized around Melville's desire to satisfy the appetites of his reading public.

We can partially reconstruct his original purpose from the novel as we have it, for chapters 2–22 constitute a distinct kind of narrative within the whole. I would call them the first act in the drama of *Moby-Dick* as a literary performance. These are the chapters in which Ishmael figures prominently as an active character within the story he tells, and they always come as a surprise to readers who know the novel only by its forbidding reputation. My students, for instance, have all heard that *Moby-Dick* is unreadable—then they start reading it, and discover to their delight that it's very entertaining. In chapters 2–22 Melville relies on the narrative strategy of *Redburn*: the motif of "his first voyage." Although Ishmael has been to sea before, on a merchantman, he is "wholly ignorant of the mysteries of whaling" (57); thus Melville can vigorously exploit the comedy of his novitiate as a "candidate for the pains and penalties of whaling" (8). Though as a narrator Ishmael is much less amateurish than Wellingborough Redburn, whose naivete often borders on puerility, as a protagonist he is every bit as green. "Comical" is a word Melville uses in this stage of the narrative about as insistently as he will use "noble" in the stage that follows to describe the milieu Ishmael has entered, and Ishmael's structural role (as the novel consciously acknowledges in chapter 5) is to "afford stuff for a good joke" (29). His good-humored misadventures with New Bedford landlords and pagan harpooneers and Nantucket owners Melville uses the same way that Mark Twain employs the persona of authorial tenderfoot, to ingratiate himself with his readers. For this perspective privileges the reader at Ishmael's expense. Redburn appealed to our sympathy; Ishmael, to our sense of humor—but in both cases the reader who overlooks the predicaments that follow from the characters' inexperience is encouraged to feel superior, is structurally forced to patronize them. It seems that Melville sought to compensate for the intractability of whaling as literary material by means of Ishmael's entertaining naivete. This shows the soundness of his judgment as a professional writer—if *Moby-Dick* had gone on in the mode of its opening chapters, it would certainly have been among the most popular of his books—but it is also worth noting that, whenever he "calculated for popularity" (to use his phrase for *Pierre*),[33] he instinctively emphasized the childishness of his autobiographical protagonists. Redburn, the Ishmael of chapters 2–22, the Pierre of the first half of his novel: their engaging innocence of the world they are portrayed as entering makes them candidates for the reader's adoption.

Yet while Melville felt America would take his books to her bosom only if he infantilized his literary self, he had already grown sick of the strategy. Not even in *Redburn* could he wholeheartedly maintain this pose, which, since it is designed to insure the affection and support of his audience, he was right to call "beggarly."[34] As many critics have observed, *Redburn*'s narrative tone in inconsistent; the point that remains to be made is that the inconsistencies are symptomatic of Melville's struggle with his own needs for the space in which the novel is being written. Most of the time Wellingborough, in his wide-eyed, droopy helplessness, bears a close resemblance to the young girls, the Ellens and Gertys, of the period's best-selling novels. Melville may have hated writing it, but Wellingborough is supposed sincerely to say: "At that time I did not know what to make of these sailors; but this much I thought, that when they were boys, they could never have gone to the Sunday School; for they swore so, it made my ears tingle, and used words that I never could hear without a dreadful loathing."[35] As the ostensible narrator too, Wellingborough keeps calling attention to his artlessness: losing track of his subject, apologizing for his digressions, offering his remarks about his story's other characters very timidly: "As I am sometimes by nature inclined to indulge in unauthorized surmisings about the thoughts going on with regard to me, in the people I meet, especially if I have reason to think they dislike me; I will not put it down for a certainty that what I suspected concerning this Jackson . . . was really the truth" (*R*, 58). Un-author-ized is exactly the right word for what Melville felt he had to do to himself in order to regain his audience's approval; his fourth book was a deliberate act of imaginative regression. *Redburn* proceeds as if it were by as well as about a child, a literary ingenue.

Not much later, however, Wellingborough can consider making jokes about constipated sailors "who at sea will doctor themselves with calomel" and still remain on duty in the rigging (*R*, 90). Although in this instance he "forebear[s]," one can sense that Melville is getting restive with the complacent, sentimental smile he has worked to paste on his genteel reader's face. In this rebellious mood he violates his characterization as well as his reader's sense of decorum. At moments Redburn is sly, knowing, artful, even sarcastic about his own filial piety, his most fundamental trait as a created character. As in *Typee*, Melville moves toward thematic confrontation with his society, pushing Redburn out from behind his Sunday school persona, allowing him to accuse the culture whose conventional values he has been flattering: "We talk of the Turks, and abhor the cannibals; but may not some of *them*, go to heaven, before some of *us*?" (*R*, 293).

Wellingborough remains a child of the genteel culture, dutifully going back to his mother and sisters at the end, just as Melville hopes his novel will make its way into other Victorian homes. The transformations of his tone remain inchoate and occasional—brief eruptions that testify to Melville's resentment at the part he had written for his narrator to play. As one such moment reveals, what he hates is feeling forced to carry his readers where they expect to go. For most of the novel, as "the son-of-a-gentleman," Wellingborough identifies with his readers and asks for their commiseration at his plight among those uncouth, unchurched seamen. At the end of chapter 24, however, thinking of elegant "cabin passengers" making their way to Europe, he attacks his readers directly. The professed purpose of the passage is to speak on the lowly sailor's behalf. Yet the irrational violence of it indicates that Melville is less concerned with class sympathies than determined to remind the ladies and gentlemen in his audience who is really in charge:

> And they little think, many of them, fine gentlemen and ladies that they are, what an important personage, and how much to be had in reverence, is

the rough fellow in the pea-jacket, whom they see standing at the wheel, now cocking his eye aloft, and then peeping at the compass, or looking out to windward.

Why, that fellow has all your lives and eternities in his hand; and with one small and almost imperceptible motion of a spoke, in a gale of wind, might give a vast deal of work to surrogates and lawyers, in proving last wills and testaments.

Ay, you may well stare at him now. . . . (*R*, 117)

This presupposes, of course, an improbable, suicidal recklessness on the part of that helmsman. Nor can we imagine Wellingborough ever speaking in this tone. This is Melville's voice, speaking directly to his reader ("Ay, *you* may well"), angry with the course he felt compelled to plot for *Redburn*, impatient to assert himself. Yet, typically, the only alternative he can think of to sailing under others' orders is as self-destructive as it is self-assertive. Only at moments does he rebel against the expectations of his readers in *Redburn*. On the whole its literary space remains dominated by his need for their approval. Yet the "Lee Shore" mood betrayed in this passage—to seize the tiller and sail defiantly into ruin—defines the impulse he had already given in to in *Mardi*, and the one that decided the ultimate course of *Moby-Dick*.

Melville finished *Redburn* in fewer than ten weeks, and pushed himself through *White-Jacket* still more quickly. It is as if he did not want to give himself a chance to subvert his design to write these books specifically for popularity. Both were selling well during the spring of 1850, the first period in which he worked on *Moby-Dick*. But he put the manuscript aside to move his family to Pittsfield, and by the time he resumed it several months later, his intentions had begun to change. As first-time readers of the novel realize soon after chapter 22, what marks the first major shift in Melville's ambition is the effective disappearance of Ishmael as an active character, for as we noted, his inexperience was the resource Melville relied on to amuse us. After chapter 22, only rarely do we see Ishmael as one sailor among the crew of the *Pequod*; as far as the literal whaling voyage is concerned he becomes almost invisible, and strangely silent. Yet at the same time his voice takes over the novel, which itself gets launched on a new voyage at precisely this point. The first paragraph of chapter 24, "The Advocate," announces the abrupt end of Ishmael's novitiate, and the start of ours: "As Queequeg and I are now fairly embarked in this business of whaling; and as this business of whaling has somehow come to be regarded among landsmen as a rather unpoetical and disreputable pursuit; therefore, I am all anxiety to convince ye, ye landsmen, of the injustice hereby done to us hunters of whales" (108).

Almost certainly, here we have the "*Moby-Dick*" that Melville began to reconceive and rewrite when he went back to his manuscript in the fall of

1850, after writing about Hawthorne that summer. The clearest single note he strikes in that essay is his advocacy of the idea of genius. Its penultimate paragraph asserts his faith "that, in all men, hiddenly reside certain wondrous, occult properties" that "may chance to be called forth here on earth" (*PT*, 253). "The Advocate" ends on the same note: Ishmael refers to an "as yet undiscovered prime thing in me," and brings this to bear directly on Melville's immediate situation by citing "precious MSS. in my desk" (112). Reading Hawthorne, and especially writing to advocate Hawthorne for his service to the cause of American literature, had aroused Melville's own instinct for greatness. When he went back to his book about whaling, he could no longer defer his quest for genius to any desire merely to entertain the reader. The tenderfoot's part he had assigned to Ishmael, however, could not be reconciled with this quest. Thus Melville inverts his narrator's previous relationship to his audience. This is the most fundamental change enacted at the start of chapter 24. The ironic limitations on Ishmael's role are all lifted.[36] He is promoted to a full-fledged "hunter of whales," while the readers who had been privileged to enjoy his "comical predicament[s]" (26) are now made to feel benighted themselves. As "landsmen," we take over Ishmael's part. *Moby-Dick* becomes *our* first voyage: toward the "highest truth" that resides "in landlessness" (107). The novel's "I" transforms itself from an ingratiating young man into an omniscient narrative presence, initiated, privileged, knowledgeable in the truths that mere "landsmen" are ignorant of. In the abruptly liberated, suddenly authorial accents of the voice that begins speaking to us here, we can hear Melville putting in his bid for genius.[37]

His primary conscious concern in the next portion of his manuscript—chapters 24–40, the second act of its drama as a performance—is to set the stage by endowing his characters with the aesthetic stature appropriate to tragedy. As we saw in the chapter on Southwestern Humor, the anxieties of American culture made the ground across which Melville was moving in this attempt to "approach Shakespeare" disputed terrain; as Ishmael concedes in chapter 33, "in this episode touching Emperors and Kings, I must not conceal that I have only to do with a poor old whale-hunter" (148). But since throughout this sequence of chapters Melville is advocating "republican progressiveness"—American figures, American values—he could theoretically have presumed an essentially sympathetic American audience. Yet psychically he could not. Right in the first paragraph of "The Advocate," his readers are presumptively guilty of "injustice" to him; when in chapter 26 he appeals to "thou great democratic God," it is to defend himself against "all mortal critics" (117), as if the whole world were against him. It is in these chapters that the reader first starts to play an explicit role in the novel, and the part Melville assigns us is an unmistakably hostile one. "The Advocate" ends with a series of direct exchanges between Melville's narrator and his audience. It begins:

> But if, in the face of all this, you still declare that whaling has no aesthetically noble associations connected with it, then am I ready to shiver fifty lances with you there, and unhorse you with a split helmet every time.
> The whale has no famous author, and whaling no famous chronicler, you will say. (111)

"The whale has no famous author" is our first line in *Moby-Dick*! and it indicates as plainly as his military metaphor how violently charged was the space in which Melville performed for the public.

In his quest for genius as an American author, it was not finally Shakespeare, or the achievement of European literature, with which Melville had to contend. It was instead his audience; that is, it was his own "anxiety" (to use the most prominent word in "The Advocate's" first paragraph) about the unappreciative audience that begins heckling him by the end of that chapter. So *Moby-Dick* would have to change again. Neither plot nor character could carry the burden that weighed most on Melville's mind; there were no terms he could imagine in which the novel could speak for itself and still be faithful to his pursuit of greatness. He would have to speak for that himself, in his own voice, addressed directly to the audience that loomed between him and his goal. Thus the drama of Melville's own performance displaces the Shakespearian one he had prepared us for. Ahab's tragic quest remains the source of what narrative momentum the novel has, but with chapters like "Cetology" (chapter 32) and "The Whiteness of the Whale" (chapter 42) the book begins to abandon a narrative mode. It becomes expository instead: the two most important characters are Melville and his reader; the plot—his determination to carry that reader out to *see*. The Ishmael who presides over chapters 55–105 is neither a first-person participant nor a "tragic dramatist," but a Romantic prophet. Telling a story gives way to an impassioned effort to tell the truth. Ishmael becomes the vehicle by which Melville aspires to become the kind of genius he describes in the essay, whose mind is a plummet that probes "the very axis of reality" (*PT*, 244). In effect, Ishmael resumes the role of "school-master" he had resigned for a berth in the forecastle (6); more accurately, Father Mapple's symbolically shaped pulpit gives way to the *Pequod* itself, from which Ishmael as prophet seeks "to preach the Truth to the face of falsehood" (48).

It is at this stage that most readers tend to part company with *Moby-Dick*. Those of us who love the novel should not blame them too hastily. We have heard that all masterpieces are demanding, and one of the orthodoxies of modern criticism is that the majority of readers will prove inadequate to such demands. Melville himself often fell back on that bitter consolation. The demands that *Moby-Dick* makes on its readers, however, are almost perversely exacting. By the middle chapters, it not only refuses to scratch the novel reader's itch for a story; it has already twice violated the expectations Melville himself set up. First Ishmael and Queequeg effectively disappear, and with them the narrative of Ishmael's first voyage; then Ahab and Starbuck, and with them the drama we have reoriented ourselves to appreciate. Moreover, readers must adjust to their own changing status. We must accept our demotion to "landsmen"; we must give up our seat as a spectator (first of a comedy, then of a tragedy) for the equivalent of a desk in school or a pew in church. Yet there is nothing arbitrary about the pattern of these demands. Through all these changes the novel is responding to and acting out the urgencies of Melville's private and public drama as a performing artist. "To preach the Truth to the face of falsehood": to that high argument Melville decided to consecrate himself. In another phrase from Mapple's sermon he bids farewell to the whaling book he had initially planned to write: "Woe to him who seeks to please rather than to appal!" (48) In one last phrase, he sums up the new ambition to which *Moby-Dick* would be dedicated: "Delight is to him . . . who against the proud gods and commodores of this earth, ever stands forth his own inexorable self" (48). Instead of impersonating the kind of writer people seemed to expect him to be and infantalizing his self for the sake of pleasing them, he would stand forth his self as artist and prophet.

And who are the gods and commodores of this earth? Who but the reviewers and readers who by this point in his career had come to seem (to borrow a phrase from Ahab) the wall shoved near to Melville. "Under no conceivable circumstances," he wrote Duyckinck while still smarting from the failure of *Mardi,* can a writer ever "be at all frank with his readers."[38] "For in this world of lies," he protests in the Hawthorne essay, "Truth is forced to fly like a scared white doe in the woodlands" (*PT,* 244). Projecting his own anxieties onto literary history, he felt that even Shakespeare had to wear a "muzzle" on his soul, indeed declared that even Solomon "a little *managed* the truth with a view to popular conservatism."[39] These exaggerations point up how much of his own experience Melville invested in the stand Ahab takes on "The Quarter-Deck," when he shoves aside Starbuck's pieties with the claim that "Truth hath no confines" (164). But whereas in *Mardi* he had gone questing for imaginative freedom by leaving his readers behind, in *Moby-Dick* he girded himself to struggle for greatness by encountering his contemporary audience directly, to create a masterpiece in and through their immediate presence, to wrestle with them as well as with his material. Regarded from this point of view, the middle chapters of the novel—the third act of *its* drama—are its most humanly compelling ones.

Although in the long history of *Moby-Dick*'s reputation, the cetological chapters were the last to attract much sustained attention, recent criticism has moved them to the center of the book's achievement. This has been due particularly to the phenomenologists, who read them as a brilliant rendering of the existential quest for meaning amid the complex welter of experience.[40] My only reservation about this reading is that it presumes the wrong context for Ishmael's quest—the context of twentieth-century doubt—and thus overlooks the deepest motive that drives Ishmael's quest forward. The novel's last word is "orphan" (573), a summing up of the human condition that resonates through much modern art and thought. But Melville was a child of his time and place, and the background against which Ishmael's voice defines his quest is the "popular conservatism" of nineteenth-century faiths. As in *Walden* Thoreau locates his life in the woods in antithesis to the "shams and delusions" that are worshipped in the village, so Ishmael defines the "highest truth" that resides in "landlessness" against the assumptions of his contemporary audience. He identifies his expository context exactly in "The First Lowering," where amidst "the audacious seas" he reminds his reader that "you live under the blessed light of the evangelical land" (223). What gets lost when *Moby-Dick* is lifted out of this context is an appreciation of how Ishmael's most earnest project is rhetorical rather than epistemological: if he is concerned with the act of seeing, he is still more concerned with the art of saying, getting others to see. By making this distinction we can identify the source of the novel's amazing power in those middle chapters: Melville's anxiety-ridden aspiration to what in the Hawthorne essay he calls "the great Art of Telling the Truth" (*PT*, 244). This is a phrase that phenomenology would have to reject as hopelessly naive. Nonetheless to Melville it was a summons to greatness, the leviathan he had shipped for.

Chapter 42, "The Whiteness of the Whale," is by all acounts the central statement of Ishmael's quest. It is also typical of the cetological chapters as a group in that it explicitly organizes Ishmael's encounter with meaning in terms of his transaction with his readers. As its opening sentences make clear, his heaviest burden here is the same as the "anxiety" he admitted at the start of "The Advocate"—the anxiety to "convince" us:

> What the white whale was to Ahab, has been hinted; what, at times, he was to me, as yet remains unsaid.
> ... and yet so mystical and well nigh ineffable was it, that I almost despair of putting it in a comprehensible form ... and yet, in some dim, random way, explain myself I must, else all these chapters might be naught. (188)

This is the dilemma faced by all the Romantic prophets whenever they faced an audience. Jonah was sent directly by God. Father Mapple has the Bible on which to found his message. But Ishmael, to use Pierre's phrase, seeks to "gospelize the world anew, and show them deeper secrets than the Apocalypse" (*P*, 273); Ishmael is writing what Thoreau calls a "newer testament," for which there is no external sanction. He can appeal to Romanticism's one great authority—"in a matter like this," he cautions, "subtlety appeals to subtlety, and without imagination no man can follow another into these halls" (192)—but in fact this leaves him where he began, with the problem of the reader's receptiveness. In chapter 42 Ishmael claims to speak of "the common, hereditary experience of all mankind" (192) and democratically addresses himself to the widest possible American audience, referring to "most men," the "unsophisticated Protestant of the Middle American states," the "untravelled American" (192). As a work of the Romantic imagination written for "the common apprehension" (193), *Moby-Dick* must be (to cite Emerson's sole criterion for truth) its own evidence: its vision must compel and justify itself to the reader's mind, or else be "naught." After laboring throughout the chapter to open his reader's mind to the problem of whiteness as the problem of a universe that remains to be resolved, Melville ends "The Whiteness of the Whale" with a question that is both rhetorical and real, real because on its answer depends the fate of his rhetorical quest: "Wonder ye then at the fiery hunt?" (195)

It took more faith for Ishmael to hunt his audience in this fashion than for Ahab to go after his whale, for Melville had to lower for the truth in the face of all his accumulated grievances and doubts about his contemporary audience. "We" speak again in chapter 42, and once again our tone is harshly negative: "But thou sayest, methinks this white-lead chapter about whiteness is but a white flag hung out from a craven soul" (194). Like our first line in the novel, this interjection attacks Melville's surrogate *personally*; the issue is not whether whaling is respectable or whiteness paradoxical so much as what kind of writer and man Ishmael is. The ad hominem nature of these remarks may help us understand why Melville had so little respect for the logic of literary form:[41] in his mind the work of fiction was a vulnerable extension of his self, inseparable as a form from the whole problem of his identity. This sense of being locked in a personal confrontation with an adversary reader is the key to the structure and strategies of the book's cetological chapters. It explains why, beginning with that first paragraph of "The Advocate," the reader figures so prominently in Ishmael's prose. The eighty middle chapters of *Moby-Dick* probably contain more direct references to the reader—as "you," "ye," "thee," and "thou"—than any other nineteenth-century novel.

By the third act in the drama of its performance, all the supernumeraries have been pushed to the side of the stage. The issue is now between Melville and his audience, as figured in the rhetorically immediate relationship the dynamic of the novel creates between the "I" of Ishmael and the "you" of its landsman reader. Like a preacher for whom every moment is Sunday morning, every object the pretext for a sermon, Ishmael comes at us again and again. With his style, his wit, his imagination, his oratorical prowess, and his inexhaustible energy as his resources, he takes up each different part of the whale, the ocean, or the whaleship as an empirical point of reference from which to take soundings of the cosmos. The cetological chapters open out onto the largest prospects, but at the center of each is invariably the reader's innocence; this completes the inversion of the opening chapters, which had used *Ishmael's* innocence about whaling as their narrative premise, by making our innocence the occasion for *Moby-Dick*. Literally the landsman is innocent about the whaleman's world, so each chapter begins by patiently describing what "Brit" is, or what "The Line" looks like, or what whalemen mean by "The Battering Ram." So vividly does Ishmael manage these expositions that by the time they finish the novel, most readers feel they could hunt a whale themselves—but of course Ishmael is after still bigger game. In each chapter, having opened his text, he proceeds to interpret it as a piece of "veritable gospel cetology" (xvii). As he moves from what, say, "Brit" is to what it means, he ascends that neoplatonic scale Emerson outlines in *Nature*, where natural facts are symbolic of spiritual ones. Each of these chapters repeats in miniature the larger movement of *Moby-Dick*, for if Ishmael begins by deferring to his reader's needs, Melville does not let him stop until he has satisfied his own, which is to "preach truth" by probing "the very axis of reality," and so put forward again and again his legitimate claim to "genius."

The rhetorical plot of these chapters is finally *against* their reader's innocence, the unexamined complacencies of their belief. Ishmael speaks to "the evangelical land" about the truths of the unsounded ocean, "which is the dark side of this earth, and which is two thirds of this earth" (424). He comes to announce a reality that is well represented by what he says about Fedallah: "He was such a creature as civilized, domestic people in the temperate zone only see in their dreams" (231). He seeks to carry such people back beyond their acquired preconceptions about life to "the ghostly aboriginalness of earth's primal generations, . . . when all men . . . eyed each other as real phantoms, and asked of the sun and the moon why they were created and to what end" (231). He is the prophet, that is, of experiential truth confronting the face of conventional falsehood. Whaling is literally the quest for light, but the paradox that underlies most of the cetological chapters is that the vision they arrive at sheds darkness back onto the landsman's everyday life. Sworn to appal rather than to please, Ishmael (in "Brit") restores "that sense of the full awfulness of the sea which aboriginally belongs to it" (273); or (in "The Line") points out the terrors that encompass us even as we read *Moby-Dick*, "seated before your evening fire with a poker, and not a harpoon, by your side" (281); or (in "The Battering Ram") insists that truth is always "terrific": "For unless you own the whale, you are but a provincial and sentimentalist in Truth. But clear Truth is a thing for salamander giants only to encounter; how small the chances for the provincials then? What befel the weakling youth lifting the dread goddess's veil at Sais?" (338). As Melville's readers may have known, he was stricken senseless, and despaired for the rest of his life—which puts an unbearably steep price on spiritual knowledge. Thus although these chapters are so many homilies, sermons on "leviathanic revelations" (134), they aim to initiate readers, not to save them—except, we could say, from the sentimental provincialisms of their civilized, domestic culture.

The setting and characters of *Typee* are even more remote from Melville's audience's experience, but one of the secrets to his first book's popularity is the way he uses metaphor to domesticate the unfamiliar. The "Ti," for instance, is the hut where the Typee men gather around the chief and the priests of the tribe; it is taboo to women; it is where the ostensible cannibal feast occurs. But in three consecutive paragraphs Tommo refers to it as "a sort of Bachelor's Hall" and as "a kind of savage Exchange, where the rise and fall of Polynesian Stock was discussed," and he points out that men gather there "in the same way that similar characters frequent a tavern in civilized countries" (*T*, 157). There are several hundred similar analogies throughout the book, and they all have the same effect: to reassure Melville's reader that he or she already knows the world, that this exotic new realm can be explained and contained by referring it to the experience of the average American. In *Moby-Dick*, on the other hand, metaphor works in just the opposite way: instead of privileging the world the reader already knows and using it to disarm the unknown, now the "outlandish" world (298) through which the *Pequod* voyages is the authoritative point of reference, and the analogies Melville uses it to make continually defamiliarize the known. After describing the feeding frenzy of the sharks at the carcass of a dead whale, for instance, Ishmael warns the reader that "if you have never seen that sight, then suspend your decision about the propriety of devil-worship" (293). Or in the chapter on the sperm whale's brow, "The Prairie," he says that "gazing on it, in that full front view, you feel the Deity and the dread powers more forcibly than in beholding any other object in living nature" (346). Where *Typee* reassures and reconfirms the assumptions the reader brings to it (and I can think of no better generalization about the way popular literature works),[42] *Moby-Dick* is a work of vision that continually challenges its reader to reconceive the known, to reexamine even her most fundamental assumptions—about God, the devil, life itself—by the new light that "this whaling world" (321) sheds on the human condition. Instead of privileging the reader's experience, metaphor in *Moby-Dick* proceeds on the basis that Ishmael makes explicit in chapter 45, where he tells us flatly that "most landsmen" are "ignorant . . . of the wonders of the world" (205). "I put that brow before you," he announces at the end of "The Prairie," challenging his reader's preconceptions with equal explicitness; "Read it if you can" (347).

Yet while we must note how Melville's cetology consistently subverts the "popular conservatism" of his time, it would be wrong to suggest that the vision of these chapters is exclusively dark or sharkish. One of the great achievements of this "third act" of *Moby-Dick* is the plurality of moods and ideas that the persona of Ishmael can coherently be made to entertain and express. Impossible to paraphrase, this intricate richness can only be indicated by sketching a sample sequence of chapters:

91 — "THE PEQUOD MEETS THE ROSE BUD"
A spirited narrative version of a stock form of American humor: a Yankee diddling a foreigner.[43]

92 — "AMBERGRIS"
An essentially comic exposition of a moral paradox: that rotting decay produces the sweetest perfume.

93 — "THE CASTAWAY"
The grim narrative of Pip's fate when left "in the middle of such a heartless immensity" as the ocean; it ends by fiercely stating a much more threatening paradox: "So man's insanity is heaven's sense" (414).

94 — "A SQUEEZE OF THE HAND"
The first chapter about Ishmael himself since 72; here *he* feels restored to a sense of "attainable felicity," forgetting "all about our horrible oath" in a mood of contagious geniality (416).

95 — "THE CASSOCK"
A short, obscene, impious joke about the whale's penis (referred to obliquely) and "pulpits," "bible leaves," and "an archbishoprick" (420).

96 — "THE TRY-WORKS"
Again about Ishmael, at the ship's tiller for the first and last time in the novel; it begins as a narrative, but becomes a secular sermon on darkness, fire, and sunlight—one of the book's most eloquent passages, displaying a lyrical intensity and a metaphysical complexity unmatched by any novelist's prose until Conrad's.

Like the rhythms of the *Pequod*'s voyage "round the world" (237) through alternating storms and calms, Ishmael's *Moby-Dick* refuses to rest in any one attitude, either toward life at one extreme or toward its contemporary audience at the other. There is a tendency among postmodernist critics to treat this plurality as a species of nihilism, to decide that this multiplicity adds up to chapter 99, "The Doubloon." There, as Pip puts it, "I look, you look, he looks; we look, ye look, they look"

(434)—but no one can *see*, because everyone is trapped inside his own relativistic and solipsistic perspective, and so "reality" or "truth" remains unknowable and potentially bereft of meaning. This is not the end at which the cetological chapters aim, but the phenomenologists are right to call attention to the complexity of Ishmael's vision. What enables him alone to survive the "fiery hunt" is surely his mature intellectual willingness to abide with paradox, beautifully symbolized on this long book's last page when he floats away from the catastrophe on a coffin that is also a life buoy. To me, the most impressive instance of Ishmael's adroitness at keeping two opposite ideas in his field of vision involves his reader, of whom he can say at the end of chapter 89, drawing the largest circle around himself he can imagine, defining the true goal of the cetological chapters, "And what are you, reader, but a Loose-Fish and a Fast-Fish, too?" (398)

Given the exigencies of Melville's temperament and career, it is not surprising that *Moby-Dick*'s middle chapters would leave plot and characterization behind so that he could step in front of his story to engage his audience directly. His readers as Fast-Fish, stuck blindly to their society's proprieties and compelled to condemn a writer who would not "intercept" his "full articulations,"[44] had come to seem the wall that shut him away from the imaginative kingdom he felt entitled to. Ishmael, however, the Ishmael who asserts himself without once taking his eye off the reader, Ishmael was Melville's effort to open a door in that wall. As we can tell from the oratorical pitch at which he sustains it, this performance was under tension all the time. If a chapter like 91 relaxes into a straightforward attempt to entertain its American audience, we need read no further than chapter 95 to remember Melville's reservoir of hostility and resentment, for if they could have gotten his joke about "The Cassock," most contemporary readers would have been thoroughly appalled. The dozen or so dirty jokes that he insinuates into the novel are so many gestures of defiance, refusals to share the book's space with others. Yet the dirtiest jokes are well disguised; they seem to be written more for his private benefit—perhaps as a means to relieve the tension of his performance—than to offend his readers. Nearly all the rest of the time, in these middle chapters Melville is writing as well and as frankly as he knows how, in an imaginative space that is rhetorically and psychologically as public as a lyceum hall, in a voice that is summoned into existence by the audience it speaks to.

The cetological chapters are informed by Melville's liberating conviction that at last he is finding sea-room, not just to tell the truth in, but also to use all his gifts—narrative, descriptive, comic, declamatory—as a writer, to drop his plummet through the deepest depths of thought, to push language to the furthest reaches of expression; in short, to practice "the great *Art* of Telling the Truth." This is what is surprising about the novel's "third act": that Melville found the faith to cast the drama of his relationship with his audience on the high ground of Romantic prophecy, to recast the antagonism between I and you as the creatively productive give-and-take of dialectic argument. The Ishmael who is "all anxiety" to address us in these chapters believes he can "convince" us. He is Melville's act of faith in the imagination—ours as well as his own. In chapter 104, just before Ishmael's garrulous presence exits from the book, Melville allows him to exult in what has happened:

> One often hears of writers that rise and swell with their subject, though it may seem but an ordinary one. How, then, with me, writing of this Leviathan? Unconsciously my chirography expands into placard capitals. Give me a condor's quill! Give me Vesuvius' crater for an inkstand! Friends, hold my arms! For in the mere act of penning my thoughts of this Leviathan, they weary me, and make me faint with their outreaching comprehensiveness of sweep, as if to include the whole . . . universe, not excluding its suburbs. Such, and so magnifying, is the virtue of a large and liberal theme! We expand to its bulk. To produce a mighty book, you must choose a mighty theme. (456)

Yet what produced the mightiness of *Moby-Dick* was not so much its theme as its occasion: the fecundating drama of performance. The book's constant references to "you" and "ye," to "thee" and "thou," serve Melville the way touching the earth aided Antaeus. They serve continually to renew his quest for literary greatness, though the presence of those readers is both the source of his energy and the antagonist he is wrestling with. Ishmael draws here a picture that every admirer of Melville must cherish: the portrait of an artist who for once feels empowered to take imaginative possession of life, who for once can refer to the audience that hovers round him at his manuscript as "friends." As a metaphysical voyage toward the truth, Ishmael's circumnavigation of the cosmos does lead him back almost to the point of his departure. In terms of Melville's creative aspirations, however, toward the goal of being appreciated for the truth he is trying to tell, the whiteness of the whale has become a vast blank surface on which *to write*. Ishmael's many-sided expansiveness is not offered as a symptom of nihilism, but rather as an invigorating, infectious example of the mind's inexhaustible powers. He cannot conquer them, but he can artistically and intellectually fight all "mortally intolerable truth[s]" (107) to a tie.

As a mind performing its feats amid the ambiguous vicissitudes of life, Ishmael is not just trying to dazzle us with his virtuosity. Step by step through the cetological chapters, almost sentence by sentence, he invites us to join him on the stage. "Without imagination," we cannot take even the first step with him into "the immense Remote, the Wild, the Watery, the Unshored" (486). To go to "see" with him, we must give up our complacent preconceptions about life. And such voyaging, he reminds us several times, is always risky. But the human possibility that Ishmael enacts, to convert our antagonists into an occasion for our own accomplishments, is what Melville offers his readers in exchange for the conventional certainties he cuts them adrift from: a chance to "expand" in the same fashion to the full scope of their powers, to dive as Loose-Fish and keep themselves afloat amid the terrors and immensities of the sea. Ishmael's hand is always extended to us. Indeed, the pronouns in that passage where he celebrates the mightiness of the book he has written in our presence are unusually generous, even for Ishmael. It is an impersonal "one" who only "hears of writers." "You," however, should aspire "to produce a mighty book." At this furthest limit of Ishmael's egalitarian good fellowship, the division between genius and the masses has dissolved. At the end of chapter 104, Ishmael provisionally bestows on his reader, who had been a mere "landsman," the noblest, most honorific titles in his vocabulary: "In this Afric Temple of the Whale I leave you, reader, and if you be a Nantucketer, and a whaleman, you will silently worship there" (458).

Although readers cannot suspect it at the time, Ishmael is about to leave them, and the disappearance of his engaging voice after chapter 105 marks the beginning to the novel's fourth, tragic "act." But before turning to that, I would like to look specifically at chapter 96, "The Try-Works," as the culminating example of Melville's achievement in act 3. With this chapter we reach the end of the long process that begins on "The Mast-Head" (chapter 35). The whale has been sighted, lined, killed, hoisted to the ship's side, stripped, and cut up; the trying-out is the final step that transforms blubber into light-producing oil. Melville suggests the climactic significance of this chapter in another way as well: it is the only point in the whole voyage when Ishmael stands at the *Pequod*'s tiller as the helmsman.

The chapter begins empirically, describing the try-works, then "go[es] back for a moment" to the time they "were first started on this present voyage":

> By midnight the works were in full operation. We were clear of the carcase; sail had been made; the wind was freshening; the wild ocean darkness was intense. But that darkness was licked up by the fierce flames, which at intervals forked forth from the sooty flues. . . . The burning ship drove on, as if remorselessly commissioned to some vengeful deed. (422)

Already narrative begins to give way to exposition, although in this one case Melville is subjecting his own story to interpretation. The extended description that follows of the scene on board the *Pequod* makes the interpretive implications more and more explicit: fierce flames forking forth from sooty flues are followed by (to cite only about one-third of the examples) pagan harpooneers with pronged poles pitching hissing masses into snaky flames while telling unholy tales of terror; even their laughter "forks upward" like the flames (423). As if all this were not enough, Melville finally calls the ship itself a "red hell."

Contemporary readers would certainly have found that last line redundant, for if there was any literary language they knew well, it was this diction of Christian allegory. Melville describes this scene in the "sooty" terms that Stowe uses to set the moral scene at Simon Legree's plantation, or that Hawthorne employs whenever he wants to put the meaning of an episode beyond ambiguity. A writer more practiced than Melville in using the dialect of the popular culture would doubtless have shown a bit more restraint—but what is striking here is that he is so obviously trying to wed his vision to the terms his audience was most familiar with. And though he lays them on too thickly, he does reinvigorate the clichés of this vocabulary by grounding them not in derived preconceptions but in the immediate realm of Ishmael's experience. Stowe's readers know evil when they see it because they have been told what evil is. Ishmael, however, has long since thrown off all cultural prejudgments; if he tells us something is evil (which is what the diction of this description, of course, does), it is because he has come to that conclusion for himself.

In "The Try-Works" he tells us as much, although to bring the reader with him through the process he reverses the epistemological order. First he brings his description to an interpretive close: "the rushing Pequod, freighted with savages, and laden with fire, and burning a corpse, and plunging into that blackness of darkness, seemed the material counterpart of her monomaniac commander's soul" (423). Then he gives us the experiential basis on which he grounds this interpretation: "So seemed it to me, as I stood at her helm, and for long hours silently guided the way of this fire-ship on the sea" (423). By bringing the narrative back to Ishmael, and putting Ishmael in the authoritative role of helmsman, Melville finds the emblematic means to confess his own kinship with the satanism of Ahab's fiery hunt, even to admit that he is tempted by it: "The continual sight of the fiend shapes before me, capering half in smoke and half in fire, these at last begat kindred visions in my soul" (423). What happens next is the single most decisive of all the things that occur to Ishmael aboard the *Pequod*. All he does is turn around, but it is a conversion. Waking from the demonic vision he realizes he has been enchanted by "this unnatural hallucination of the night," been "inverted" at the tiller, and he turns back just in time to prevent "the fatal contingency" of capsizing the ship (424). If Ishmael saves himself here by turning *from* the self-destructive satanism of Ahab's quest, he completes the movement, as the rest of the chapter reveals, by turning *to* his reader.

In his subtly nuanced discussion of "The Try-Works," R.W.B. Lewis calls the three paragraphs with which it concludes "stanzas."[45] He is right to want to call attention to the lyric intensity and suppleness of Melville's prose in this passage, but in fact the chapter is structured less as a poem than as a sermon; just as Father Mapple ended his sermon by applying the lesson of Jonah to his listeners' lives, so Ishmael seeks to apply to his readers the meaning of the discoveries he has made. Admittedly, the popular poetry of Victorian America blurred the distinction between poems and sermons, but by thinking of this chapter as a sermon we gain an appreciation of just how explicitly rhetorical it is. Indeed, its concluding paragraphs begin with a series of apostrophes: "Look not too long in the face of the fire, O Man! . . ." (424). Ishmael brings himself back from an absorption in Ahab's demonism by means of this address, for if Ahab's madness enrolls him among "the congregation of the dead" (425), Ishmael will speak to the congregation of his living readers. As a moral helmsman, he will try to guide their way through this darkness.

His peroration brilliantly conducts us through a series of paradoxes. On the one hand, through Ishmael Melville here rejects the stand that Ahab takes against the human condition: "there is a woe that is madness" (425). Thus he resists the fatal enchantment of the fire. On the other, though, he does not simply confirm any popular conservatisms. He can sound very conventional, even like Hawthorne's Hilda, when he says that "the glorious, golden, glad sun [is] the only true lamp" (424), but he goes on at once to lead his reader back toward the tragic vision of *Moby-Dick*, the "wisdom that is woe":

> Nevertheless . . . The sun hides not the ocean, which is the dark side of this earth, and which is two thirds of this earth. So, therefore, that mortal man who hath more of joy than sorrow in him, that mortal man cannot be true—not true, or undeveloped. With books the same. The truest of all men was the Man of Sorrows, and the truest of all books is Solomon's, and Ecclesiastes is the fine hammered steel of woe. "All is vanity." ALL. This wilful world hath not got hold of unchristian Solomon's wisdom yet. (424)

This passage insists on much more problematic terms than the description of the *Pequod* as a "red hell" that Melville uses as the text for his sermon. "More of joy than sorrow"—this was the unofficial motto of Victorian American culture, and the conclusion arrived at by all its best-selling literature. To that assumption Melville says, No. Although the chapter returns at the end to its audience, it continues to privilege Ishmael's private experience. Yet Melville is seeking out a way to mediate between his own vision and his audience's preconceptions. Solomon is "unchristian," but as a biblical figure he can serve as a kind of middle ground between the highest truth that Melville preaches and the a priori values of the "wilful world" that is his congregation. There is another detail to note too: "This wilful world hath not got hold of unchristian Solomon's wisdom *yet*." It may be that not all is vanity. This passage may not be in vain. The mortals to whom he preaches may be "undeveloped," but the emphatic implication of that "yet" is that the willful world can learn, can come to sea to see the truth. In this chapter as a whole, as in the cetological chapters as a group, Melville is "trying-out" the assumptions of his culture. It is, indeed, that "yet" that sustains them all: his faith that he is speaking not in vain, that by burning away their facile innocence in the passion of his oratorical prose he can make them wise. The note on which the chapter ends may look like a non sequitur, until we realize that its deepest concern, like that of the other cetological chapters, is with the drama of performing, for this chapter about fire, darkness, evil, and woe ends on a note of triumphant celebration: "There is a wisdom that is woe; but there is a woe that is madness. And there is a Catskill eagle in some souls that can alike dive down into the blackest gorges, and soar out of them again and become invisible in the sunny spaces" (355). This refers to air space rather than sea-room, but the point is the same. By disporting in this metaphor, Melville is celebrating the visionary and imaginative freedom he has achieved in *Moby-Dick*'s third act: to find and to tell the deepest truths.

Actually, I only wish this were the note on which the chapter finally ends. There is one more sentence, and it turns the eagle's triumph into a grousing exile; it does not turn *to* the audience, it turns *on* them: "And even if he for ever flies within the gorge, that gorge is in the mountains; so that even in his lowest swoop the mountain eagle is still higher than other birds upon the plain, even though they soar" (425). It is in vain for me to wish to say to Melville: You didn't need to add that. First you suggest we too can be developed, can be Catskill eagles (an image that is very hospitable to us American readers). But now you say we can't. You condemn us to the plains, no matter how we try to soar, as if the final proof of your genius is that we can't or won't follow you. . . .

This was in fact the most fundamental of Melville's convictions about his quest for greatness as a writer. As he wrote to Hawthorne in June 1851: "Though I wrote the Gospels in this century, I should die in the gutter." He is writing just before going to New York to "finish [the novel] up in some fashion or other" while the opening chapters were being set in type, and it is in this letter, at just this point in the composition of *Moby-Dick*, that he announces the failure of the faith that had sustained Ishmael's garrulity as a prophet: "What I feel most moved to write, that is banned, —it will not pay. Yet, altogether, write the *other* way I cannot. So the product is a final hash, and all my books are botches."[46] From this we could perhaps have guessed the "fashion" in which Melville would choose to finish the novel, for the figure of his botched books points straight toward crippled Ahab and his defiant rage against the source of his disfigurement. As late as "The Try-Works" Melville could resist the spell that Ahab exercized upon his mind, but this sense of kinship with Ahab's victimization at length prevailed.

After chapter 105, the novel's mood and strategy change again. If the eighty middle chapters are characterized by Ishmael's engaging expository voice, in the last thirty (chapters 106–135) that voice falls silent; following a last brief reference to himself in chapter 111, Ishmael as prophet disappears even more completely than Ishmael as character had. *Moby-Dick*'s commentators have had little to say about this last change, except to suggest that Melville aptly stops digressing in order to move straightforwardly toward the strong narrative finish. Yet this is hardly accurate. Until the last three chapters about "The Chase," *Moby-Dick* is still very talky—but it is Ahab, who was not supposed to "speak much" (79), who does the talking.[47] Even in chapters whose titles lead us to expect more of Ishmael's expatiations, chapters like "The Forge" or "The Log and Line," Ahab's voice is essentially the only one we hear. And by retiring Ishmael to bring Ahab to the front of the book's stage,[48] Melville abruptly withdraws from the kind of dialogic encounter with the audience that Ishmael had established—for Ahab's voice, although grandiloquent, is arhetorical, self-absorbed, impatient with anything but his own preoccupations. Ahab speaks in solipsistic monologues, as the novel itself admits in chapter 108, when Ahab first starts speaking at length: "who's he speaking to, I should like to know?" the *Pequod*'s carpenter asks himself as Ahab goes on and on (470).

Only in these chapters does *Moby-Dick* deserve its reputation for unreadability. Because it speaks at us, not with us, not even to us, Ahab's voice quickly grows tiresome. At one point it speaks immediately at us; Ahab lifts his shaggy, seamed face up from the world of the novel to address Melville's audience directly: "Lo! ye believers in gods all goodness, and in man all ill, lo you! see the omniscient gods oblivious of suffering man . . ." (522). It is a startling moment, and it can serve to measure the difference between Melville's approach to us through Ishmael and his approach through Ahab: the anxiety to convince us gives way to this scornful contempt for us.

One could talk about what happens at the end of the novel in several different ways. We could emphasize the collapse of the distance that Ishmael had enabled Melville to keep between himself and the part of the self he invested in Ahab's "quenchless feud." Or we could note how the terms of Ahab's representation change when he moves back to the center: the opening accounts use a psychological vocabulary to describe him—mad, crazy, monomaniac, and so on—whereas the last thirty chapters describe him in theological terms—as satanic. "The Try-Works" anticipates this shift in its treatment of Ahab's defiant rage and ceaseless woe as both "infernal" and "mad," but "The Try-Works," although it climaxes Ishmael's engagement with Ahab's quest, is not the novel's last word on satanism. That is actually to be found in a still later letter to Hawthorne, written after Melville had been to New York to start *Moby-Dick* through the press and just as he was finishing the manuscript. "This is the book's motto (the secret one)," he tells Hawthorne, "Ego non baptiso te in nomine—but make out the rest yourself."[49]

Since Melville had just mentioned "the hell-fire in which the whole book is broiled," Hawthorne probably had no trouble filling in the blank. When he later read *Moby-Dick*, he would have learned that this is also Ahab's motto, howled "deliriously" in "The Forge" while baptizing his harpoon "in nomine diaboli" (489). While it is grossly inaccurate to say that the "whole" of the novel glows with hellfire, Melville's simplification all too plainly indicates how he had come to associate Ahab's defiant blasphemy with his own stance as the author of *Moby-Dick*. "But make out the rest yourself": even though he is addressing Hawthorne, the one other American for whose genius and vision Melville had utter respect, he cannot keep a kind of Ahablike contempt for explaining himself to others from inflecting his own voice. The clearest indication we have about the state of mind in which he finished the novel is still more derisive. "Concerning my own forthcoming book," he wrote Sarah Morewood, a sympathetic neighbor in the Berkshires, "Dont you buy it—dont you read it, when it does come out. . . . Warn all gentle fastidious people from so much as peeping into the book—on risk of a lumbago & sciatics."[50] Having begun over a year and a half earlier to write a novel that would appeal to Victorian America, he winds up bragging about how he has defied them all—although of course for a professional writer to warn people against buying his book is exactly as self-destructive as Ahab's refusal to turn back from his quest.

What *Moby-Dick* winds up eulogizing in its "last act" is defiance. Eulogizing is the right word, for even though Ahab does not die until the end, the narrative makes it clear long before the *Pequod* sights the white whale that his quest will fail. By that point, however, the question that the narrative will answer has been transposed into starker terms: it is not, can Ahab defeat Moby Dick? but how will he bear up to the inevitability of his defeat? Indeed, since his quarrel is with life, it has been obvious from the

outset that Ahab can only fail. But it remains for Melville to show us, as
he does vividly in the chapters called "The Chase," that Ahab's will will
not surrender, that he'll hurl himself in the teeth of his quest's inevitable
failure and thus define *his* "inexorable self" by this self-destructive act.
The whale's omnipotence and Ahab's indomitableness—the whole range
of the novel, and of the cosmos it surveys, has shrunk to these two fixed
points, which remain fixed for the whole last act. In his final speech—or
rather, his final self-absorbed soliloquoy—Ahab insists that *nothing has
changed*:

> "Oh, now I feel my topmost greatness lies in my topmost grief. Ho, ho!
> from all your furthest bounds, pour ye now in, ye bold billows of my whole
> foregone life, and top this one piled comber of my death! Towards thee I
> roll, thou all-destroying but unconquering whale; to the last I grapple with
> thee; from hell's heart I stab at thee; for hate's sake I spit my last breath at
> thee. Sink all coffins and all hearses to one common pool! and since neither
> can be mine, let me then tow to pieces, while still chasing thee, though tied
> to thee, thou damned whale! *Thus*, I give up the spear!" (571)

But this speech also registers how much the novel as a whole has
changed. Ahab is only talking to his own doomed life and that damned
whale, but Melville has not forgotten the audience for whom he stages
this ultimate encounter. I have said that Ahab's voice has none of the
creative play in it that Ishmael's has, but in his very last line he makes the
book's fiercest pun. "*Thus*, I give up the spear": Victorian American readers would have needed no annotator's help to recognize the allusion to
Jesus' death on the cross: "he bowed his head and gave up his spirit"
(John 19:30; Luke 23:46). Uncle Tom and Dimmesdale also die with
Christ's words on their lips, but Melville's use of that convention here is
still more blasphemous than Ahab's baptism of his harpoon "in nomine
diaboli." In making this moment the summit of Ahab's heroism, Melville
is hurling his defiance directly at his readers: at their New Testament, at
their Christianity, at their most sacred values. It is one thing, through
Ishmael, to put the whale's brow before us as an enigmatic symbol of the
Deity, or to make unchristian Solomon's wisdom the truest truth he
knows, or to leave us in an African whale temple; in these cases Melville
sets up a dialectic between his vision and the falsehood to which he is
preaching. But the terms he lays down in Ahab's final speech admit no
dialectical interplay whatever. Ahab as Antichrist, Antichrist as hero:
given Melville's culture, no more defiant final note is imaginable.

But Melville wrote this speech for Ahab precisely because it was the
most defiant note that the terms of his culture made available. From the
start of his career, from the half dozen censorious reviews of *Typee*, he
knew that contemporary readers were prepared to grant him a good deal

of imaginative freedom, except when it came to what one reviewer of *Moby-Dick* referred to as "sneering at the truths of revealed religion."[51] *Moby-Dick* actually received generally good reviews, but one of the most constant objections was to Melville's "irreverence."[52] The reviewer for the *Literary World*, who was probably Evert Duyckinck, Melville's friend and former mentor, put it this way: "We do not like to see what, under any view, must be to the world the most sacred associations of life violated and defaced."[53] You would think Melville would have been prepared for this, considering the way he had gloated about the book's secret motto. Indeed, as in *Mardi*, he had practically forced the reviewers to react this way. But here again we have to confront the dividedness of Melville's ambitions. The evidence that Hershel Parker has assembled suggests that it was precisely Melville's anger at the complaints *Moby-Dick* aroused, particularly Duyckinck's response, that changed the course of *Pierre*, the novel he was writing when the reviews starting coming in: he decided to make Pierre an author to give himself an occasion, as William Charvat puts it, to make "the reader the villain" of that book.[54] The reviews of *Pierre* were much more hostile, although not more so than Melville is in the second half of that book toward novels, readers, and reviewers in America. The widespread condemnation and virtual unsalability of *Pierre* was the decisive event in Melville's career as a novelist, leading him to abandon the conflicted desire for both fame and infamy that had fueled his productivity and botched his novels.

But to come back to the question at hand: what changed the course of *Moby-Dick*? What prompted Melville, in the last quarter of the novel, to identify himself so thoroughly with Ahab's narcissistic rage against the universe?[55] Why did he end up with only Ahab's shrill note of defiance to sound, after he and Ishmael had found so many more supple, more productive ways to assert an inexorable self? As opposed to what Parker can tell us about the composition of *Pierre*, there is no evidence to suggest that anything happened in the first half of 1851 to embitter or anger Melville with his prospects as a writer while deciding in what fashion he would finish *Moby-Dick*. But here *Pierre* itself can help. All criticism, remember, would come too late for Pierre. Reading his reviewers may have precipitated Melville's feeling of futility about ever being allowed to write his way, but that feeling was already in his bones, for the novel anticipates Pierre's fate as a writer when it traces his experience as a son. The Ishmael we meet at the novel's start is a lot like Pierre at home in Saddle Meadows; he is defined by his ability to please the reader, just as Pierre's identity has been determined by the pattern of his mother's expectations. But then through Ishmael Melville decides to show the world how much greater he is than the role its expectations have created for him. For the space of the cetological chapters he sustains his faith that he can do two things at once: be true to all the powers inside himself and also reach his audience. But the faith on which these chapters sail—that others' expectations can be reshaped—always had to compete, within Melville himself, with the deeper, underlying insecurity on which Pierre's hopes run aground: that he will only be loved or appreciated as long as he conforms to others' expectations. This doubt is always on the verge of rage, not just against the world, but against his own desire to please or even reach that world. It is this rage that Melville surrendered to in *Moby-Dick*: projected through Ahab as the incarnation, not just of his defiance, but of his quest for self-destruction as the only final proof of autonomy, of independence, of his refusal to surrender. Of course Ishmael, with his willingness to abide constraints and limits on the self, is finally much freer than Ahab, who is held captive by his unrealizable demand for absolute sovereignty. But Ishmael is freer than Melville himself could finally be.

Long as this chapter is, I must end it by admitting my own inescapable constraints. I cannot hope to "prove" that the whale that crippled Ahab is ultimately the audience that botched Melville's books, or that the drama *Moby-Dick* enacts was scripted by Melville's earliest life—that the aboriginal "you" he pleases, then wrestles with, then despairingly defies in his conflicted quest for greatness, is a transformation of his mother. But I can offer one last textual imaging of this pattern, though like Ishmael I must rely on a give-and-take relationship with you. Give me, then, the assumption that chapter 23, "The Lee Shore," was written very late in the course of the novel's composition, perhaps just before Melville started the book through the press. If you agree with me about the four acts of *Moby-Dick*, then I think you will readily agree that the mood of "The Lee Shore" belongs with the last act. Call the first act Ingratiation, the second Advocacy, the third Prophecy, and the fourth Defiance. Structurally chapter 23 falls between the first two acts, and in the brief space of its four paragraphs it rehearses the characteristics of them all, but it ends by sounding the defiant note that the last act will sustain for almost ninety pages. There is, however, one piece of harder evidence for my contention: in this chapter Melville explicitly anticipates the "ocean-perishing" of the *Pequod* and all her crew (107), and the commentators agree that Melville only decided to end the book with that conclusive catastrophe much later in its composition. And there is one good reason why Melville would have added the chapter just before sending the manuscript to the printer. In chapter 3 he carefully introduces the Byronic seaman Bulkington, creating the expectation that Bulkington would play a prominent part in the narrative. Instead, Bulkington became one of those loose ends left by Melville's changing ambitions for the book, but in looking through the opening chapters to make sure they were ready for the printer, Melville

apparently decided that he owed us some further word before allowing
Bulkington to disappear from the story.

That is the gesture with which the chapter begins: acknowledging the
responsibility a novelist owes his readers. "Some chapters back" a character was introduced (106); he must now be accounted for. This is the way
Moby-Dick itself began: privileging its readers' expectations, letting them
define the shape of the story. But as in *Moby-Dick* as a whole, if the chapter begins by seeking to satisfy its audience, it goes on to challenge them
instead. Melville offers to account for Bulkington with a metaphor instead of a story: "Let me only say that it fared with him as with the storm-
tossed ship, that miserably drives along the leeward land" (106). In such
a fix, as every sailor knows, the very port the ship has been making for
becomes her adversary:

> The port would fain give succor; the port is pitiful; in the port is safety,
> comfort, hearthstone, supper, warm blankets, friends, all that's kind to our
> mortalities. But in that gale, the port, the land, is that ship's direst jeopardy;
> she must fly all hospitality; one touch of land, though it but graze the keel,
> would make her shudder through and through. With all her might she
> crowds all sail off shore; in doing so, fights 'gainst the very winds that fain
> would blow her homeward; seeks all the lashed sea's landlessness again; for
> refuge's sake forlornly rushing into peril; her only friend her bitterest foe!
> (106)

It is a brilliant image of the human condition, charged with the hyster-
ical wisdom of Nietzsche's best epiphanies. It is only as Melville elaborates it, however, that we can see how much it meant to him as an image
of his storm-tossed career as a writer. In the next paragraph, he turns
directly to his readers, the port he has been making for all the time he has
been writing the novel, the audience that could "succor" him:

> Know ye, now, Bulkington? Glimpses do ye seem to see of that mortally
> intolerable truth; that all deep earnest thinking is but the intrepid effort of
> the soul to keep the open independence of her sea; while the wildest winds
> of heaven and earth conspire to cast her on the treacherous, slavish shore?
> (107)

Melville had commenced the chapter trying to weave a loose end called
Bulkington back into the pattern of his novel. But his aggressively
arhetorical question—"Know ye, now, Bulkington?"—betrays his tetchy
impatience with the need to explain himself to anyone. How, we might
legitimately reply, can we know Bulkington, when you haven't bothered
to develop his character? It wouldn't matter if I did, Melville replies; you
could only seem to see glimpses of the truth that such men as Bulkington

and I bear witness to—and in any case, how could I explain to you without compromising the open independence of the sea I mean to sail in?

That the shore should be "slavish" as well as "treacherous" does not
follow from the logic of the conceit Melville is developing, but we can tell
why he would have been led to this elaboration. It makes perfect sense in
the context of the psychodrama that the paragraph makes explicit when
it berates its readers. He associates the land, the homeward port, with his
contemporary public and its apparent demand that the novelist conform
to their hearthstone proprieties. Indeed, this implication takes over the
image:

> But as in landlessness alone resides the highest truth, shoreless, indefinite as
> God—so, better is it to perish in that howling infinite, than be ingloriously
> dashed upon the lee, even if that were safety! For worm-like, then, oh! who
> would craven crawl to land! (107)

That the shore should be "safety" completely inverts the original terms of
the image, but Melville is no longer thinking as an ex-sailor. He is thinking as a sorely crowded writer performing for an audience that has come
to seem his bitterest foe, even while it remains the only possible friend to
his hopes for a literary career. And here he is thinking as a wounded son,
for whom the apparent safety of home masks a treacherous enslavement.
Thus he must fly all hospitality. He can no longer imagine sea-room to
tell the truth in; he can either betray himself by crawling back to land,
cravenly surrendering to others' expectations, or embrace his self-destruction by questing for landlessness "alone." In its last lines the chapter
offers Bulkington at the helm of the *Pequod* as the emblem of Melville's
plight as the author of *Moby-Dick*—and of his own heroism, for he promises Bulkington that, like Ahab, his topmost greatness lies in his topmost
grief:

> Terrors of the terrible! is all this agony so vain? Take heart, take heart, O
> Bulkington! Bear thee grimly, demigod! Up from the spray of thy ocean-
> perishing—straight up, leaps thy apotheosis! (107)

This puts the virtue of self-destructiveness beyond dispute. It is in this
mood that the novel's last act was written to exalt Ahab's suicidal rage to
higher and higher heights of heroism. And with this conclusion, the
chapter not only reenacts the movement that recurs in so many individual
passages in Melville's books, where he winds up addressing gods or dem-
igods because there is no fit mortal audience to speak to; the chapter also
reenacts the structural arc through which the four acts of *Moby-Dick*
move. At the beginning of "The Lee Shore," Melville directly addresses
his readers. At the end, in choosing to address and canonize this character
whom he never allows us to meet, Melville willfully leaves his readers out.

We are blind witnesses to a private apotheosis, just as the anguish of this passage can only be understood on the assumption of our blindness. The agony of the soul that searches for truth is presented as a martyrdom at the hands of the public who would rather have him crawl back to them, but whose promised succor is as treacherous as Mary Glendenning's apparently doting smile. By turning away from us to embrace Bulkington, by making it "better" to perish in that howling infinite, Melville deliberately exiles himself from any human community to enroll instead in what, in "The Try-Works," Ishmael rejects as "the congregation of the dead." This congregation—which includes Ahab, Pierre, and Bartleby as well— is the only fit communion for the intrepid soul. Human communities can only enslave and betray it.

"All's o'er, and ye know him not!" (*P*, 362): so ends *Pierre*. This is not Melville's admission that he has somehow failed to communicate the truth; it is his resentful accusation of our unworthiness to ever know the truth. Both *Moby-Dick* and *Pierre* end apocalyptically, with the effective destruction of the world each book creates; all perishes, tragically but gloriously, with the apotheosis of the great soul whose greatness, let me say again, comes to be defined by his choice to perish. We can look at Melville's career and call it a tragic perishing as well, at least until the revival in the 1920s retrieved the example of his genius for us. Since Melville's story was resurrected in the modernist era, however, it has been with the assumption that his fate was inflicted on him by a culture unworthy of his genius. This was the mood in which he himself ended his attempt to write fiction for and tell truth to America; he dedicated *The Confidence-Man* (1857) "to victims of Auto da Fe," those souls who were persecuted and finally condemned because they would not cravenly crawl before the inquisitorial will of the majority. The fate of Melville's career, however, was determined more by his needs than by his audience's expectations. We might say it was determined by *his* expectations of them, which he made into a prophecy that fulfilled itself. His career was martyred to his own anxieties, just as Pierre seems to woo his mother's, and finally to exult in the public's rejection of him. What happens at the end of "The Lee Shore" is what happens at the end of *Moby-Dick*, and what had happened by the end of Melville's brief, anguished career—he denies that his readers can play any role, except to stand for what he must defy.

Chapter IX

CONCLUSION: "WHO AIN'T A SLAVE?"

Publication—is the Auction
Of the Mind of Man—

Thought belong to Him who gave it—
Then—to Him Who bear
Its Corporeal illustration—Sell
The Royal Air—

In the Parcel—Be the Merchant
Of the Heavenly Grace—
But reduce no Human Spirit
To Disgrace of Price—
        —Emily Dickinson

AFTER FINISHING *Moby-Dick* in a defiant burst of "wickedness," Melville knew he had written a great book, but also one that would not earn many of those dollars on which his career as a professional novelist depended. The apocalyptic violence of the novel's final flurry had apparently emptied him, for the time being, of the rage out of which Ahab had sprung. When Hawthorne's wife Sophia wrote to compliment him on the achievement of *Moby-Dick*, he replied with genuine amazement that she "should find any satisfaction in that book . . . for as a general thing, women have small taste for the sea." He promised that his next novel would not make so steep a demand on her good will: "My Dear Lady, I shall not again send you a bowl of salt water. The next chalice I shall commend, will be a rural bowl of milk."[1] By comparing this reference to *Pierre* with the way he had written to Sarah Morewood about *Moby-Dick* just four months earlier, we can see that Melville's mood had swung back to the desire to court his contemporary audience. In the first half of *Pierre* he tries to steer directly toward their appetites and expectations; as he told Richard Bently, it is "very much more calculated for popularity than anything you have yet published of mine—being a regular romance, with a mysterious plot to it, & stirring passions at work."[2] When we read the opening chapters of *Pierre*, there is no mistaking Melville's uneasiness with the forms and conventions of "regular romance," but still more conspicuous is his determination to align his imaginative vision with the categories of popular fiction.

This mood did not last either. About halfway through the novel Melville abruptly decided to make Pierre an American author, and all the various narrative and emotional issues he had begun *Pierre* to explore gave way to the one passion that, by 1852, stirred Melville most deeply: the tragedy of his own fate as a performing writer. *Pierre* essentially became the story of "Pierre at His Book"—the martyred victim to his high-souled quest for truth. And what is Pierre's book about? When Melville summons us to "peep over the shoulder of Pierre, and see what it is he is writing there, in that most melancholy closet," we find Pierre commanding *his* reader to look on Vivia, his "author-hero," at work on *his* book—another martyr to the literary "pursuit of . . . virtue and truth": "'Cast thy eye in there on Vivia; tell me why those four limbs should be clapt in a dismal jail—day out, day in—week out, week in—month out, month in—and himself the voluntary jailer! Is this the end of philosophy? This the larger, and spiritual life?'"[3] We find out nothing about the book that "Vivia" is writing, but it is not unlikely that he too is at work on a novel about an American (perhaps named "Herman Melville") writing a novel about writing a novel as the ultimate act of tragic heroism. What makes the novelist's fate a tragic martyrdom, of course, is the blindness of the audience whom he must address: "I hate the world, and could trample all lungs of mankind as grapes, and heel them out of their breath, to think of the woe and the cant, —to think of the Truth and the Lie!" This is from Pierre's novel, but might as well be from Vivia's—or Melville's. "The Truth" is what the writer seeks; "the Lie" is all his culture wants to see.

Melville ends this section of *Pierre* by noting that although Pierre is "quite conscious" of "his fatal condition," he is powerless to avoid or alter it. Certainly both his personal experience and the cultural circumstances of his time and place made it inevitable that Melville would write directly about the difficulty of writing for an American audience. In a sense the collapse of *Pierre* into this obsession with its own creation literalizes, with melodramatic explicitness, the subject of this study: the way the major texts of the American Renaissance are *about* the drama of their own performance. But let us for a moment lift our eyes from Vivia, Pierre, and Melville. For we should note how much is lost when Melville decides that of all possible subjects the truest for an American novel is just all that is "hard and bitter in his lot" as an American novelist. The same kind of loss can be felt in the Dickinson poem I've put at the head of this chapter. According to Thomas H. Johnson's dating, this poem was written in 1863, the same year as the Emancipation Proclamation. Much of the greatness of Dickinson's imagination lies in the compelling greediness of her appropriation of other people's experiences as the measure of her own inward richness, but on this occasion she surely claims too much. What the poem gains in force by its analogy between the writer in the literary marketplace and the slave on the auction block is, I think, overbalanced by a larger loss: the diminishment of the fact of selling and buying people and the human content of their lives to this self-referential, self-pitying metaphor.

"Who ain't a slave?" asks Ishmael at the start of *Moby-Dick*.[4] The answer depends on how you define "slave," but given the definition that was strictly enforced in America when Melville wrote this line, we should be very leery of the answer that Melville, like Dickinson, implies. Literature as a performing art imposes a number of constraints on the autonomy of the writer; how many constraints, and how tightly they bind or chafe the imagination, depends mainly on the writer's own ambitions. The writer, however, ain't a slave, though Melville often felt so, as in that passage from "The Lee Shore" where he canonizes his refusal to crawl back to the "slavish shore." Indeed, his one sustained treatment of slavery can be read as another reflection, an ironic one, of his "hard and bitter" fate as an American writer.

"Benito Cereno" was among the last of the fictions that Melville wrote for publication.[5] After the decisive critical and popular failure of *Pierre*, he had been forced to turn to the magazines, writing and selling fifteen short stories and sketches between 1853 and 1856. In *Moby-Dick* and *Pierre*, his big, ambitious novels, Melville had consecrated himself to "the great Art of Telling the Truth," but as a magazinist he perfected the deceptive art of the ironist. His audience was still acutely present to him as he wrote, but his chief pleasure now lay in misleading them: satisfying the "superficial skimmer of pages"[6] while insinuating his own terrific truths about the human condition so subtly that such a reader would remain oblivious to them.

"Benito Cereno" is a particularly complex instance of this technique. As an ostensibly two-part story, it first creates and then exposes one ironic pattern. Its first half is the narrative of Amasa Delano's experience on board the ship *San Dominick*; although written in the third person, the narrative sticks closely to Delano's perspective, to his interpretations of the puzzling phenomena he witnesses. The irony—his misreading of events—is then apparently revealed and emended in the second half: a first-person narrative in the form of the legal deposition of Benito Cereno, captain of the *San Dominick* and presumably a privileged witness (just as a legal deposition, taken under oath, is presumably a privileged narrative form) to what "really" happened. First the puzzle, then the solution; first the text, then the interpretation. Melville invites his reader to jump to this conclusion in the comment the narrative makes on Cereno's testimony: "If the Deposition have served as the key to fit into the lock of the complications which precede it, then, as a vault whose door has been flung back, the San Dominick's hull lies open to-day" (114). Even most modern readers are satisfied with this account. First the lock, then the key. But Melville used the subjunctive: "*If* the Deposition . . .". Readers who accept Cereno's account as definitive fail to remember the story's earlier use of a lock and a key as "significant symbols" (63), for in that earlier scene it turns out that what looks like a key hanging around Cereno's neck "by a slender silken cord" (63) is actually an emblem of his lack of freedom, while the man who wears the padlock is in fact his captor. It is Amasa Delano who refers to the lock and key as "significant symbols, truly," although he fails to see what they truly symbolize. It is also at this point in the tale that we are told that Delano is "a man of such native simplicity as to be incapable of . . . irony" (63).

To such an exegete of experience, one "incapable" of irony, "Benito Cereno" is a two-part story, wholly told when Cereno's testimony clarifies the enigmas of the narrative that precedes it. But the deposition is another lock. The ultimate failure of such a reading is to realize that "Benito Cereno" is really a three-part story—in which the third part is withheld. Delano's perspective governs the first part and Cereno's the second, but there is a third main character: Babo, the slave who led the revolt aboard the *San Dominick*, who never tells the story from *his* perspective. We hear Babo's voice only in the masquerade he is forced to perform to deceive Delano, in which he enacts the part of Cereno's faithful servant. Once the masquerade is exposed Babo refuses to speak at all: "he uttered no sound, and could not be forced to" (116). The reason for his silence is not given, but it is nonetheless self-evident: once the whites have suppressed his revolt, no audience available to him has any interest in his version of the truth. The court in which Cereno testifies begins with the conviction that slavery is legal and thus that a slave is either property or, if he rejects his commodification and strikes out for freedom, a criminal. Though Delano is from Massachusetts, he shares the same assumption. When he first sees blacks on board the *San Dominick*, he labels them "negro slaves, amongst other valuable freight" (48), and the instant he realizes those same blacks have assumed command of the ship he labels their behavior "fierce piratical revolt" (99). Given such assumptions, anything that Babo might say at the end, if heard at all, would only be held against him.

In "Benito Cereno" Melville identifies most deeply with Babo, and with the "voiceless end" to which his quest for freedom brought him (116). The tale itself signals this by repeatedly referring to Babo as the author, not just of the revolt but of the narrative that comprises the first half. Babo is "the plotter from first to last" (112), who creates "the invented story" (109): "the fictitious story dictated to the deponent [Cereno] by Babo, and through the deponent imposed upon Captain Delano" (110). Since the same story is "imposed" by Melville upon his reader, Babo thus becomes his double. Onto Babo Melville imposes his frustrations as a "plotter" of stories, the frustrations that we hear in his comment to Duyckinck: "What a madness & anguish it is, that an author can never—under no conceivable circumstances—be at all frank with his readers."[7] For even as the author of "the fictitious story," Babo is still enslaved by the demands of the performance, which is to say, by the assumptions and prejudgments of Delano, the audience for the story. What the tale does best, in fact, is to explore the pattern of Delano's responses as an American "reader," whose preconceptions can be manipulated but not challenged, much less changed. Through the irony of his account of the relationship between Delano's preconceptions and his misperceptions, Melville perhaps finds some compensation for his anguish at the way his contemporary audience's assumptions had come to seem the wall shoved between him and his literary aspirations. But he is no longer interested in trying to get around or through that wall. Babo can lie to his audience, reconfirming its unexamined beliefs and re-enslaving himself in the process, but there is no point in telling the truth. Babo's masquerade thus rehearses the bleak trope Melville elaborated at length in his last novel, where "the plotter" becomes *The Confidence-Man* and all fictitious stories con games, just as Babo's "voiceless end," his self-imposed withdrawn silence (like Bartleby's and Hunilla's), anticipates Melville's own determination to quit writing stories entirely.

I realize that "Benito Cereno" is a much more complex text than my reading of it has suggested. What it ultimately "says" about slavery, about blacks, about Delano remains hotly contested by the commentators.[8] The particular kind of ambiguity the tale leaves us with is, in fact, at the heart of my point in referring to it as part of my conclusion. My reading of it is a criticism of it. By writing about slavery in 1855—about a northern white, a "southern" slaveholder, and a slave who aspires to freedom— Melville engaged the central issue of his culture, the most anguished conflict of the time and place. My specific criticism is against the narrowness of his appropriation of the slave's condition as a veiled metaphor for his own fix as a writer. The Melville we admire was not always so self-absorbed; his protests in *Typee* against the exploitation of the South Sea islanders and in *White-Jacket* against the autocratic usages of the Navy, and the democratic humanism of his representation of Queequeg, for example, all attest to his wanting to use fictitious stories for larger moral ends, to serve some greater cause than his own grievances. Yet even if you are reluctant to agree that what drew Melville to the tale he tells in "Benito Cereno" was the image of his own rhetorical "enslavement" he saw reflected in Babo's performance and fate, you might agree that we should still regret "Benito Cereno." Aesthetically it is among his most accomplished fictions, but as an irony it still leaves a lot to be desired. The people who read it in *Putnam's* in 1855 may have been made to doubt the adequacy of Delano's naively racist assumptions about blacks, though not necessarily, since that depends on rereading the tale, or at least rethinking it, not something magazine readers in the nineteenth century were likely to do. And they almost certainly would have seen no reason to question the apparent finality of Delano's own second "reading" of the experience: that if blacks are not contented servants, they are fiends. That one of America's most brilliant imaginations felt in 1855 that the only way to write about slavery was ironically (however one decides to interpret the irony) seems a shabby commentary, not just on Melville's earlier hopes as a writer but on the human role of serious literature. There is no point in blaming Melville for the loss of faith in the communicative power of art that, like Pierre, he was powerless to prevent. But it does seem appropriate to register our dismay.[9]

For a different way of measuring what is lost in "Benito Cereno," we can compare it to the one work of fiction Frederick Douglass wrote. Published two years before Melville's tale, "The Heroic Slave" is also a long short story based on an actual revolt on board a slave ship.[10] The most obvious difference is that, while Melville's tale begins after the revolt has occurred and focuses its attention on the "white" response to it, Douglass spends the first three-fourths of his tale leading up to the revolt as a means of establishing the slave's moral and psychological right to rebel in the cause of his own freedom. Douglass was one American writer who had literally been a slave. For him writing was a liberating, not an enslaving act. But of course as a black man writing for an almost entirely white audience, he had at least as much reason as any of the writers I have discussed to feel anxious about the demands of literary performance. Like "Benito Cereno," in fact, the focus of "The Heroic Slave" is on the white audience's response: the tale is written in the third person, but in each of its four sections the narrative's perspective is that of a white man. The point of view in the first three parts is that of Mr. Listwell, a northerner who is in some respects like Amaso Delano; he is Douglass's version of a representative Yankee gentleman. The point of view in the last part is that of Tom Grant, the first mate of the ship on which the revolt occurred, and thus someone whose relationship to the events of the revolt is analogous to Benito Cereno's. Douglass's identification with Madison Washington, the slave who leads the uprising, is even more undeniable than Melville's with Babo, but both stories acknowledge in their very structure the way writing differs from doing as a means of acting on the world: whatever a writer hopes to accomplish with words is at the mercy of the audience's reaction.

Here we should recall how Douglass, as a boy about nine years old, first realized he wanted to learn to read and write. Mrs. Auld, his mistress in Baltimore, had begun teaching him the alphabet, but when Mr. Auld "found out what was going on," he "at once forbade [her] to instruct me further." The vehemence of Auld's assertion that "learning would *spoil* the best nigger in the world" was what convinced Douglass that literacy was "the pathway from slavery to freedom." It was the force of Auld's opposition that, as Douglass puts it in his autobiography, inspired him: "What he most dreaded, that I most desired. What he most loved, that I most hated. That which to him was a great evil, to be carefully shunned, was to me a great good, to be diligently sought" (47–48). This is like Thoreau's declaration at the start of *Walden* that "the greater part of what my neighbors call good I believe in my soul to be bad," although arrived at in considerably more extreme circumstances. As a slave in a slaveholding society, Douglass can only define himself in these antithetical terms: as the negation of the white culture's values and beliefs. The gap that originally existed between Douglass—his sense of his self, his vision, his ambitions and hopes—and the larger culture was much wider than any with which either Melville or Thoreau had to contend.

But for Douglass, not only was literacy a means to his own freedom; literary performance was a way to close that gap. From the moment that, as a child who had taught himself to read, he found a copy of *The Columbian Orator* and read there a dialogue between "a master and his slave" in which the slave's arguments talk the master into emancipating him, Douglass remained convinced of "the power of truth over the conscience of even a slaveholder" (52–53). And the power of truth, for Douglass, is the power of words, as an orator or author can use them—and as an audience can feel them. This is actually the story that "The Heroic Slave" dramatizes.[11] It begins with Mr. Listwell accidentally overhearing Madison Washington speaking aloud to himself in the woods of Virginia. Washington utters his "complaints and griefs" as a slave to "the vacant air" (305) because he cannot believe that anyone would be willing to hear and sympathize with them. But though Washington never knows Listwell is there, his words *create* an appreciative audience. List-well listens well. At first he is moved to listen only by curiosity, but he is converted by the act of listening. He says to himself: "'From this hour I am an abolitionist. I have seen enough and heard enough, and I shall go to my home in Ohio resolved to atone for my past indifference to this ill-starred race, by making such exertions as I shall be able to do, for the speedy emancipation of every slave in the land'" (305). This process is dramatized again in the story's last part, which recounts Washington's shipboard rebellion in the words of the slave ship's white first mate, who is describing the revolt a few months later to an audience of other white sailors. Tom Grant would seem to be a tougher audience than Listwell. He was, after all, an officer on a slave ship, and his own life had been directly threatened by the armed and defiant Washington. When the slaves break free of the hold to take over the ship, he sees them as "fiends from the pit" (344); after watching them kill both the captain and the slaveholder and seeing Washington at the ship's helm, Grant's first resolve is to retake the ship "or die in the attempt" (345). But as soon as the "murderous villain," "the imp at the helm," knocks Grant down and speaks to him, two new men are born: Grant is converted from antagonist to admiring audience, and Madison Washington is converted from villain to hero. As Grant declares: "'I felt little disposition to reply to [his] speech. By heaven, it disarmed me. The fellow loomed up before me. I forgot his blackness in the dignity of his manner, and the eloquence of his speech. It seemed as if the souls of both the great dead (whose names he bore) had entered him'" (345).

Aesthetically, "The Heroic Slave" demands much less of its reader than "Benito Cereno." Douglass's commitment to the cause he is serving by writing the story makes using any but the most obvious kind of irony, for instance, out of the question. The text's rhetorical strategy is transparently plain: by using these white consciousnesses to organize the story, Douglass is doubling his contemporary reader; by having both Listwell and Grant listen to Washington's words, and through that transaction come to recognize the black man's greatness and right to liberty, Douglass enacts his design on that reader inside the text itself. But "The Heroic Slave" is far from unsophisticated as a performance. Ultimately it makes enormous demands on its contemporary white reader. As Robert Steptoe points out, for example, Douglass's Washington is clearly intended to reply to and subvert the racialist assumptions of *Uncle Tom's Cabin*: that mulattoes like George Harris can be fiery, manly, and independent, but pure blacks like Uncle Tom are innately childlike and submissive.[12] Even more ambitiously, Douglass sought to persuade an audience that had already shown itself capable of sympathizing with the suffering of slaves to admire and applaud the heroism of a black militant, a slave who rejects his suffering to fight for self-determination. Two white men are killed in the revolt Washington leads, and he is unrepentantly prepared to kill the rest of the crew rather than lose the freedom he has won. Even though he is writing for a white audience predisposed to abolitionism, Douglass is trying to push them to take a dramatic conceptual leap: hating the evil of slavery was one thing, but appreciating the righteousness of a violent slave insurrection was another, and far more threatening to white consciousness. Yet Douglass knew that until America was prepared to grant (that's the pun in Tom Grant's name) blacks the same right of rebellion that it had enshrined in its founders, they would continue to be marginalized by the culture. "The Heroic Slave" must strike us as an act of faith: faith in "the power of truth," in Douglass's own powers as a literary performer, and finally in the moral resources there for him to draw on in the conscience of white, middle-class America as an audience.[13]

The revolutionary power that Douglass aspires to, however, springs dialectically from restraint, from the acceptance of limitation. This is what the modern reader notices immediately as the conventionality of "The Heroic Slave." Its third-person narrator seems thoroughly at home amid the pieties of Victorian America. He actually begins the narrative with a tribute to "the Old Dominion" as "the mother of statesmen" (299). When his story takes him into the rowdy company of a barroom, he promises to spare the genteel sensibility of his audience: "It would not be proper here to give the reader any idea of the vulgarity and dark profanity which rolled, as 'a sweet morsel,' under these corrupt tongues" (329). His first description of Madison Washington, stylistically at least, has much in common with Stowe's cliché-ridden description of little Eva St. Clare: "His face was 'black, but comely.' His eye, lit with emotion, kept guard under a brow as dark and as glossy as the raven's wing. His whole appearance betokened Herculean strength; yet there was nothing savage or forbidding in his aspect. A child might play in his arms, or dance on his shoulders" (303). More than one kind of concession is made here to the audience's expectations: "black *but* comely" even privileges a certain degree of white racism.

As an armed black man who kills white men, Washington's appearance and actions mount a radical assault on bourgeois American assumptions, but the story's representation of him pays devout homage to those assumptions. Even Washington's own voice speaks the language of the tribe of Douglass's white, middle-class audience. Here are the first words Listwell overhears from the plaintive, soliloquizing voice in the wilderness: "'What, then, is life to me? it is aimless and worthless, and worse than useless. Those birds, perched on yon swinging boughs, in friendly conclave, sounding forth their merry notes in seeming worship of the rising sun, though liable to the sportsman's fowling-piece, are still my superiors. They *live free* . . .'" (301). This voice, as improbable as Ahab's, is defined by the ears that will hear it. Like the voice of Emerson's essays, it is intended to create a home for itself by insinuation. A price is paid when Douglass denies Washington his individuality in this way: contemporary Afro-American novelists, by seeking ways to express Afro-American experience in its own idioms, are only now beginning to balance the account. Yet one can also recognize the gain from Douglass's point of view. Washington wins freedom through violent action. But social freedom for Douglass and his fellow blacks in this country was ultimately dependent upon the place they could occupy in the consciousness of the larger white culture. The success of Douglass's revolt against the status quo depends upon converting his audience: that is the revolution his story dramatizes—the effect of Washington's grandiloquent words on the whites who hear them and repeat them to other white listeners. The various concessions Douglass makes to his audience are rhetorically strategic. A writer who wants to *move* an audience must *reach* them first. This is the dialectic that binds a writer's imagination and an audience's preconceptions.

It was Melville, not Douglass, who saw this bond as a form of bondage. I admit that this comparison between a real ex-slave and a popular white writer who saw his popularity as an enslavement is an almost invidious one, but I have my own rhetorical strategy. I'm trying to unsettle our late-twentieth-century assumptions. If as literary critics we regret anything, it is more likely to be the concessions we hear in Douglass's voice than Melville's ironic withdrawal into voicelessness.[14] Babo's silence speaks to us with more power than Washington's eloquence. One reason we admire "Benito Cereno" and ignore "The Heroic Slave" is that we have inherited the modernists' conviction about the place of art in the larger culture. Here is the way Pope Ezra Pound, writing in one of the "little magazines" that emerged at the beginning of this century to redeem literature from the kind of magazine that Melville had been driven to write for, laid down the first commandment for "The Serious Artist":

> If an artist falsifies his report as to the nature of man, as to his own nature, as to the nature of his ideal of the perfect, as to the nature of his ideal of this, that or the other, of god, if god exist, of the life force, of the nature of good and evil, if good and evil exist, of the force with which he believes or disbelieves this, that or the other, of the degree in which he suffers or is made glad; if the artist falsifies his reports on these matters or on any other matter in order that he may conform to the taste of his time, . . . to the conveniences of a preconceived code of ethics, then that artist lies. If he lies out of deliberate will to lie, if he lies out of carelessness, out of laziness, out of cowardice, out of any sort of negligence whatsoever, he nevertheless lies and he should be punished or despised in proportion to the seriousness of his offence.[15]

Thou shalt make no concessions to your audience.

Pound's pronouncement is predicated upon the assumption that the only thing a serious artist can be serious about is art, that the work of literature has to aspire to be its own achievement, that there is no value in ever trying to address and change the taste of his time or her audience's preconceived codes. To the extent that writers allow their imaginative vision to be dialectically shaped by their audience's values, they lie. We can find traces of Pound's scorn for the taste of a time even in the formula that Hans Robert Jauss derives from his theoretical concern with the "dialogical" interaction between literary texts and contemporary readers. To Jauss the distance between a particular work and a particular audience's "horizon of expectations" is what "allows one to determine its artistic character."[16] It is not quite clear from Jauss's account what kind of distance he is thinking of, whether thematic distance, such as Douglass's attempt to make a black militant heroic in the eyes of white readers, counts for as much as aesthetic distance, such as Melville's use of a third-person ironic narrative form. One wonders how Jauss's equation could handle, for instance, *Uncle Tom's Cabin*, so deeply divided between its political radicalism and its aesthetic conventionality. And in any case, why should a work of literature's "artistic character" be made to depend precisely on its rejection or defiance of the cultural status quo? Jauss's distinction between "entertainment" and "art" reflects our own critical "horizon of expectations" as heirs to the split modernism established when it separated the kingdom of serious literature from the republic of letters.

The way the legacy of the American Renaissance has generally been interpreted is also the product of this conditioning. Melville, for instance, was first "revived" in the era of high modernism, and part of his claim on modern attention has been that of the great artist undone by a benighted audience. "Significantly, Melville received less critical and popular support than any other major American writer of his day or since, nor did he court it": so claims Ann Douglas in her recent study of Victorian-American culture.[17] The assertion is demonstrably false; even putting aside Douglas's last claim and considering only her first, which can be empirically tested, Melville's books as a group received much more "critical and popular support" than Thoreau's, Whitman's, Poe's, or even Hawthorne's. But there is no mistaking the "significance" that this version of Melville's career has for postmodern students of American literature. Douglas calls her last chapter "Herman Melville and the Revolt against the Reader," and in it she raises Melville's brilliant martyred mind up, the way Melville leaves Babo's voiceless head on a pole, to level its accusing stare at the failures of American culture:

> Melville soon acknowledged his ambition—to write great books which would fully utilize the most demanding and ambiguous material America offered; but he flatly proclaimed that there were few in America to aid or appreciate his attempt. Melville regarded the reception of his books as a test which would ascertain what genuine masculinity, or, as he tacitly defined it, what health and independence of mind, remained in American culture. The content and style of his work were to register his increasingly bitter disillusion with his experiment. Melville's subject came to be his readers, and his disappointment with them.[18]

As I hope I have shown in my previous chapter, Douglas is certainly right when she says that for Melville public-ation was a process of testing, but it is wrong to accept the unreasonable terms he himself laid down for the experiment. In fact, his audience responded to each of his book's exactly as he wanted them to; the real conflict, as I also hope I've shown, was in what he wanted in the first place.

But we have shifted the blame for Melville's frustrations entirely onto the culture. We have valorized the failure of his "failed" books. We have in fact treated Melville's agony as exemplary; what can be heard in an account like Douglas's is the assumption that "great books" cannot succeed "in America," that America always destroys its artists. We are less comfortable with the achievements of writers like Stowe, Douglass, and Hawthorne, who wrote books that profoundly challenge the preconceptions of their audience but do so in the publicly available aesthetic terms. It would seem naive to protest that *Moby-Dick* and *Walden* are brilliant books that, because they rely on such idiosyncratic and even arbitrary terms, because they made too many conflicting demands on their audience, could not reach their culture at all, and thus could not do anything for or against their culture's vision—because we don't expect great books to "do" any kind of cultural work. This is a great loss. We do not have to accept it as inevitable, though when we assume that the popular failure of writers like Melville and Thoreau measures only the failure of their culture, we at least implicitly endorse the idea of its inevitability. If my study does anything, I hope it will complicate and enrich our sense of a writer's relationship to his or her audience. There are always two parties to that relationship.

It was by addressing themselves to the American public that the writers of the American Renaissance thrived and suffered, suffered and thrived. We must not forget that in some sense they did thrive. It would be impossible to disentangle what we as late-twentieth-century readers value and admire in the texts of the American Renaissance from the specific, mid-nineteenth-century rhetorical circumstances in which they were produced. Nor can we appreciate their achievements if we proceed on the modern assumption that, as Wallace Stevens puts it in "Of Modern Poetry," the writer addresses "an invisible audience." For all these American authors, their audience was almost palpably present when they sat down to write. And to their performances before that audience they brought their own needs, as human beings seeking to define their selves through the act of performance. However they sought to define their selves, they needed what in any case they could not escape—their sense of an American audience.

NOTES

CHAPTER I
THE ANXIETY OF PERFORMANCE

1. The essential neglect of its public nature is the most serious flaw in Freud's account of the creative process. His misconception appears clearly in "The Relation of the Poet to Day-Dreaming" (1908), where he establishes "the hypothesis that imaginative creation, like day-dreaming, is a continuation of and substitute for the play of childhood." Dreams and daydreams, however, occur in private—unless, that is, the dreamers are in therapy and know when they fall asleep that their dreams will be "published" the next day for the analyst. Playing and artistic creation, on the other hand, take place in a space that is shared with and visible to others. This aspect enters into Freud's account only in his distinction between primary needs and the aesthetic elaborations of art as a "secondary process," by means of which a authors enlist an audience's interest in their private fantasies. But Freud is certainly wrong when he claims that although "a child does not conceal his play from adults, . . . his playing is quite unconcerned with them." For young children especially, while playing is deeply responsive to private needs, it is also profoundly shaped by an awareness of the parental figures in whose presence the child plays; in other words, the drama of playing itself as a performance creates its own set of psychic needs, which must be incorporated into the play. Since Freud's day, psychoanalytic theory has devoted more attention to the psychology of the ego as a way to complement Freud's emphasis on the psychology of the unconscious. Particular useful for literary criticism is D. W. Winnicott's idea of the "play ground," the site of an individual's earliest cultural experiences and the prototype of the place where all such experiences occur. It is the space between the young child still in the process of acquiring an ego and the parental figures who preside over that process. The "area of experiencing" thus defined belongs neither to the inner world (psyche) nor to the outer one (reality), but is the setting of the dramatic transactions between the two. Surely this is where literature also occurs; it explains what we mean when we recognize that writing is both utterly private and thoroughly public. Thus our account of the way a writer is trying to define his or her identity through the creative process needs to include the inescapably primary role played by the presence of the audience in this process. Daydreamers need only satisfy themselves, but the terms on which writers meet their own needs are inseparable from the responses they provoke from "the Other" whom we call their audience. (See Sigmund Freud, "The Relation of the Poet to Day-Dreaming," in *On Creativity and the Unconscious*, ed. Benjamin Nelson [New York: Harper & Row, 1958], pp. 44–54; and D. W. Winnicott, *Playing and Reality* [London: Tavistock, 1971].)

2. Washington Irving, *The Sketch Book* (1820; rpt., New York: Putnam, 1857), p. 256.

3. James D. Wallace, *Early Cooper and His Audience* (New York: Columbia University Press, 1986).

4. See the original preface to *The Pioneers*, by James Fenimore Cooper (1823; rpt., New York: Holt, Rinehart and Winston, 1959), p. xxv.

5. Cooper to Horatio Greenough, 13 June 1833, in *The Letters and Journals of James Fenimore Cooper*, ed. James Franklin Beard (Cambridge, Mass.: Harvard University Press, 1960–68), 2:384.

6. Cooper to John Whipple, 14 January 1834, in *Letters and Journals of Cooper*, 3:28—and Cooper, *A Letter to His Countrymen* (New York: John Wiley, 1834), p. 99.

7. Stephen Railton, *Fenimore Cooper: A Study of His Life and Imagination* (Princeton, N.J.: Princeton University Press, 1978).

8. Cooper, *The Crater; or, Vulcan's Peak* (1848; rpt., New York: James G. Gregory, 1854), p. 493.

9. *The Journals and Miscellaneous Notebooks of Ralph Waldo Emerson*, 14 vols., ed. William H. Gilman et al. (Cambridge, Mass.: Harvard University Press, 1960–), 7:98.

10. Susan R. Suleiman, "Introduction: Varieties of Audience-Oriented Criticism," in *The Reader in the Text*, ed. Suleiman and Inge Crosman (Princeton, N.J.: Princeton University Press, 1980), p. 3.

11. For a good general introduction to contemporary reader-response theorists (particularly Jonathan Culler, Stanley Fish, Norman Holland, and Wolfgang Iser) see Elizabeth Freund, *The Return of the Reader: Reader-Response Criticism* (London: Methuen, 1987). For an example of how American literature can be approached from this perspective, see Steven Mailloux, *Interpretive Conventions: The Reader in the Study of American Fiction* (Ithaca, N.Y.: Cornell University Press, 1982); Fish, Culler, and Iser's work provide Mailloux with the basis for his own approach.

12. Walter J. Ong, "The Writer's Audience is Always a Fiction," *PMLA* 90 (1975): 9–21.

13. Wordsworth, "Essay, Supplementary to the Preface" (1815), in *Selected Poems and Prefaces by William Wordsworth*, ed. Jack Stillinger (Boston: Houghton Mifflin, 1965), p. 481.

14. Samuel Taylor Coleridge, *Biographia Literaria* (1817; rpt., London: Dent Everyman, 1965), p. 169. Two different but related versions of the "implied reader" are developed by Wolfgang Iser (see *The Implied Reader* [Baltimore, Md.: Johns Hopkins University Press, 1974] and *The Act of Reading: A Theory of Aesthetic Response* [Baltimore, Md.: Johns Hopkins University Press, 1978]) and Wayne Booth (*The Rhetoric of Fiction* [Chicago: University of Chicago Press, 1961]).

15. Emerson, *Journals and Miscellaneous Notebooks*, 5:304–5.

16. Hans Robert Jauss, "Literary History as a Challenge to Literary Theory," in *Toward an Aesthetics of Reception*, trans. Timothy Bahti (Minneapolis: University of Minnesota Press, 1982), p. 22.

17. Jacques Leenhardt, "Toward a Sociology of Reading," in *Reader in the Text*, p. 214.

18. See George Santayana, "The Genteel Tradition in American Philosophy" (1911), in *Winds of Doctrine: Studies in Contemporary Opinion* (New York: Scribner's, 1913), Fred Patee, *The Feminine Fifties* (New York: Appleton-Century, 1940); Ann Douglas, *The Feminization of American Culture* (New York: Knopf, 1977). For an interesting exploration of the ways gender-oriented anxieties shaped the quest for identity undertaken by the authors I study here, see David Leverenz, *Manhood and the American Renaissance* (Ithaca, N.Y.: Cornell University Press, 1989); especially in chapter 1, " 'I' and 'You' in the American Renaissance," Leverenz's analysis runs parallel to and often complements my focus on performance anxieties.

19. See William Charvat, *Literary Publishing in America; The Cost Books of Ticknor and Fields and Their Predecessors, 1832–1858,* ed. Charvat and Warren S. Tryon (New York: Bibliographical Society of America, 1949); and especially *The Profession of Authorship in America, 1800–1870: The Papers of William Charvat,* ed. Matthew J. Bruccoli (Columbus: Ohio State University Press, 1968). In this last book, which remained unfinished at his death, Charvat demonstrates with force and insight how much literary criticism can do with the fruits of his literary scholarship. I came across Charvat's book at the early stages of my own thinking on audience; it helped me in more ways that I can acknowledge to appreciate the full dimensions of the kind of performance nineteenth-century American writers were involved in, and it is good to see that Charvat's achievement is finally beginning to get the recognition it has long deserved. See, for instance, Lawrence Buell, *New England Literary Culture: From Revolution through Renaissance* (Cambridge: Cambridge University Press, 1986), especially p. 7. In *Early Cooper and His Audience,* Wallace makes extensive use of the empirical methodology Charvat pioneered.

20. Nina Baym, *Novels, Readers, and Reviewers: Responses to Fiction in Antebellum America* (Ithaca, N.Y.: Cornell University Press, 1984). See also William Charvat, *The Origins of American Critical Thought, 1810–1835* (Philadelphia: [University of Pennsylvania Press], 1936).

21. All three quotations in this paragraph are from Harold Bloom, *The Anxiety of Influence: A Theory of Poetry* (New York: Oxford University Press, 1973), pp. 91, 26, 91.

22. Ultimately, it seems, although Bloom does not elaborate this notion, the poet is struggling with his own mortality; see *Anxiety of Influence,* p. 10. Richard Poirier has elaborated this idea; in *The Performing Self* what defines the drama of literary performance is the presence of death (New York: Oxford University Press, 1971), pp. 86–111.

23. For an account of the American Renaissance based on Bloom's archetype, see Robert Weisbuch, *Atlantic Double-Cross: American Literature and British Influence in the Age of Emerson* (Chicago: University of Chicago Press, 1986).

24. Bloom, *Anxiety of Influence,* p. 32.

25. It is conspicuous, for example, that Milton's voice is most palpably present in Wordsworth and Coleridge's work precisely where their thought is least conventional. I am thinking particularly of chapter 13 of the *Biographia Literaria,* which Coleridge omitted on the ground that "the public" was not ready to enter-

tain its original vision; to introduce the abridged version of that chapter he does include, he cites a long passage from *Paradise Lost*. Similarly, when Wordsworth came to announce his radical prophetic project in the "Prospectus to the Recluse," he couched his credo in so many Miltonic echoes that his assertion about the secular possibility of regaining paradise could seem wholly continuous with Milton's doctrinally orthodox account of how paradise was lost. Bloom argues that Wordsworth here is contending with Milton, but I think an equally good case can be made for the point that Wordsworth is "conspiring with" Milton's voice to try to co-opt the theological ground that both Milton and Wordsworth's audience occupy.

26. Bloom can ignore this anxiety even when directly confronted by it. He cites the following passage from Emerson's journal (21 July 1837) as an instance of "Emerson's acute apprehension of the sorrows of poetic influence": "Courage consists in the conviction that they with whom you contend are no more than you. If we believed in the existence of strict *individuals*, natures, that is, not radically identical but unknown[,] immeasurable, we should never dare to fight." This is an egregious "misreading"; there isn't a trace of the meaning Bloom avers in the passage he cites. "They with whom" Emerson is thinking about contending are not his literary precursors but very definitively the people in his potential audience, the mid-nineteenth-century Americans who seem unreceptive, indeed hostile, to his announcement of the godhead within. (See Bloom, *A Map of Misreading* [New York: Oxford University Press, 1975], p. 163.)

27. Emerson, *Journals and Miscellaneous Notebooks*, 7:180–81.

28. Henry Nash Smith, *Democracy and the Novel: Popular Resistance to Classic American Writers* (New York: Oxford University Press, 1978), pp. 8–9.

29. This kind of humanizing of the dynamic between texts and contemporary readers is the most exciting contribution of Cathy N. Davidson's *Revolution and the Word: The Rise of the Novel in America* (New York: Oxford University Press, 1986).

30. Ong, "The Writer's Audience," pp. 16–17. He refers to periods of "major audience readjustment," citing the "mature medieval" and the Elizabethan periods as examples. I think he would agree, however, that in this process authors also have to adjust.

31. Erich Auerbach, "The Emergence of a Literary Public in Western Europe," in *Literary Language and Its Public in Late Latin Antiquity and the Middle Ages* (1958; rpt., London: Routledge & Kegan Paul, 1965), pp. 237–52.

32. Ian Watt, *The Rise of the Novel* (London: Chatto & Windus, 1957), especially chapter 2, "The Reading Public and the Rise of the Novel" (pp. 36–61).

33. Raymond Williams, "The Romantic Artist," in *Culture and Society, 1780–1950* (New York: Columbia University Press, 1958), pp. 30–48.

34. See Amy Cruse, *The Englishman and His Books in the Early Nineteenth Century* (New York: T. Y. Crowell, 1930); Arthur Simmons Collins, *The Profession of Letters: A Study of the Relation of Author to Patron, Publishers and Public, 1780–1832* (London: G. Routledge & Sons, 1928); Q. D. Leavis, *Fiction and the Reading Public* (London: Chatto & Windus, 1932); R. K. Webb, *The British Working Class Reader, 1790–1848: Literacy and Social Tension* (London: Allen & Unwin, 1955), Richard D. Altick, *The English Common Reader: A Social History*

of the Mass Reading Public, 1800–1900 (Chicago: University of Chicago Press, 1957); Louis James, *Fiction for the Working Man, 1830–1850* (New York: Oxford University Press, 1963); Jon P. Klancher, *The Making of English Reading Audiences, 1790–1832* (Madison: University of Wisconsin Press, 1987).

35. In addition to the work of Charvat and Baym's study of reviews, there have been several source studies of the popular culture in Victorian America. See Carl Bode, *The Anatomy of American Popular Culture, 1840–1861* (Berkeley and Los Angeles: University of California Press, 1959); and Russel Blaine Nye, *The Unembarrassed Muse: The Popular Arts in America* (New York: Dial Press, 1970) and *Society and Culture in America, 1830–1860* (New York: Harper & Row, 1974). More explicitly concerned with literary culture are Patee, *Feminine Fifties*; Douglas, *Feminization of American Culture*; Smith, *Democracy and the Novel*; Jane Tompkins, *Sensational Designs: The Cultural Work of American Fiction, 1790–1860* (New York: Oxford University Press, 1985); Michael T. Gilmore, *American Romanticism and the Marketplace* (Chicago: University of Chicago Press, 1985); and David S. Reynolds, *Beneath the American Renaissance: The Subversive Imagination in the Age of Emerson and Melville* (New York: Knopf, 1988). As yet, however, no one has attempted a sociological study of "the American reading public." One impressive sign that this neglect is being redressed is the collection of essays in *Reading in America: Literature and Social History*, ed. Cathy N. Davidson (Baltimore, Md.: Johns Hopkins University Press, 1989). Davidson collects twelve articles dealing with various aspects of literacy, readership, and the economics of book production in America from colonial times to the present.

36. Coleridge, *Biographia Literaria*, p. 34.

37. See Watt, *Rise of the Novel*, pp. 37–40. Even in America in the 1850s, as Henry Nash Smith reminds us, the public that read even the best of the best-selling books was "still only a tiny fraction of the total population" (*Democracy and the Novel*, p. 8).

38. See Leavis, *Fiction and the Reading Public*, p. 130: "The change may be noticed, for instance, in the difference between the tone of the *Tatler* and of the *Idler*, the one talking at his ease to a circle of friends, and the other consciously raising his voice for the benefit of a public assembly."

39. Moore, diary entry in 1834 about a conversation with Wordsworth, quoted in ibid., p. 188.

40. The *Oxford English Dictionary* cites Addison, writing in 1702, as the first to use the phrase "republic of letters."

41. For a brilliant account of the way literature was commodified, see Williams, "The Romantic Artist." In *American Romanticism and the Marketplace*, Gilmore analyzes the way this process affected the major texts of the American Renaissance.

42. Samuel Johnson, *The Lives of the Poets* (1781; rpt., New York: Holt, Rinehart and Winston, 1952), p. 446.

43. Interestingly, best-seller lists were not published until the end of the century. They first appeared in America in 1895. See James D. Hart, *The Popular Book: A History of America's Literary Taste* (New York: Oxford University Press, 1950), pp. 184–85, and Richard D. Altick, "The Reading Public in England and

America in 1900," in *Writers, Readers, and Occasions* (Columbus: Ohio State University Press, 1989, p. 224).

44. Quoted by Leavis, *Fiction and the Reading Public*, p. 188.

45. Emerson, *Journals and Miscellaneous Notebooks*, 14:28.

46. It is worth comparing this simple declaration of faith to Wordsworth's similar but more tortured conclusion to the 1800 preface to *Lyrical Ballads*. There he too acknowledges the common reader's power to decide the achievement of his poetic "experiment," but he carefully instructs that reader in how to acquire taste before exercising his or her inherent right. In chapter 2 I discuss more fully the tension in Romantic thought between democratic metaphysics and the practical concern with the reading public.

47. See Charvat, *Profession of Authorship in America*. Chapter 8 of Bode's *Anatomy of American Popular Culture*, "The Spread of Print," gives a good empirical account of how "the people and the printed word came together" in the American Renaissance (p. x, see also pp. 109–16). See also "The Great Revolution in Publishing," chapter 13 of Frank Luther Mott's *Golden Multitudes: The Story of Best Sellers in the United States* (New York: Macmillan, 1947), pp. 76–79.

48. Smith, *Democracy and the Novel*, p. 8.

49. A good start toward such a study is Ian Jack's "descriptive" survey, *The Poet and His Audience* (Cambridge: Cambridge University Press, 1984).

50. Coleridge, *Biographia Literaria*, p. 34. Leavis agrees with this assessment; talking about the first decades of the nineteenth century, she notes that "there was still only one public, which through the reviews took its standards from above" (*Fiction and the Reading Public*, p. 144).

51. Melville, "Hawthorne and His Mosses," in *The Piazza Tales and Other Prose Pieces, 1839–1860*, ed. Harrison Hayford et al. (Evanston and Chicago: Northwestern University Press & The Newberry Library, 1987), p. 247.

52. See Baym, *Novels, Readers, and Reviewers*, pp. 44–45.

53. *Putnam's Monthly Magazine* 8 (December 1856): 655.

54. This deference shows up clearly, for example, in the reviews that Melville's books received across the course of his uneven career. Let me just quote two instances. The first is from a review of *Mardi*: "So we must confess to the slightest possible prejudice against the Paradise of Typee. But we would give all due credit to books that won the plaudits of the people so widely." The second, from a review of *Pierre*: "Ambiguities there are, not a few, in this new work by a popular author; but very little doubt can there be, touching the opinion which the public will entertain of its merits." These are reprinted in *Melville: The Critical Heritage*, ed. Watson G. Branch (Boston: Routledge & Kegan Paul, 1974), pp. 179, 298.

There remained all through the period a Whig attitude toward literature and the popular audience. It is well represented by someone like Edward T. Channing, a Harvard professor and regular contributor to the conservative *North American Review*. His reviews assume that it is the prerogative of the learned critic "to direct the public judgment" about literary merit. Even Channing, however, acknowledged the influence of what Cooper called "the community power" in America's democracy: "In the ancient republics, the orator might control the audience, but now we see the audience controlling him." (Channing, *Lectures Read to the Seniors in Harvard College*, ed. Dorothy I. Anderson and Waldo W.

Braden [1856; rpt., Carbondale: Southern Illinois University Press, 1968], p. 17; Cooper, *The Crater*, p. 324.)

55. Hawthorne, *The Scarlet Letter* (Columbus: Ohio State University Press, 1962), p. 127.

56. "Readers By the Million," *Harper's New Monthly Magazine* 19 (November 1859): 838–40.

57. See Richard Poirier's *A World Elsewhere: The Place of Style in American Literature* (New York: Oxford University Press, 1966). Poirier's analyses and mine take a similar textual characteristic as a starting point: what he refers to as the "kind of drama, . . . as interesting as the drama involving the characters" (p. 91), enacted on the surface of American works. But while he occasionally refers to the role played by the reader in the works he examines, he locates the conflict he is interested in in a fairly abstract context: the American self versus the larger environment.

58. Fuller, "American Literature" (1846), in *Margaret Fuller: An American Romantic*, ed. Perry Miller (New York: Anchor Books, 1963), pp. 233, 245–46.

59. See Stephen Railton, "Jim and Mark Twain: What Do Dey Stan' For?" *Virginia Quarterly Review* 63 (Summer 1987): 393–408. For an illuminating discussion of art as performing in the period after the American Renaissance, including an analysis of *Huckleberry Finn*, see Phillip Fisher, "Appearing and Disappearing in Public: Social Space in Late-Nineteenth-Century Literature and Culture," in *Reconstructing American Literary History*, ed. Sacvan Bercovitch (Cambridge, Mass.: Harvard University Press, 1986), pp. 155–88.

60. Wallace Stevens, *The Necessary Angel: Essays on Reality and the Imagination* (New York: Vintage, 1951), p. 29.

CHAPTER II
EMERSON AS ORATOR

1. "Self-Reliance," in *The Collected Works of Ralph Waldo Emerson*, vol. 2 *Essays: First Series*, ed. Joseph Slater, Alfred R. Ferguson, and Jean Ferguson Carr (Cambridge, Mass.: Harvard University Press, 1979), p. 40. Subsequent references to this volume are indicated in the text parenthetically by volume and page number. References to vol. 1, *Nature, Addresses, and Lectures*, ed. R. E. Spiller and A. R. Ferguson (Cambridge, Mass.: Harvard University Press, 1971), are indicated in the text parenthetically by the page number only.

2. *The Journals and Miscellaneous Notebooks of Ralph Waldo Emerson*, 14 vols., ed. William H. Gilman et al. (Cambridge, Mass.: Harvard University Press, 1960–), 4:324; see also 5:219, 449. Subsequent references to the journals are cited in the text parenthetically as *JMN*, followed by volume and page numbers.

3. See David Robinson, *Apostle of Culture: Emerson as Preacher and Lecturer* (Philadelphia: University of Pennsylvania Press, 1982), p. 4. This is a good study of the development of Emerson's thought, especially of the way it grew out of contemporary Unitarianism. On this topic, see also Lawrence Buell, *Literary Transcendentalism: Style and Vision in the American Renaissance* (Ithaca, N.Y.: Cornell University Press, 1973).

4. H. N. Smith, "Emerson's Problem of Vocation: A Note on *The American Scholar*," *New England Quarterly* 12 (March 1939): 52–67.

5. From a very different interpretive perspective, Eric Cheyfitz reaches a similar conclusion about the role of eloquence for Emerson: "This is the final marriage, the marriage of the orator and the mob. From this marriage issues the final miracle: a 'whole' appears, resurrected, erected from the refuse of its 'unregarded parts'" (*The Trans-Parent: Sexual Politics in the Language of Emerson* [Baltimore, Md.: Johns Hopkins University Press, 1981], p. 109).

6. Samuel Taylor Coleridge, *Biographia Literaria* (London: Dent, 1956), pp. 42–43.

7. Wordsworth, 1802 preface to *Lyrical Ballads*, in *William Wordsworth: Selected Poems and Prefaces*, ed. Jack Stillinger (Boston: Houghton Mifflin, 1965), p. 455. Except for one passage noted below, all quotations from Wordsworth are from this edition of his prose. In the order in which I cite them, they can be found on the following pages: 480, 456, 459, 463.

8. Wordsworth, "Prospectus to *The Recluse*," in ibid., p. 46.

9. "Society," in *The Early Lectures of Ralph Waldo Emerson*, 3 vols., ed. Stephen Whicher et al. (Cambridge, Mass.: Harvard University Press, 1959–1972), 2:109.

10. See Stanley Cavell, "Thinking of Emerson," in *The Senses of Walden: An Expanded Edition* (San Francisco: North Point Press, 1981), pp. 136–37.

11. Coleridge, *Biographia Literaria*, p. 136.

12. Shelley, preface to *Prometheus Unbound*, in *Percy Bysshe Shelley: Selected Poetry and Prose*, ed. Kenneth Neill Cameron (New York: Holt, Rinehart and Winston, 1951), p. 303.

13. The best history of the lyceum movement in America is Carl Bode's *American Lyceum: Town Meeting of the Mind* (Carbondale: Southern Illinois University Press, 1956).

14. *The Correspondence of Thomas Carlyle and Ralph Waldo Emerson*, 2 vols., ed. Charles Eliot Norton (Boston: Osgood, 1883), 1:88.

15. Emerson, "Eloquence," in *The Complete Works of Ralph Waldo Emerson*, ed. E. W. Emerson, 12 vols. (Boston: Houghton Mifflin, 1903), 7:66.

16. In *Emerson's Fall: A New Interpretation of the Major Essays* (New York: Continuum, 1982), B. L. Packer subtly and sympathetically explores the way Emerson's public works repeatedly engage this fact of the human condition: our sense of the fallenness of the world and the alienation of the self. She briefly connects this with the aspirations and needs of Emerson's eloquence; see pp. 131ff.

17. Emerson, "Eloquence," p. 65.

18. Ibid., p. 63.

19. For an account of the Puritan jeremiad, see Perry Miller, *The New England Mind*, vol. 2, *From Colony to Province* (Cambridge, Mass.: Harvard University Press, 1953), pp. 27–39. In *The American Jeremiad* (Madison: University of Wisconsin Press, 1978), Sacvan Bercovitch reexamines the dynamic of the Puritans' use of the form and traces its continuing centrality to American culture and literature through the American Renaissance.

20. Elizabeth Peabody, "Emerson as Preacher," in *The Genius and Character of Emerson*, ed. F. B. Sanborn (Boston: Osgood, 1885), p. 158.

21. Perry Miller provides the texts with which to retrace the controversy in his anthology, *The Transcendentalists* (Cambridge, Mass.: Harvard University Press, 1950), pp. 157–246. See also the ten contemporary responses (from August 1838 to January 1839) reprinted in *Critical Essays on Ralph Waldo Emerson*, ed. Robert E. Burkholder and Joel Myerson (Boston: G. K. Hall, 1983), pp. 31–66.

22. See Conrad Wright, "Emerson, Barzillai Frost, and the Divinity School *Address*," in *The Liberal Christians: Essays on American Unitarian History* (Boston: Beacon Press, 1970), pp. 41–61.

23. Loring's journal comments about "Holiness" are quoted by Eleanor M. Tilton, "Emerson's Lecture Schedule—1837–1838—Revised," *Harvard Library Bulletin* 21 (Oct. 1973): 389–90. Tilton calls "Holiness" "alarmingly unorthodox" (383), but as this kind of misunderstanding among its listeners suggests, its unorthodoxy was at best but vaguely proclaimed. Emerson's own dissatisfaction with the lecture is indicated by his rejection of it for *Essays, First Series*. There, although he reused the two preceding lectures, "Prudence" and "Heroism," he rewrote "Holiness" as "The Over-Soul."

24. Emerson, *Early Lectures*, 2:341.

25. Ibid., pp. 347–50.

26. In 1849, revising "The Divinity School Address" for republication in *Nature, Addresses, and Lectures*, Emerson deleted this infelicitous repetition and the repetitious "Be to them a man" from the passage on p. 90. By then the psychic need that prompted these insistent iterations lay behind him. Since most reprintings of the address use the 1849 text, however, the pattern of its insistence has been somewhat obscured.

27. Quoted by Peabody, "Emerson as Preacher," p. 159.

28. Joel Porte, *Representative Man: Ralph Waldo Emerson in His Time* (New York: Oxford University Press, 1979), p. 156. In his analysis of the address Porte assumes that Emerson's intention was to shock his audience, an assumption that governs most of the critical commentary on it. An exception, however, is Stephen E. Whicher, who notes that "the address itself was calculated to give no offense, on grounds of vocabulary at least, to a Unitarian audience" (*Freedom and Fate: An Inner Life of Ralph Waldo Emerson* [Philadelphia: University of Pennsylvania Press, 1953], p. 74).

29. Ware's letter is printed in James Eliot Cabot's *Memoir of Ralph Waldo Emerson*, 2 vols. (Boston: Houghton, Mifflin, 1887), 2:689.

30. "In composition the *What* is of no importance compared with the *How*" (*JMN*, 5:304–5): in this sentence Emerson gives us the formula that should govern our formal explications of his texts. Yet while the organization of *Nature*, for example, has often been analysed, no one has noticed that, although this work was not intended for a live performance, it too is ultimately organized around Emerson's strategic concern with his audience. For instance, he begins by defining "Nature" as "Commodity," even though this meant that the essay had, as he admitted in a letter, "one crack in it not easy to be soldered or welded," because commodity "is the only use of nature which all men apprehend" (11). The crack is between objective and subjective, external and internal realities, and Emerson could have avoided it by beginning with the ideas he establishes in the section called "Idealism." But while all people appreciate commodity, "the frivolous

make themselves merry with the Ideal theory" (29); that is, Emerson began with "Commodity" to try to get all readers up on the first rung of *Nature*'s ascending ladder. (See Emerson to William Emerson, 8 August 1836, in *The Letters of Ralph Waldo Emerson*, 6 vols., ed. Ralph Rusk [New York: Columbia University Press, 1939], 2:32.)

31. Cabot, *Memoir of Emerson*, p. 690. Gay Wilson Allen points out in his biography that for "meet dissent" Emerson had initially written "offend"—this is a typical revision, in the direction of conciliation (*Waldo Emerson* [New York: Viking, 1981], p. 320).

32. Quentin Anderson, *The Imperial Self* (New York: Knopf, 1971), pp. 22–23.

33. Perry Miller quotes Norton's article from *The Boston Daily Advertiser* (27 August 1838) in his anthology, *The Transcendentalists*, p. 196.

34. "Religion," in *Early Lectures*, 3:276–77.

35. *Letters of Emerson*, 2:162.

36. *Correspondence*, 1:220–21.

37. James Russell Lowell, *My Study Windows* (Boston: Osgood and Company, 1871), p. 381.

38. Peabody, *Genius and Character*, p. 172.

39. Lowell, *Study Windows*, p. 377. John McAleer has gathered together a wide range of contemporary accounts of Emerson's performance as a lecturer in *Ralph Waldo Emerson: Days of Encounter* (Boston: Little, Brown, 1984), pp. 484–93.

40. Henry Nash Smith retells the story of Mark Twain's complex performance in *Mark Twain: The Development of a Writer* (1962; rpt., New York: Atheneum, 1972), pp. 92–112.

41. By "best" I mean the most honest and humanly compelling, even (to use Emerson's own frame of reference) the most useful as a guide to the problems and possibilities of our lives. But for an intelligent attempt to establish the achievement of the journals as an aesthetic one, see Lawrence Rosenwald, *Emerson and the Art of the Diary* (New York: Oxford University Press, 1988).

42. *Early Lectures*, 3:95, 97.

43. "Hypocrisy" was the word Emerson used, in the journal entry I used as the epigraph to chapter 1, to describe the writer's self-conscious situation: "The child is sincere, and the man when he is alone, if he be not a writer, but on the entrance of the second person hypocrisy begins" (*JMN*, 4:314).

44. Quoted by W. A. Swanberg, *Jim Fisk: The Career of an Improbable Rascal* (New York: Scribner's, 1959), pp. 212–13.

CHAPTER III
THOREAU'S *WALDEN*

1. *The Journal of Henry D. Thoreau*, ed. Bradford Torrey and Francis H. Allen, 14 vols. (Boston: Houghton Mifflin, 1906), 1:485. Princeton University Press is currently reissuing the journals as part of *The Writings of Henry D. Thoreau*. For entries before 1848, I have compared Torrey and Allen's text against the two

Princeton journal volumes that have thus far appeared, under the general editorship of John C. Broderick. Where a substantive difference existed, I have followed the reading of the Princeton editors. But for the sake of consistency, all references to journal entries in the text are cited from the 1906 edition parenthetically as *J*, followed by volume and page numbers.

2. So noted Prudence Ward, a friend of Thoreau's family and a member of the audience at his lecture, in a letter quoted by Walter Harding in *The Days of Henry Thoreau* (New York: Knopf, 1965), p. 188. As Harding points out, it was very unusual for a lyceum lecturer to give such an encore performance.

3. Ibid., p. 189. See also J. Lyndon Shanley, *The Making of Walden* (Chicago: University of Chicago Press, 1957), pp. 18–19.

4. Shanley, *Making ot Walden*, p. 27.

5. *Walden*, ed. J. Lyndon Shanley (Princeton, N.J.: Princeton University Press, 1971), p. 3. All subsequent references to *Walden* are from this edition, cited parenthetically in the text by page number.

6. For a very different analysis of Thoreau's "implied reader" and the role he plays in the text of *Walden*, see Steven G. Kellman, "A Conspiracy Theory of Literature: Thoreau and You," *Georgia Review* 32 (Winter 1978): 808–19. See also Steven Fink, "Thoreau and His Audience in 'Natural History of Massachusetts,'" in *The American Renaissance: New Dimensions*, ed. Harry R. Garvin (*Bucknell Review* 23 [1983]): 65–80.

7. See Shanley, *Making of Walden*.

8. *The Journals and Miscellaneous Notebooks of Ralph Waldo Emerson*, 14 vols., ed. William H. Gilman et al. (Cambridge, Mass.: Harvard University Press, 1960–), 9:9–10.

9. Emerson, "Thoreau" (1863), in "Emerson's 'Thoreau': A New Edition from Manuscript," by Joel Myerson, *Studies in the American Renaissance* (1979), p. 52.

10. Ibid., p. 39.

11. *The Correspondence of Henry David Thoreau*, ed. Walter Harding and Carl Bode (New York: New York University Press, 1958), pp. 284–85.

12. For an interesting analysis of Thoreau's punning in the context of his life history, see Michael West, "Scatology and Escatology: The Heroic Dimensions of Thoreau's Word-Play," *PMLA* 89 (October 1974): 1043–64.

13. *Walden* and "Civil Disobedience" are probably better known than any single Emersonian text. Which writer is "greater" is a matter of taste, but that hasn't kept critics from disputing it. In *Emerson and Thoreau* (Middleton, Conn.: Wesleyan University Press, 1966), Joel Porte was perhaps the first critic to compare the two to Thoreau's advantage. Very recently, thinking of Stanley Cavell's book on Thoreau (*The Senses of Walden* [New York: Viking, 1972]), Harold Bloom has felt the need to reassert Emerson's priority (see Bloom's introduction to *Modern Critical Views: Henry David Thoreau* [New York: Chelsea House, 1987], pp. 1–11). My own feeling is that which writer one prefers is finally a matter of politics—social, not academic. The more seriously one is concerned about the socioeconomic ills and injustices of America, the more likely one is to valorize Thoreau, who unlike Emerson cannot be co-opted by capitalist or neo-conservative assumptions.

14. Harding, *Days of Thoreau*, p. 254. See also pp. 202, 205, 292, and especially 239, where Harding reprints an editorial from the Concord *Yeoman's Gazette* (1849) full of praise for "Our Townsman—Mr. Thoreau" as "a gentleman of rare attainments" and a promising writer. For a diverse gathering of contemporary firsthand reactions to Thoreau himself, including several reviews of the lectures from which *Walden* originated, see Harding's *Thoreau: Man of Concord* (New York: Holt, Rinehart and Winston, 1960).

15. Emerson, "Thoreau," pp. 53 and 35.

16. "Walking" (1863), in *Henry David Thoreau: The Natural History Essays*, ed. Robert Sattelmeyer (Salt Lake City, Utah: Peregrine Smith, 1980), p. 94.

17. Ibid., p. 112.

18. *Correspondence*, p. 319.

19. Consider this journal entry for 26 March 1842: "I must confess I have felt mean enough when asked how I was to act on society, what errand I had to mankind. . . . I would fain communicate the wealth of my life to men, would really give them what is most precious in my gift. . . . I have no private good, unless it be my peculiar ability to serve the public" (*J*, 1:350). Many other passages indicate this desire more or less obliquely. For example, at the end of "Walking" he reports how he "carried straightway to the village" the new blossom he had found at the top of a pine tree, "and showed it to stranger jurymen who walked the streets . . . and to farmers and lumber-dealers and woodchoppers and hunters" ("Walking," p. 133).

20. As Ruth Wheeler notes, for example, at least half of the young men of Thoreau's generation left Concord to go west (see "Thoreau's Concord," in *Henry David Thoreau: Studies and Commentaries*, ed. Walter Harding et al. [Rutherford, N.J.: Farleigh Dickinson University Press, 1972], p. 27).

21. Three important exceptions are Raymond Gozzi, "Tropes and Figures: A Psychological Study of Henry David Thoreau" (Ph.D. diss., New York University, 1957) and Richard Lebeaux, *Young Man Thoreau* (Amherst: University of Massachusetts Press, 1977) and *Thoreau's Seasons* (Amherst: University of Massachusetts Press, 1984). I have learned a great deal from their analyses of Thoreau's inner life, particularly Lebeaux's, with its Eriksonian emphasis on Thoreau's ego. On pages 44–45 and 69–70 of *Young Man Thoreau*, Lebeaux discusses Thoreau's need to test his mother's love.

22. The source of the well-known and presumably reliable anecdote about how Thoreau, at age 20, broke into tears when his mother suggested he could take up his knapsack and "go abroad to seek his fortune" is Ellery Channing's memoir, *Thoreau: The Poet-Naturalist*, ed. F. B. Sanborn (Boston: Houghton Mifflin, 1902), p. 18. According to Channing, Thoreau was not comforted until his sister Helen promised him that he could "stay at home and live with us."

23. F. B. Sanborn, who boarded at the Thoreaus', recalls that Mrs. Thoreau would frequently interrupt his conversations with Henry at the dinner table, taking over whatever subject they had been discussing. "Henry would sit silent and attentive, during the long interruption; then, as the last period closed, he would bow slightly to his mother, and resume our dialogue exactly where it had been stayed" (*The Life of Henry David Thoreau* [Boston: Houghton Mifflin, 1917], p. 320).

24. "Autumnal Tints" (1863), in *Natural History Essays*, p. 174.

25. *Correspondence*, p. 15.

26. Consider this journal entry for 28 March 1853: "My Aunt Maria asked me to read the life of Dr. Chalmers, which however I did not promise to do. Yesterday, Sunday, she was heard through the partition shouting to my Aunt Jane, who is deaf, 'Think of it! He stood half an hour yesterday to hear the frogs croak, and wouldn't read the life of Chalmers'" (*J*, 5:58). It may also have been Aunt Maria who "interfered" (as Thoreau puts it in "Civil Disobedience") and paid the poll tax to save the family from the disgrace of Henry being in jail.

27. Consider this journal entry, written during the heat of August 1854: "My attic chamber has compelled me to sit below with the family at evening for a month. . . . I must cultivate privacy" (*J*, 6:415).

28. *Correspondence*, p. 131.

29. This quest to belong, to be absorbed, would be one way to explain his increasingly obsessive study of the phenomena of nature, and his delight at the end of *Walden* in finding that nature "is mother of humanity" (308). But Thoreau reveals his longing for a nurturing family more directly as well, especially at the end of "Walking" in his moving description of the "altogether admirable and shining family" he occasionally "saw" in the pine wood at Spaulding's Farm: "They have sons and daughters. They are quite well. . . . If it were not for such families as this, I think I should move out of Concord" ("Walking," in *Natural History Essays*, pp. 131–32).

30. This is the conclusion Lebeaux reaches, after studying all the evidence about the two brothers more thoroughly than anyone else (*Young Man Thoreau*, especially pp. 60–61).

31. The phrase is from ibid., p. 196. See also all of chapter 6, where Lebeaux also cites Raymond Gozzi's conclusions about Henry's guilt.

32. Ibid., pp. 67–70.

33. It was also, of course, just far enough from home to allow his mother and sisters to visit him every Saturday, bringing food out to the pond, and for him to go back inside his parents' house at least two or three times each week. Although he devotes two chapters of *Walden* to visitors and mentions how often he went into the village, except for the coy references to his "washing and mending" (60) and to "din[ing] out occasionally" (61), he makes no acknowledgment of the role his family continued to play in his life at the pond. Learning these facts invariably shocks the students to whom I teach *Walden*; Thoreau's omission does leave his account vulnerable to "inveterate cavillers" (61). It is hard, however, to know how he could have been honest about his mother's role in his life at the pond and still sustain the myth of self-creation.

34. See Joseph J. Moldenhauer, "The Extra-vagant Maneuver: Paradox in *Walden*," *Graduate Journal* 6 (Winter 1964): 132–46. For an account of how Thoreau's rhetorical strategies derive from contemporary theories about exposition, see Richard H. Dillman, "The Psychological Rhetoric of *Walden*," *ESQ: A Journal of the American Renaissance* 25, no. 2 (1979): 79–91.

35. "Resistance to Civil Government," in *The Writings of Henry D. Thoreau, Reform Papers*, ed. Wendell Glick (Princeton, N.J.: Princeton University Press, 1973), p. 74. This is the essay most people know as "Civil Disobedience." It is

worth pointing out that this essay, like *Walden*, began as a lecture for the Concord lyceum that Thoreau wrote to answer his townspeople's questions, in this case about his reasons for going to jail.

36. See Charles Feidelson, Jr., *Symbolism and American Literature* (Chicago: University of Chicago Press, 1953), p. 137.

37. See Barbara Johnson, "A Hound, a Bay Horse, and a Turtle Dove: Obscurity in *Walden*," in *A World of Difference* (Baltimore, Md.: Johns Hopkins University Press, 1987), and Walter Benn Michaels, "*Walden*'s False Bottoms," *Glyph* 1 (1977): 132–49. Both these deconstructionist accounts argue that obscurity or ambiguity is a pervasive trait of Thoreau's book.

38. I am not claiming for Thoreau's journals what I claimed for Emerson's. Because Thoreau's resources were most fully aroused by writing for the public, his published work is consistently more powerful than his journal. As I suggested earlier, even his journal essentially elides the central story of his emotional life. But the journals do record his best moments as a communicant with nature much more fully, much less guardedly than anything he published. For two recent attempts to locate Thoreau's achievement in the many volumes of the journal, see William Howarth, *The Book of Concord: Thoreau's Life as a Writer* (New York: Viking, 1982), and Sharon Cameron, *Writing Nature: Henry Thoreau's Journal* (New York: Oxford University Press, 1985).

39. *Correspondence*, p. 214.

40. Scholars have looked for sources for these parables, but without success. See *The Annotated Walden*, ed. Philip Van Doren Stern (New York: Clarkson N. Potter, 1970), pp. 227, 444.

41. I am relying on Shanley's dating of the additions to the manuscript of *Walden*, in *Making of Walden*, pp. 72–73.

42. Many critics have approached *Walden* as essentially a work of art and explored the ways in which it establishes its own order and meanings. There are certainly reasons to see the text in this light. No one, for example, has yet discussed in the detail it deserves the role that Thoreau's lengthy exposition of the "sand foliage" that flows at the climax of "Spring" plays in reconciling, textually, all the antitheses around which the book is organized: purity and impurity, man and nature, self and the village, the eternal laws of nature and the innovations of technology, language and the human body, vitality and death, and so on. Thoreau's elaborations on the "sand foliage" were, according to Shanley, the last major additions he made to the manuscript; in them he clearly pushes at the limits of seeing and interpreting nature in order to make a "whole" out of the book's various "parts" (304–9). This quest for intratextual, self-referential unity is one that Emerson, with his experience of success with his audience, never had any reason to undertake.

43. But see Moldenhauer, "The Extra-vagant Maneuver," p. 142.

44. In *American Romanticism and the Marketplace* (Chicago: University of Chicago Press, 1985), pp. 35–51, Michael T. Gilmore goes further. He argues that in the last chapters of *Walden* Thoreau betrays his political purpose by retreating from his polemical engagement with American capitalism into a "timeless" and asocial private realm. Given Gilmore's concerns, such a complaint is perfectly justified; given Thoreau's needs, on the other hand, that he could bring

this private world into public expression is still an achievement. In a sense, it was always easier for Thoreau to attack his neighbors' lives than to express his own.

45. Shanley, *Making of Walden*, p. 30.

46. Ibid., pp. 72–73.

47. In a letter to Horace Greeley on 29 September 1860, Thoreau suggests that he is writing a book on "the Dispersion of Seeds" (*Correspondence*, p. 590). If so, he never finished it.

48. "The Succession of Forest Trees" (1860), in *Natural History Essays*, p. 91.

CHAPTER IV

STOWE'S *UNCLE TOM'S CABIN*

1. "Author's Introduction" (1878), in *Uncle Tom's Cabin* (New York: Harper & Row, 1958), p. xxi.

2. See Frank Luther Mott's account of the novel's publication and reception in *Golden Multitudes: The Story of Best Sellers in the United States* (New York: Macmillan, 1947), pp. 114–21.

3. Harriet Beecher Stowe, *Uncle Tom's Cabin; The Minister's Wooing; Oldtown Folks* (New York: The Library of America, 1982), pp. 329, 90. Subsequent references to *Uncle Tom's Cabin* will be to this edition, cited parenthetically in the text by page number.

4. See Ann Douglas, *The Feminization of American Culture* (New York: Knopf, 1977), and Henry Nash Smith, *Democracy and the Novel* (New York: Oxford University Press, 1978). For a detailed summary of the sales figures and commerical success of the various major women domestic writers in the American Renaissance, see Mary Kelley, *Private Woman, Public Stage: Literary Domesticity in Nineteenth-Century America* (New York: Oxford University Press, 1984), especially chapter 1, pp. 3–27.

5. She was still more explicit in a letter to the editor of *The National Era*, Gamaliel Bailey: "My vocation is simply that of a painter, and my object will be to hold up in the most lifelike and graphic manner possible Slavery" (quoted in Eric J. Sundquist's introduction to *New Essays on Uncle Tom's Cabin*, ed. Sundquist [Cambridge: Cambridge University Press, 1986], p. 9).

6. See Barbara Welter, "The Cult of True Womanhood: 1820–1860," *American Quarterly* 18 (1966): 151–74. In the two decades since Welter's article, antebellum American culture and the place of "woman" in it has been widely and penetratingly studied by a number of scholars. Among the most useful analyses for the student of Stowe's novel are Mary P. Ryan, *The Empire of the Mother: American Writing about Domesticity, 1830–1860* (New York: Haworth Press, 1982), and Elizabeth Ammons's "Heroines in *Uncle Tom's Cabin*," *American Literature* 49 (May 1977): 161–79, and "Stowe's Dream of the Mother-Savior," in *New Essays on Uncle Tom's Cabin*, pp. 155–95.

7. See especially Douglas's *Feminization of American Culture* and Helen Waite Papashvily, *All the Happy Endings: A Study of the Domestic Novel in America, the Women Who Wrote It, the Women Who Read It, in the Nineteenth Century* (New York: Harper & Brothers, 1956). In her study *Woman's Fiction: A Guide*

to Novels By and About Women in America, 1820–1870 (Ithaca, N.Y.: Cornell University Press, 1978), Nina Baym contests the assumptions on which analyses like Papashvily's and Douglas's are based, arguing that these women's novels engage the issue of woman's place and prospects with a subtle, even political, realism. Her case is made carefully and intelligently, but I think she is consistently too generous to the works she examines.

8. In *Beneath the American Renaissance: The Subversive Imagination in the Age of Emerson and Melville* (New York: Knopf, 1988), David S. Reynolds illuminatingly discusses the novel's "bitter" characters in terms of the conflict between "Subversive" and "Conventional" forces as he sees them at work in the period (see pp. 74–79).

9. Maria S. Cummins, *The Lamplighter* (1854; rpt., New York: John B. Alden, 1893), p. 360.

10. In the last paragraph of the novel's narrative, Stowe construes the book's titular symbol in an equally narrow way. George's concluding speech to the slaves he has freed back in Kentucky is the book's last word on Uncle Tom's cabin: "'every time you see UNCLE TOM'S CABIN . . . let it be a memorial to put you all in mind to follow in his steps'" (509). Of course George does not mean that they should go down the river and die at Legree's, but by this point Tom's actual human fate has disappeared; the only "reality" to which we can refer his life, and Stowe's symbol, is neither "living" nor "dramatic," but exclusively spiritual and allegorical.

11. See p. 307, where Stowe insists that there have been "many" children "like Eva"—"an especial band of angels, whose office it was to sojourn for a season here."

12. Two recent commentaries on the novel do a fine job of bridging the gap between our conditioned responses as twentieth-century readers and the sentimental aesthetic Stowe and her readers had in common. In *Hard Facts: Setting and Form in the American Novel*, Philip Fisher analyses the political and psychological implications of sentimentalism (1985; rpt., New York: Oxford University Press, 1987), pp. 87–127. In *Sensational Designs: The Cultural Work of American Fiction, 1790–1860* (New York: Oxford University Press, 1985), Jane Tompkins looks at the novel's sentimentalism in terms of the moral and theological values on which its effect depends. Her attempt to rehabilitate this aspect of the novel is an impressive piece of sympathetic criticism (see pp. 122–46). When she attempts, however, a similar reinvigoration of the achievement of *The Wide, Wide World*, her sympathies get the better of her critical judgment. Warner's novel is a bad book. Its appeal to its contemporary readers can be explained, but it makes a poor stick with which to castigate the patriarchal guardians of the canon. By the logic Tompkins uses to defend it, she would have to admire Mickey Spillane's best-sellers and take them just as seriously as "literature" (see pp. 147–85).

13. This is the phrase Hawthorne uses to describe Phoebe Pyncheon's sunny efficiency in doing chores around *The House of the Seven Gables*.

14. Thoreau, *Walden*, ed. J. Lyndon Shanley (Princeton, N.J.: Princeton University Press, 1971), p. 205.

15. Many of the women in the abolitionist movement had seen this already, arguing that as consumers American women had to take care to avoid the com-

plicity that came through "indulging in the luxuries" provided by an economy based on slavery. See Dorothy Sterling, ed., *Turning the World Upside Down: The Anti-Slavery Convention of American Women* (1837; rpt., New York: Feminist Press, 1987), especially pp. 19, 28. Margaret Fuller seems to have seen this too. In *Woman in the Nineteenth Century*, addressing herself to the evils of slavery and the Mexican War, she also pointedly addresses her women readers: "Women of my country! . . . have you nothing to do with this?" Like Stowe, the power she acknowledges in them is "a moral power" that "each" woman can exercise "in her own home." But Fuller asks more of those readers than Stowe saw any need for. They must speak out against "the men," who are "willing to sell shamelessly" happiness, honor, and souls, but one of the things they must say is this: "tell these men that you will not accept the glittering baubles, spacious dwellings, and plentiful service, they mean to offer you through these [money market and political power] means." (*Woman in the Nineteenth Century* [1845; rpt., New York: Norton, 1971], pp. 166–67.

16. Ann Douglas discusses the rise of feminine consumerism as another kind of compensation for the displacement of women from productive roles in the economy (*Feminization of American Culture*, pp. 69–70 and passim).

17. For an argument that Stowe's tribute to domestic pieties is actually a kind of radicalism, see Gillian Brown, "Getting in the Kitchen with Dinah: Domestic Politics in *Uncle Tom's Cabin*," *American Quarterly* 36 (Fall 1984): 503–23.

18. See also Ryan, *The Empire of the Mother*.

19. Hawthorne to William D. Ticknor, 19 January 1855, in *Nathaniel Hawthorne: The Letters, 1853–1856*, ed. Thomas Woodson et al. (Columbus: Ohio State University Press, 1987), p. 304.

20. Melville, "Hawthorne and His Mosses," in *The Piazza Tales, and Other Prose Pieces: 1839–1860*, ed. Harrison Hayford et al. (Evanston, Ill.: Northwestern-Newberry, 1987), p. 247.

21. *The Letters of Herman Melville*, ed. Merrell R. Davis and William H. Gilman (New Haven, Conn.: Yale University Press, 1960), p. 128.

22. Melville, *Pierre; or, The Ambiguities*, ed. Harrison Hayford et al. (Evanston, Ill.: Northwestern-Newberry, 1971), p. 337.

23. Thoreau, "Life Without Principle" (1863), in *Reform Papers*, ed. Wendell Glick (Princeton, N.J.: Princeton University Press, 1973), p. 158.

24. Melville, *Pierre*, p. 273.

25. Thoreau, *Walden*, p. 212.

CHAPTER V
SOUTHWESTERN HUMOR

1. For a recent analysis of the period's popular literary culture, which does a good job reminding us how heterogeneous and lively it was, see David S. Reynolds, *Beneath the American Renaissance: The Subversive Imagination in the Age of Emerson and Melville* (New York: Knopf, 1988).

2. In *Novels, Readers, and Reviewers: Responses to Fiction in Antebellum America* (Ithaca, N.Y.: Cornell University Press, 1984), Nina Baym quotes an

essay from the *North American Review* in 1853 that indicates how men became part of the audience for a popular novel: "As far as we know the early history of *The Wide, Wide World*, it was, for some time, bought to be presented to nice little girls. . . . Elder sisters were soon found poring over the volumes, and it was very natural that mothers next should try the spell. . . . After this, papas were not very difficult to convert" (p. 49). It is worth noting the assumptions here—that adult women would "naturally" read the novel, whereas adult men had to be maneuvered into doing so. The available evidence suggests that men read the great Victorian British novelists, especially Dickens and Thackeray, with the same enthusiasm as all other American readers. I am, however, concerned with American authors.

3. See Carl Bode, *The Anatomy of American Popular Culture, 1840–1861* (Berkeley and Los Angeles: University of California Press, 1959), pp. 201–18. The best-selling American essayist, however, was a woman: Sara Payson Willis, who wrote as Fanny Fern and whose various collections of essays—*Fern Leaves from Fanny's Port-Folio* (1853), *Little Ferns for Fanny's Little Friends* (1854), and so on—sold almost as many copies as *The Wide, Wide World*.

4. See Ann Douglas, *The Feminization of American Culture* (New York: Knopf, 1977), pp. 273–309.

5. Melville to Sarah Huyler Morewood, 12[?] September 1851, in *The Letters of Herman Melville*, ed. Merrell R. Davis and William H. Gilman (New Haven, Conn.: Yale University Press, 1960), p. 138.

6. A good standard history of Southwestern Humor can be found in the introduction to *Humor of the Old Southwest*, ed. Hennig Cohen and William B. Dillingham (1964; rev. ed., Athens: University of Georgia Press, 1975), pp. xiii–xxviii. Although it is now a bit out of date, this anthology includes a full bibliography of other work on the genre, including biographies and critical studies of single authors.

7. Mott's "better sellers" are those books whose sales fell just short of the criteria he uses for establishing his list of American "best sellers." See Frank Luther Mott, *Golden Multitudes: The Story of Best Sellers in the United States* (New York: Macmillan, 1947), pp. 318, 320.

8. See E. Douglas Branch, *The Sentimental Years, 1836–1860* (New York: Appleton-Century, 1934), Fred Lewis Patee, *The Feminine Fifties* (New York: Appleton-Century, 1940), and Bode, *Anatomy of American Popular Culture*.

9. James D. Hart, *The Popular Book: A History of America's Literary Taste* (Berkeley and Los Angeles: University of California Press, 1950), pp. 142–43. The only writers he mentions by name are Longstreet and Baldwin.

10. Cohen and Dillingham, eds., *Humor of the Old Southwest*, p. xiv. Their conviction that the sources on which Southwestern Humor drew were "a part of the folk heritage of the region" remains dominant. In his chapter on Harris's Sut Lovingood, for instance, Larzer Ziff refers to Southwestern Humor as "a literature of the plain folk," and in his figures of speech Ziff assumes an organic connection between the oral culture of the frontier and the humorists' texts: "the fantasies that grew straight up from the roots of their anarchic culture," and so on. See Ziff, *Literary Democracy: The Declaration of Cultural Independence in America* (1981; rpt., New York: Penguin, 1982), pp. 184, 185; see also p. 187.

11. This is true even though Europeans throughout the Old World quickly followed the example of the Grimms. The American Folklore Society was founded in 1888, modeled after and inspired by *England's* Folklore Society, which had been organized a decade earlier. But as Richard M. Dorson notes, even so "the subject languished" until the twentieth century (*American Folklore* [1959; rpt., Chicago: University of Chicago Press, 1977], p. 2). It seems that, while Europeans like the Grimms could value and seek to preserve folk traditions, educated Americans as a group were uninterested in them. This seems paradoxical, given our country's ostensible faith in "the people"—until we recall how anxious most Americans are about the charge of provincial vulgarity. In the nineteenth century especially, Americans looked east to the aristocracies of Europe for culture, even "folk culture"; it is probably safe to say that they were not simply uninterested in American folk culture, but even ashamed to appear interested. Americanists who teach in *English* departments are still familiar with this dynamic.

12. As R. M. Dorson puts it, "The humorous vein of the Crockett almanacs, Jack Downing and Sam Slick, the New York *Spirit of the Times*, Simon Suggs and Sut Lovingood, belongs to popular literature and not to folklore" (*American Folklore and the Historian* [Chicago: University of Chicago Press, 1971], p. 190).

13. James M. Cox, "Humor of the Old Southwest," in *The Comic Imagination in American Literature*, ed. Louis D. Rubin, Jr. (New Brunswick, N.J.: Rutgers University Press, 1973), p. 108.

14. Ziff, *Literary Democracy*, p. 187.

15. George Washington Harris, "Blown Up With Soda," in *Sut Lovingood's Yarns*, ed. M. Thomas Inge (New Haven, Conn.: College and University Press, 1966), p. 69.

16. Harris, "Rare Ripe Garden-Seed," in *Sut Lovingood's Yarns*, p. 174. George Washington Harris had a family pew in the First Presbyterian Church of Knoxville, and he served for many years as an elder of the church. See Milton Rickels, *George Washington Harris* (New Haven, Conn.: College and University Press, 1965), p. 27.

17. Edgar Allan Poe, "Georgia Scenes," in *The Complete Works of Edgar Allan Poe*, ed. James A. Harrison (New York: George D. Sproul, 1902), 8:265.

18. Kenneth Lynn, *Mark Twain and Southwestern Humor* (Boston: Little, Brown, 1960), p. 64. Lynn's reading of the genre, and mine, were anticipated by Louis J. Budd, who notes that "despite its varied prolixity and its plebian borrowings, printed Southern humor after 1830 produced a group of writers who stood well apart from backwoods yarning." In his discussion of Lovingood, for example, Budd points out that "Sut never escaped from the limits set by Harris" (see "Gentlemanly Humorists of the Old South," *Southern Folklore Quarterly*, 17 [December 1953], 232–40).

19. Quoted by Norris W. Yates, *William T. Porter and the Spirit of the Times* (Baton Rouge: Louisiana State University Press, 1957), p. 15.

20. Quoted in ibid., p. 45.

21. For example, here is how Porter prefaced "Jones's Fight, A Story of Kentucky—By an Alabamian": "The writer . . . is a planter of North Alabama, and a gentleman of family and fortune. . . . Few gentlemen . . . have more distinguished themselves by their wealth, enterprise and spirit" (*The Big Bear of Arkan-*

sas, and Other Sketches, Illustrative of Characters and Incidents in the South and South-West, ed. W. T. Porter [Philadelphia, 1845], p. 32). In his preface to *The Big Bear,* Porter sums up the various contributors this way: "They [the sketches and tales in the volume] were furnished for publication mainly by country gentlemen, planters, lawyers, &c. 'who live at home in ease'" (p. xii).

22. Porter, *The Big Bear,* p. vii. I think it is worth pointing out that even while speaking of the "rising literature of America," he chooses to use the British spelling of "honour."

23. Ibid.

24. Herman Melville, "Hawthorne and His Mosses" (1850), in *The Piazza Tales and Other Prose Pieces, 1839–1860,* ed. Harrison Hayford et al. (Evanston, Ill.: Northwestern-Newberry, 1987), p. 245.

25. According to the editors of the Northwestern-Newberry text of "Hawthorne and His Mosses," what Melville initially said was "Shakespeares are this day being born on the banks of the Ohio" (*The Piazza Tales,* p. 245). The editors believe that he revised this at the urging of Evert Duyckinck, who objected to some of Melville's "original nationalistic extravagances" (see p. 668) as *too* nationalistic. That Duycknick was uneasy with this particular sentence supports my point about the antidemocratic bias Southwestern Humor imposed on America's sense of who lived "on the banks of the Ohio."

26. Melville, *Moby-Dick,* ed. Harrison Hayford et al. (Evanston, Ill.: Northwestern-Newberry, 1988), p. 117. According to Robert Hopkins's analysis, Hooper's *Some Adventures of Capt. Simon Suggs* was conceived as a satire on Andrew Jackson's campaign biography and the idea that a fit president could be found among the backwoods commoners. See Hopkins, "Simon Suggs: A Burlesque Campaign Biography," *American Quarterly* 15 (Fall 1953): 459–63.

27. As Budd puts it, "it was the friction between plantation amenities and Southwestern crudities which agitated the feeling for comic incongruity" ("Gentlemanly Humorists," p. 239).

28. Porter, *A Quarter Race in Kentucky and Other Tales* (Philadelphia: Carey and Hart, 1846), p. 13.

29. Thomas Bangs Thorpe, "Bob Herring," in *A Quarter Race,* p. 141.

30. "The Big Bear of Arkansas" is probably the most widely anthologized piece of Southwestern Humor. The references here are to the story in Cohen and Dillingham's *Humor of the Old Southwest,* pp. 278–79.

31. Thorpe, "Bob Herring," pp. 130–32.

32. Henry Watterson, ed., *Oddities in Southern Life and Character* (Boston: Houghton, Mifflin, 1882).

33. Watterson, "The South in Light and Shade," in *The Compromises of Life and Other Lectures and Addresses* (New York: Fox, Duffield, 1903), pp. 68–69.

34. Henry David Thoreau, "Walking," in *The Natural History Essays,* ed. Robert Sattelmeyer (Salt Lake City, Utah: Peregrine Smith, 1984), p. 111.

35. Emerson, "The American Scholar," in *The Collected Works of Ralph Waldo Emerson: Nature, Addresses, and Lectures,* ed. R. E. Spiller and A. R. Ferguson (Cambridge, Mass.: Harvard University Press, 1971), p. 61. The Transcendentalists agreed in seeing the frontier as, symbolically at least, America's last, best hope. As Thoreau said in a letter, "the scene of our fairest dreams [lies] in the

west" (*The Correspondence of Henry David Thoreau*, ed. Walter Harding and Carl Bode [New York: New York University Press, 1958], p. 53). In the address he read at Dartmouth the year after "The American Scholar," Emerson developed the dream at more length: "Men looked, when all feudal straps and bandages were snapped asunder, that nature, too long the mother of dwarfs, should reimburse itself by a brood of Titans, who should laugh and leap in the continent, and run up the mountains of the West with the errands of genius and love" ("Literary Ethics," in *Nature, Addresses, and Lectures*, p. 100). As Orestes Brownson wrote James Freeman Clarke, who moved from Boston to Louisville to found the *Western Messenger*, which he hoped would serve as the trumpet of revolution sounded in the West: "All the elements of humanity exist with you on a scale as gigantic as that of your physical nature; and when they shall have been moulded into an harmonious and perfect whole, they will form the true MAN of which there has been on earth but one prototype" (quoted by Perry Miller, *The Transcendentalists* [Cambridge, Mass.: Harvard University Press, 1950], p. 448). I have not been able to find any record of the Transcendentalists' reactions to the way Southwestern Humor reported on the frontier.

36. Joseph G. Baldwin, *The Flush Times of Alabama and Mississippi: A Series of Sketches* (1853; rpt., Gloucester, Mass.: Peter Smith, 1974), p. 64. This book was probably the most popular of all the works in the genre.

37. Porter, *The Big Bear*, p. viii.

38. For a recent description of the Victorian American obsession with appearance and status that made etiquette books another genre of best-selling literature, see Karen Halttunen, *Confidence-Men and Painted Women: A Study of Middle-Class Culture in America, 1830–1870* (New Haven, Conn.: Yale University Press, 1982), especially chapter 3, "Sentimental Culture and the Problem of Fashion," and chapter 4, "Sentimental Culture and the Problem of Etiquette" (pp. 56–123). As Halttunen puts it, "running through these rules [as laid down in the etiquette manuals] was the primary law of middle-class politeness: gentility was the exercise of perfect physical and emotional self-restraint" (p. 96).

39. Larzer Ziff, in his discussion of Sut, says much the same thing: "he is a free spirit, the true alter ego of his creator; he expresses the passionate subrational forces repressed in the mechanically skilled Presbyterian elder, and he expresses them all the more forcefully for Harris's successful repression of them in his own life" (*Literary Democracy*, p. 186). But Ziff's larger discussion of Sut, and Southwestern Humor in general, essentially contradicts his insight here, because he insists on seeing the genre as an expression of forces "buried in the psyche of [the] folk," rather than the gentlemen (p. 185). He finally sees Sut's violence as "the unconscious reaction of the proletarian in a society in which the rules operate to make him pay while others profit" (p. 192).

40. See the "Historical Note" to the Northwestern-Newberry edition of Melville's *Piazza Tales*, p. 491.

41. "Somebody in My Bed," in *A Quarter Race in Kentucky*, pp. 168–71.

42. Edmund Wilson, in his discussion of Sut, notes this larger pattern: "it is plain that a sense of frustration—'flustratin' is one of Sut's favorite words—is at the root of the ferocious fantasies in which, in the character of Sut, [Harris] likes to indulge himself" (*Patriotic Gore* [New York: Oxford University Press, 1962],

p. 516). Wilson is specifically referring to Harris's economic frustrations; in his quest for gentility on the expensive model established by the plantation aristocracy, Harris was almost always in debt, and frequently on the verge of bankruptcy. Such materialistic overreaching was typical of the humorists as a group.

43. Yates, *William T. Porter*, p. 128.

CHAPTER VI
HAWTHORNE'S *SCARLET LETTER*

1. Hawthorne, "The Custom-House," in *The Scarlet Letter*, ed. William Charvat et al. (Columbus: Ohio State University Press, 1962), p. 31. Subsequent references to "The Custom-House" and to *The Scarlet Letter* will be to this edition, which is vol. 1 of the Centenary Edition of the Works of Nathaniel Hawthorne, cited parenthetically in the text by page number.

2. I do not say this to contest the argument Ann Douglas develops so persuasively in *The Feminization of American Culture* (New York: Knopf, 1977): that by the middle of the nineteenth century the American clergy felt excluded from positions of power within a society that was increasingly devoted to the marketplace. I am only referring to the rhetorical dynamic of the sermon itself. Even here, as Douglas points out, ministers often felt compelled to make concessions to the appetites of a congregation that was beginning to be redefined as an audience, and whose attention, even attendance, had to be won.

3. Hawthorne, "Preface" to the 1851 edition of *Twice-Told Tales*, ed. Roy Harvey Pearce et al. (Columbus: Ohio State University Press, 1974), p. 6. In *The Shape of Hawthorne's Career* (Ithaca, N.Y.: Cornell University Press, 1976), Nina Baym also explores Hawthorne's fiction in terms of the dialectic between "his sense of himself and his sense of an audience" (p. 83). Her account was especially useful to me in its first three chapters, which explore the various authorial identities he rehearsed in his short fiction. Two other recent critics who have analysed Hawthorne's art in terms of its engagement with an audience are Kenneth Dauber, *Rediscovering Hawthorne* (Princeton, N.J.: Princeton University Press, 1977), especially pp. 87–118, and Edgar A. Dryden, *Nathaniel Hawthorne: The Poetics of Enchantment* (Ithaca, N.Y.: Cornell University Press, 1977), pp. 120–28. This issue is also treated insightfully in Gordon Hutner's *Secrets and Sympathy: Forms of Disclosure in Hawthorne's Novels* (Athens: University of Georgia Press, 1988).

4. In *The Imperial Self* (New York: Knopf, 1971), Quentin Anderson similarly distinguishes Hawthorne from Emerson, Whitman, and Henry James on the basis of his allegiance to the fact of society, to the presence of other human consciousnesses. Anderson's analysis of *The Scarlet Letter* is one of the best accounts of the novel that we have (see pp. 59–87).

5. See Michael T. Gilmore's analysis of Hawthorne's novel in *American Romanticism and the Marketplace* (Chicago: University of Chicago Press, 1985).

6. Hawthorne, "Preface" to *Twice-Told Tales*, p. 3.

7. See Frederick Crews's analysis of Brand and of Hawthorne's guilt-ridden concern with "The Sin of Art," in *The Sins of the Fathers: Hawthorne's Psychological Themes* (New York: Oxford University Press, 1966).

8. Hawthorne, "Ethan Brand," in *The Snow-Image and Uncollected Tales*, ed. Roy Harvey Pearce et al. (Columbus: Ohio State University Press, 1974), pp. 83, 85. Subsequent references to "Ethan Brand," found in vol. 11 of the Centenary Edition of the Works of Nathaniel Hawthorne, are cited parenthetically in the text by volume and page number.

9. Lewis Mumford, *Herman Melville: A Study of His Life and Vision* (1929, rpt., New York: Harcourt, Brace & World, 1962). Mumford corrected the error for the 1962 revised edition of his biography.

10. "Main-street," in *The Snow-Image*, p. 73.

11. This is the epithet he used to sum up "the influences of my situation and customary associates" in a letter to Longfellow from the customhouse, 11 November 1847, in *Nathaniel Hawthorne: The Letters, 1843–1853*, ed. Thomas Woodson et al. (Columbus: Ohio State University Press, 1985), p. 215.

12. *Letters, 1843–1853*, p. 270.

13. Hawthorne to James T. Fields, 11 December 1852, in *Letters, 1843–1853*, p. 624. Hawthorne's 1855 letter about that "damned mob" is cited in chapter 4.

14. I am quoting from his "Preface" to *The Snow-Image*, where he defines himself as "a person, who has been burrowing, to his utmost ability, into the depths of our common nature, for the purposes of psychological romance" (*The Snow-Image and Uncollected Tales*, p. 4).

15. "Young Goodman Brown," in *Mosses from an Old Manse*, ed. Roy Harvey Pearce et al. (Columbus: Ohio State University Press, 1974), p. 87.

16. This is the title of Crews's chapter in *The Sins of the Fathers* on Hawthorne's representations of the artist. In her study of *Hawthorne's View of the Artist* (n.p.: State University of New York, 1962), Millicent Bell, working from entirely different assumptions than Crews's Freudian ones, reaches an essentially similar conclusion—that for Hawthorne, being an artist is a potentially "cursed" choice (see p. 204).

17. Hawthorne to L. W. Mansfield, 19 March 1850, in *Letters, 1843–1853*, pp. 324–25.

18. James R. Mellow also suggests that these "moments in Dimmesdale's private drama . . . approach autobiography for Hawthorne" (*Nathaniel Hawthorne in His Times* [Boston: Houghton Mifflin, 1980], pp. 306–7).

19. *Uncle Tom's Cabin* also acknowledges this issue right at the start, when Stowe reassures her reader that not even her "desire to be graphic in our account" will "induce us to transcribe" the "various profane expressions" that Haley, the slave trader, uses in his conversation (New York: The Library of America, 1982), p. 11. Unlike Hawthorne, however, Stowe has no reason to be bothered by the words she cannot use. As Leslie Fiedler pointed out, the word "adultery" never once appears in Hawthorne's novel, even though the Puritan children can shout it at Hester in the streets of Boston (*Love and Death in the American Novel*, rev. ed. [New York: Dell, 1966], p. 228).

20. Hawthorne to Fields, 15 January 1850, in *Letters, 1843–1853*, p. 305.

21. While all the contemporary reviews I have been able to find acknowledge the greatness of the novel and the delicacy with which Hawthorne handles its theme, a number agreed with Orestes Brownson's opinion that "it is a story that should not have been told." Arthur Cleveland Coxe, writing in a religious periodical, was the most alarmed: "Is the French era actually begun in our literature?"

(See *Hawthorne, The Critical Heritage*, ed. J. Donald Crowley [London: Routledge & Kegan Paul, 1970], pp. 176, 182).

22. For example, Harriet Beecher Stowe tells how, after writing the first episode of *Uncle Tom's Cabin*, "her husband being away, she read it to her two sons of ten and twelve years of age" ("Author's Introduction" [1878], in *Uncle Tom's Cabin* [New York: Harper & Row, 1965], p. xix). Hawthorne also wrote for children, in *The Whole History of Grandfather's Chair*, *A Wonder Book for Boys and Girls*, and *Tanglewood Tales*. He did so for a number of reasons, but doubtless one was that he wanted to keep alive a distinction that was often blurred in his time, especially by the most popular novelists (including Warner) and poets (including Longfellow): a distinction between adult and children's literature, between speaking to kids and addressing the facts of adult life. He did not want art to become another toy for children, like the doll and the hobbyhorse he mentions alongside the center table books in the parlor. (One of the ultimate ironies about the fate of *The Scarlet Letter* is that, while Hester's sin and punishment give the Puritan children a "half-holiday" from school [54], since the 1920s it has regularly been required reading for American school children—even though in general they are still too young to comprehend the issues of the story.)

23. Hawthorne to Fields, 20 January 1850, in *Letters, 1843–1853*, p. 308.

24. See Sacvan Bercovitch, "The A-Politics of Ambiguity in *The Scarlet Letter*," *New Literary History* 19 (Spring 1987): 629–54.

25. See Anderson, *The Imperial Self*, p. 66.

26. Tom, for instance, twice has a vision of little Eva being translated directly, in a radiant cloud of glory, into heaven (*Uncle Tom's Cabin*, pp. 368, 406–7), and George L. Aiken's incredibly popular 1852 dramatization of Stowe's novel ends with an amazing piece of stagecraft, though it's a conventional enough piece of piety. Here is the whole of act 5, scene 1: "Gorgeous clouds, tinted with sunlight. Eva, robed in white, is discovered on the back of a milk-white dove, with expanded wings, as if just soaring upward. Her hands are extended in benediction over St. Clare and Uncle Tom, who are kneeling and gazing up to her. Impressive music. —Slow curtain."

27. Of course, the Hawthorne work that (as he put it in 1838) "awakened the interest of a larger number of readers, than any of his subsequent productions" was just such a sentimental work: "The Gentle Boy" (1832). But he remained uneasy about its popularity. (See the preface he wrote for an 1839 edition of the tale, illustrated by his fiancée, Sophia Peabody, quoted in *Twice-Told Tales*, pp. 567–68.)

28. See the last two chapters of Jane Tompkins's *Sensational Designs: The Cultural Work of American Fiction, 1790–1860* (New York: Oxford University Press, 1985).

29. Hawthorne uses this same gambit again to begin his next novel, *The House of the Seven Gables*, where the opening chapters are devoted to Hepzibah Pyncheon's struggle to subsist in the wide, wide world. I agree with Michael Gilmore's point that in dramatizing Hepzibah's need to "market" herself Hawthorne is refracting his own situation as a professional writer (*Romanticism in the Marketplace*, pp. 73–74), but I would add that it's an indication of Hawthorne's shrewdness as a professional that he refracts his situation onto a woman.

30. An exception is the only other woman present at the opening scene with a child in *her* arms, who can sympathize with Hester (see pp. 51, 54). Stowe also uses this same configuration in introducing her reader to Tom. Like Hawthorne, she knows she has to make exceptional claims on her readers' sympathies (for Tom's blackness, like Hester's sexuality, makes it easy for them to see him as an "other"). Before showing us Tom, she locates him amid the details of kitchen, cooking, wife, and children that her readers identified as their province—and only a few moments are allowed to pass before Tom has a baby girl on *his* lap (*Uncle Tom's Cabin*, pp. 32–39). As Elizabeth Ammons puts it, Stowe reconceives Tom as a classic Victorian *heroine*: see her "Heroines in *Uncle Tom's Cabin*," *American Literature* 49 (May 1977): 161–79.

31. It might seem that Hester's ultimate stance in the novel, once she has come back inside the pale of civilization and resigned her will to the operations of Providence, is too much like the way Stowe disposes of her dark heroine, Cassy, in *Uncle Tom's Cabin*. But there is always this crucial difference: Stowe does not ask her readers to learn anything about themselves (except what they must repress) from Cassy's dark eyes, whereas Hawthorne requires his readers to keep the rendezvous with Hester in the woods and to learn from her "the hidden mysteries" of our own existences.

32. He switches to the present tense in all the passages that discuss the public as a judge; see p. 127, for example, where he talks about the interpretations of "an uninstructed multitude."

33. See Frank Kermode, *The Classic* (New York: Viking, 1975): "in Hawthorne the reader's share is always a great one. . . . [Hawthorne's] texts, with all their varying, fading voices, their controlled lapses into possible inauthenticity, are meant as invitations to co-production on the part of the reader" (pp. 105, 113).

34. For a particularly rich, although ahistorical, reading of the novel for its ultimate ambiguity, its play of determinacy and indeterminacy, see Evan Carton, *The Rhetoric of American Romance* (Baltimore, Md.: Johns Hopkins University Press, 1985), pp. 191–216. See also Norman Bryson, "Hawthorne's Illegible Letter" (1983), in *Nathaniel Hawthorne's "The Scarlet Letter,"* ed. Harold Bloom (New York: Chelsea House, 1986), pp. 81–95.

35. Hawthorne to Horatio Bridge, 4 February 1850, in *Letters, 1843–1853*, p. 312.

36. "Ethan Brand," in *The Snow-Image and Uncollected Tales*, p. 99.

37. Hawthorne to Bridge, 4 February 1850, in *Letters, 1843–1853*, p. 311.

38. Hawthorne to J. T. Fields, 20 January 1850, in *Letters, 1843–1853*, p. 307.

39. Melville, "Hawthorne and His Mosses," p. 253.

40. The best account of the novel's reception is William Charvat's "Introduction" to the 1962 centenary edition of *The Scarlet Letter*, pp. xv–xxviii, especially p. xvi. In *The School of Hawthorne* (New York: Oxford University Press, 1986) Richard H. Brodhead explores in detail the process by which American literary culture, beginning in the 1850s, canonized Hawthorne, but he almost entirely ignores the sustained effort Hawthorne made in his texts to speak to his available audience.

CHAPTER VII
POE'S PSYCHOLOGY OF COMPOSITION

1. Edgar Allan Poe, "The Tell-Tale Heart," *Collected Works of Edgar Allan Poe*, ed. Thomas Ollive Mabbott, 3 vols. (Cambridge, Mass.: Harvard University Press, 1978), 3:792. Throughout this chapter, references to Poe's tales are from this edition, cited parenthetically in the text. Because the pages are numbered consecutively throughout the volumes, only the page numbers are provided. I also rely heavily on Poe's nonfiction prose, his essays and reviews. A good selection has recently been made available to the modern reader in *Edgar Allan Poe: Essays and Reviews*, ed. by G. R. Thompson (New York: Library of America, 1984); wherever possible I refer to that edition, cited parenthetically in the text as *ER*, followed by the page number. The remaining passages from Poe's nonfiction prose are quoted from *The Complete Works of Edgar Allan Poe*, ed. James A. Harrison, 17 vols. (New York: George D. Sproul, 1902); references to this source are cited parenthetically by volume and page numbers.

2. Poe uses this image more than once. See *ER*, 14; and *Edgar Allan Poe: Marginalia*, ed. John Carl Miller (Charlottesville: University Press of Virginia, 1981), p. 205.

3. Daniel Hoffman, *Poe, Poe, Poe, Poe, Poe, Poe, Poe* (1972; rpt., Garden City, N.Y.: Anchor Press, 1973), p. 91.

4. Poe's earliest references to "unity" were in three reviews printed in *The Southern Literary Messenger* for December 1835 and January and June 1836 (see 8:74–75, 126; 9:46). The second of these refers the idea to Schlegel (see also 11:78–79). Schlegel's own discussion of "unity of interest" can be found in *A Course of Lectures on Dramatic Art and Literature*, trans. John Black, rev. A.J.W. Morrison (London: Henry G. Bohn, 1846), p. 243.

5. N. Bryllion Fagin, *The Histrionic Mr. Poe* (Baltimore, Md.: Johns Hopkins Press, 1949), p. 165.

6. For an attempt to see Poe's aesthetic use of effect as very subtle in its implications, see Louis A. Renza, "Poe's Secret Autobiography," in *The American Renaissance Reconsidered*, ed. Walter Benn Michaels and Donald E. Pease (Baltimore, Md.: Johns Hopkins University Press, 1985), pp. 58–89.

7. For a very different interpretation of what this line means, but one that is equally concerned with the response of the reader, see Shoshana Felman, "On Reading Poetry: Reflections on the Limits and Possibilities of Psychoanalytical Approaches," (1980), in *Modern Critical Views: Edgar Allan Poe*, ed. Harold Bloom (New York: Chelsea House, 1985), pp. 119–39.

8. One exception is Michael Williams, who in " 'The *language* of the cipher': Interpretation in 'The Gold-Bug,' " *American Literature* 53 (January 1982); 646–60, reads the tale's action as a narrative exploration of reading as the quest for meaning.

9. *Marginalia*, p. 199.

10. *The Letters of Edgar Allan Poe*, ed. John Ward Ostrom, 2 vols. (Cambridge, Mass.: Harvard University Press, 1948), 1:7. Subsequent references to Poe's letters are cited parenthetically in the text as *L*, followed by volume and page numbers.

11. See Joseph Wood Krutch, *Edgar Allan Poe: A Study in Genius* (New York: Knopf, 1926), especially pp. 20–39, and Edward H. Davidson, *Poe: A Critical Study* (Cambridge, Mass.: Harvard University Press, 1957), p. 49.

12. *Marginalia*, p. 142.

13. In his essay "Poe's Vision of His Ideal Magazine," Lewis P. Simpson aptly refers to this quest as Poe's "intense desire . . . to impose order on the disorder of America's literary situation" (*The Man of Letters in New England and the South* [Baton Rouge: Louisiana State University Press, 1973], p. 133).

14. Michael Allen, *Poe and the British Magazine Tradition* (New York: Oxford University Press, 1969), pp. 183–84. For an elaboration of Allen's argument, and an equally good account of the role that Poe's concern with audience plays in his texts, an account that I think complements mine, see Jonathan Auerbach, "Poe's Other Double: The Reader in the Fiction," *Criticism* 24 (Fall 1982): 341–61.

15. David S. Reynolds, *Beneath the American Renaissance: The Subversive Imagination in the Age of Emerson and Melville* (New York: Knopf, 1988), p. 43.

16. See Leslie Fiedler's well-taken point: "That image of the true artist destroyed by a money-grubbing society begins with the mythifying of Edgar Allan Poe. . . . That Poe . . . failed not because [he] despised lucre and shunned the marketplace, but precisely because [he was] so desperately committed to the American dream of 'making it,' the legend does not permit us to remember" (*What Was Literature? Class Culture and Mass Society* [New York: Simon and Schuster, 1982], pp. 29–30).

17. Allen, *Poe and the British Magazine Tradition*, p. 165.

18. See Auerbach, "Poe's Other Double," p. 353.

CHAPTER VIII
MELVILLE'S *MOBY-DICK*

1. See A. Robert Lee, "*Moby-Dick*, The Tale and the Telling," in *New Perspectives on Melville*, ed. Faith Pullin (Kent, Ohio: Kent State University Press, 1978), pp. 86–127. Lee's essay also examines the reader's role in Melville's novel, but it abstracts that dynamic from Melville's contemporary rhetorical situation.

2. Herman Melville, "Hawthorne and His Mosses" (1850), in *The Piazza Tales and Other Prose Pieces, 1839–1860*, ed. Harrison Hayford et al. (Evanston, Ill.: Northwestern-Newberry, 1987), p. 252. Subsequent references to this essay are cited parenthetically in the text, as *PT*, followed by the page number.

3. *Moby-Dick*, ed. Harrison Hayford et al. (Evanston, Ill.: Northwestern-Newberry, 1988), p. 571. Subsequent references to *Moby-Dick* in this chapter are cited, by page number, parenthetically in the text.

4. Melville to John Murray, 15 July 1846, in *The Letters of Herman Melville*, ed. Merrel R. Davis and William H. Gilman (New Haven, Conn.: Yale University Press, 1960), p. 39.

5. Melville to Lemuel Shaw, 6 October 1849, in *Letters*, p. 92.

6. Melville to Nathaniel Hawthorne, 1[?] June 1851, in *Letters*, p. 130.

7. Melville, *Typee: A Peep at Polynesian Life*, ed. Harrison Hayford, Hershel

Parker, and G. Thomas Tanselle (Evanston, Ill.: Northwestern University Press, 1968), pp. 76, 97. Subsequent references to *Typee* are cited parenthetically in the text as *T*, followed by the page number.

8. William Charvat, *The Profession of Authorship in America, 1800–1870: The Papers of William Charvat*, ed. Matthew J. Bruccoli (Columbus: Ohio State University Press, 1968), p. 204; see also pp. 263–64.

9. This was Melville's own "Odious word" for the way he revised the book: Melville to Evert Duyckinck, 28 July 1846, in *Letters*, p. 43.

10. "I am more than ever impressed with the thought, that the permanent reputation as well as the present popularity of Typee will be greatly promoted by the revision to which it has just been subjected": Melville to John Murray, 30 July 1846, in *Letters*, pp. 43–44.

11. Nina Baym sums up the way Melville fictionalized *Typee* in "Melville's Quarrel with Fiction," *PMLA* 94 (October 1979): 911. Baym's article contains a number of illuminating insights into the dynamic of his relationship with his audience. For a very different approach to these issues, including the question of "fictionalization" in *Typee*, see Carolyn Porter, "Call Me Ishmael, or How to Make Double-Talk Speak," in *New Essays on Moby-Dick*, ed. Richard H. Brodhead (Cambridge: Cambridge University Press, 1986), pp. 73–108.

12. Merrell R. Davis provides a good account of Melville's active concern over the reviewers' reservations about *Typee* in *Melville's Mardi: A Chartless Voyage* (New Haven, Conn.: Yale University Press, 1952), pp. 16–28.

13. Herman Melville, *Mardi*, ed. Harrison Hayford et al. (Evanston, Ill.: Northwestern-Newberry, 1970), p. xvii. Throughout this chapter, references to *Mardi* are cited parenthetically in the text as *M*, followed by the page number.

14. Charles Gordon Greene, unsigned review, Boston *Post*, 18 April 1849; quoted in *Melville: The Critical Heritage*, ed. Watson G. Branch (Boston: Routledge & Kegan Paul, 1974), p. 156. Lest we confuse Melville's response to the critics with their response to him, it is important to note the point the Hugh W. Hetherington makes in *Melville's Reviewers, British and American: 1846–1891* (1961; rpt., New York: Russell & Russell, 1975): despite Melville's bitter sense of rejection, twenty of the thirty American reviews of *Mardi* in 1849 "expressed only satisfaction" with the novel (p. 131). Given the vicious attack on reviewers that Melville launches in chapter 180, not to mention the unevenness of the novel itself, the critics were very generous.

15. Charvat, *Profession of Authorship in America*, p. 271.

16. Melville to Evert Duyckinck, 14 December 1849, in *Letters*, p. 96.

17. Melville to Lemuel Shaw, 6 October 1849, in *Letters*, p. 91.

18. Melville, *Journal of a Visit to London and the Continent . . . 1849–1850*, ed. Eleanor Melville Metcalf (Cambridge, Mass.: Harvard University Press, 1948), p. 23.

19. Melville to Nathaniel Hawthorne, 1[?] June 1851, in *Letters*, p. 128.

20. See the concluding chapter of Ann Douglas's *Feminization of American Culture* (New York: Knopf, 1977): "Herman Melville and the Revolt against the Reader." In *American Romanticism and the Marketplace* (Chicago: University of Chicago Press, 1985), Michael T. Gilmore is more attentive than Douglas to Melville's own mixed feelings as an aspirant for popular support, but like Douglas

he ultimately locates the source of Melville's professional failure in the culture, especially in "the conditions of production and exchange emergent under capitalism" (p. 151).

21. Melville, *Journal*, p. 18.

22. Melville to Nathaniel Hawthorne, 1[?] June 1851, in *Letters*, p. 129.

23. Herschel Parker, "Why *Pierre* Went Wrong," *Studies in the Novel* 8 (Spring 1976): 20.

24. Melville, *Pierre; or, The Ambiguities*, ed. Harrison Hayford et al. (Evanston, Ill.: Northwestern University Press, 1971), p. 282. Subsequent references to *Pierre* are cited parenthetically in the text as *P*, followed by the page number.

25. Melville to Richard H. Dana, Jr., 6 October 1849, in *Letters*, p. 93; Melville to Nathaniel Hawthorne, 1[?] June 1851, in *Letters*, p. 130. One can also add what Melville says in *Pierre* about Pierre's early, popularly successful works, which he refuses to republish in a collected edition: "the probability was, that his future productions might at least equal, if not surpass . . . those already given to the world. He resolved to wait for his literary canonization until he should at least have outgrown the sophomorean insinuation of the Law; which, with a singular affectation of benignity, pronounced him an 'infant'" (*P*, 250).

26. In *Hawthorne, Melville and the Novel* (Chicago: University of Chicago Press, 1976), Richard Brodhead persuasively analyzes *Pierre* as the record of Melville's loss of faith in the forms of fiction (see pp. 182–93). See also Edgar A. Dryden, "The Entangled Text: Melville's *Pierre* and the Problem of Reading," *Boundary 2* 7 (Spring 1979): 145–73.

27. Melville to Richard Dana, Jr., 1 May 1850, in *Letters*, p. 108; Melville to Richard Bentley, 27 June 1850, in *Letters*, p. 109.

28. Leon Howard tells this story fully and incisively in *Herman Melville* (1951; rpt., Berkeley and Los Angeles: University of California Press, 1967), pp. 162–79.

29. Even in "The Town Ho's Story," Melville's frame for this tale-within-the-tale allows him to focus on performance and audience response. See Heinz Kosok, "Ishmael's Audience in 'The *Town Ho*'s Story," *Notes and Queries* 14 (February 1967): 54–56.

30. Howard Vincent, *The Trying Out of Moby-Dick* (Boston: Houghton Mifflin, 1949), p. 23. Beginning with George R. Stewart's "The Two *Moby-Dicks*" (*American Literature* 25 [January 1954]: 417–48), a number of commentators have tried to establish the history of the novel's growth during the year and a half that Melville worked on it. In "The Composition of *Moby-Dick*" (1975, in *On Melville: The Best from American Literature*, ed. Louis J. Budd and Edwin H. Cady [Durham, N.C.: Duke University Press, 1988], pp. 203–20), James Barbour reviews the conjectures of previous scholarship on this topic, then offers his own taxonomy of the "three" stages in its growth and reshaping. Barbour's analysis is then the occasion for Robert Midler's "The Composition of *Moby-Dick*" (*Emerson Society Quarterly* 23 [1977]: 203–16), in which he points out how impossibly complex is the attempt to assign different parts of *Moby-Dick* to different, specific stages of composition. I agree with Midler's caution, and should say explicitly that I don't intend my "four act" schema to imply four discretely written, separately datable chunks within the novel that we have. Melville obviously re-

vised earlier sections while writing later ones. I do want to contend that Melville's ambitions in the book and for the book progressed, during the year and a half he wrote it, through the arc of intention that can be referred to by the four "acts" I discuss.

31. Melville to R. H. Dana, Jr., 1 May 1850, in *Letters*, p. 108.

32. Melville to Richard Bentley, 27 June 1850, in *Letters*, p. 109.

33. Melville to Richard Bentley, 16 April 1852, in *Letters*, p. 150.

34. What can you expect, Melville asks Duyckinck in December 1849, from a writer who must sell books to pay bills? "What but a beggarly 'Redburn!'" (*Letters*, p. 95).

35. Melville, *Redburn: His First Voyage*, ed. Harrison Hayford, Hershel Parker, G. Thomas Tanselle (Evanston, Ill.: Northwestern University Press, 1969), p. 34. Subsequent references to *Redburn* are cited parenthetically in the text as *R*, followed by the page number.

36. See Harrison Hayford, "Unnecessary Duplicates: A Key to the Writing of *Moby-Dick*," in *New Perspectives on Melville*, p. 148.

37. I am simplifying to keep this necessarily messy argument as neat as I can. In the absence of the manuscript of *Moby-Dick*, we must continually speculate, but I am sure that many of the passages in chapters 2–22 were added after Melville went back to the novel in the fall, and thus reflect the new design with which he carried on the novel beginning in chapter 24—which is to say that we actually "hear" Ishmael's more authoritative voice often before chapter 24 signals his new status explicitly. But I stand by the point of my simplification: that Ishmael's structural place in the novel is very different in chapters 2–22 than it is from chapter 24 on. (I will come back to chapter 23.)

38. Melville to Evert Duyckinck, 14 December 1849, in *Letters*, p. 96.

39. Melville to Duyckinck, 3 March 1849, in *Letters*, p. 80; Melville to Hawthorne, 1[?] June 1851, in *Letters*, p. 130.

40. See Paul Brodtkorb, Jr., *Ishmael's White World: A Phenomenological Reading of Moby-Dick* (New Haven, Conn.: Yale University Press, 1965).

41. As Baym puts in, in his full-length fictions Melville repeatedly "breached [a] genre contract with his readers" ("Melville's Quarrel with Fiction," p. 912).

42. This is essentially what Jauss means by "entertainment art" that reconfirms an audience's "horizon of expectations": see *Toward an Aesthetics of Reception*, trans. Timothy Bahti (Minneapolis: University of Minnesota Press, 1982), p. 25.

43. At least two favorable contemporary reviews of *Moby-Dick* printed this chapter as an extract that would be particularly entertaining to their readers. See *Moby-Dick as Doubloon: Essays and Extracts, 1851–1970*, ed. Hershel Parker and Harrison Hayford (New York: Norton, 1970), pp. 36, 64.

44. Melville to Evert Duyckinck, 3 March 1849, in *Letters*, p. 80.

45. R.W.B. Lewis, *The American Adam* (Chicago: University of Chicago Press, 1955), p. 134.

46. Melville to Hawthorne, 1[?] June 1851, in *Letters*, pp. 128–29.

47. Among the book's contemporary reviewers, one of the most frequent reservations was about Ahab's long-windedness (see *Moby-Dick as Doubloon*, pp. 6, 11, 15, 46, 50, 54, 80).

48. This is literally what the novel does. "AHAB(*advancing*)" (470): with this return to the use of stage directions early in chapter 108, the novel introduces Ahab in the role he will play until the end. Formally, the last act of the novel looks more dramatic than the third; in it Melville recurs again to the stage play devices he had incorporated in the second act. There are a couple of legitimately dramatic scenes in this portion, of which the best is "The Symphony's" dialogue between Ahab and Starbuck. But these devices are superficial efforts to create the appearance of a human drama that cannot emerge; Ahab's will, to which the novel no longer offers any internal challenge, is too predominant. The third act, although devoid of such theatrical devices as stage directions, remains the one truly dramatic portion of the novel; the conflict between "Ishmael" and his reader remains the one authentic human drama.

49. Melville to Hawthorne, 29 June 1851, in *Letters*, p. 133.

50. Melville to Sarah Morewood, 12[?] September 1851, in *Letters*, p. 138.

51. New York *Commercial Advertiser*, 28 November 1851, in *Moby-Dick as Doubloon*, p. 53.

52. See *Moby-Dick as Doubloon*, pp. 9, 66, 82–83, 85.

53. *Literary World*, 22 November 1851, in *Moby-Dick as Doubloon*, p. 51.

54. Parker, "Why *Pierre* Went Wrong," and Charvat, *Profession of Authorship*, p. 252.

55. I borrow this term from Heinz Kohut, who mentions Ahab briefly in his essay "Thoughts on Narcissism and Narcissistic Rage" (*The Psychoanalytic Study of the Child* 27 [1972], 360–400). For an analysis that transposes Melville's identification with Ahab's "wickedness" into more strictly Freudian psychoanalytic terms, see Henry A. Murray's "*In Nomine Diaboli*" (1951), in *Melville: A Collection of Critical Essays*, ed. Richard Chase (Englewood Cliffs, N.J.: Prentice-Hall, 1962), pp. 62–74. Murray reads Ahab's quenchless feud with the whale as the rage of an "insurgent Id" against the repressive force of the superego, but he moves closer to my emphasis by identifying the superego with "the upper-middle class culture of [Melville's] time." But where Murray sees the novel's rhetorical violence as a "wicked book" as the result of "the frustration of Eros," I would put Kohut's etiology instead: "the archaic rage of the narcissistically vulnerable."

CHAPTER IX

CONCLUSION

1. Melville to Sophia Hawthorne, 8 January 1852, in *The Letters of Herman Melville*, ed. Merrell R. Davis and William H. Gilman (New Haven, Conn.: Yale University Press, 1960), p. 146.

2. Melville to Richard Bentley, 16 April 1852, in *Letters of Melville*, p. 150.

3. Melville, *Pierre; or, The Ambiguities*, ed. Harrison Hayford et al. (Evanston, Ill.: Northwestern-Newberry, 1971), pp. 302–3. All quotations from *Pierre* in this and the next paragraph are from these pages.

4. Melville, *Moby-Dick*, ed. Harrison Hayford et al. (Evanston, Ill.: Northwestern-Newberry, 1988), p. 6.

5. For the most definitive account of the tale's composition and publication,

see Merton M. Sealts, Jr., "Historical Note" to Melville's *The Piazza Tales and Other Prose Pieces: 1839–1860*, ed. Harrison Hayford et al. (Evanston, Ill.: Northwestern-Newberry, 1987), pp. 457–533. Subsequent references to "Benito Cereno" are to this edition, cited by page number parenthetically in the text.

6. See Melville, "Hawthorne and His Mosses," in *Piazza Tales and Other Prose Pieces*, p. 251.

7. Melville to Evert Duyckinck, 14 December 1849, in *Letters of Melville*, p. 96.

8. For a full and, as far as I can tell, impartial survey of the various commentaries on "Benito Cereno," see the chapter on the tale in Lea Bertani Vozar Newman's *Reader's Guide to the Short Stories of Herman Melville* (Boston: G. K. Hall, 1986), pp. 95–154.

9. In his new historicist reading of the tale's relationship to contemporary arguments and anxieties about slavery and slave rebellions, Eric J. Sundquist calls "Benito Cereno" "politically volatile," but I am suggesting that that is exactly what it cannot be, given Melville's displacement of slavery into the realm of metaphor and his replacement of narrative with ironic structures. See Sundquist, "*Benito Cereno* and New World Slavery," in *Reconstructing American Literary History*, ed. Sacvan Bercovitch (Cambridge, Mass.: Harvard University Press, 1986), pp. 93–122.

That Melville was unhappy with the thought that his work could no longer aspire to play a constructive role in the larger culture—more unhappy than modern critics generally are—is clear in the book he published after ending his career as a novelist in 1857 with *The Confidence-Man*. After the Civil War he tried appearing before the American public again, as a poet; the first book he published in that role, *Battle-Pieces and Aspects of the War*, published by Harpers in 1866, is characterized, as Ann Douglas puts it, by "the felt spirit of expectancy, of summons to a waiting audience" (*The Feminization of American Culture* [New York: Knopf, 1977], p. 390). In the prose "Supplement" with which he concludes the volume, Melville reassumes the role of truth-teller to the nation; speaking directly to his readers, he pleads for a spirit of reconciliation and reason to attend the work of reuniting the country. He is unmistakably still anxious about telling the truth, but just as clearly, he is hopeful that the American public will appreciate the truth he has to tell.

10. Douglass's tale initially appeared in *Frederick Douglass' Paper* (4–25 March 1853), then was republished in *Autographs for Freedom*, ed. Julia Griffiths (Boston: John P. Jewett, 1853), pp. 174–239. Michael Meyer reprints it in his edition of *Frederick Douglass: The Narrative and Selected Writings* (New York: Modern Library, 1984), pp. 299–348. My references are to Meyer's edition, cited parenthetically in the text, as are the two references to Douglass's autobiography, *The Narrative of the Life of Frederick Douglass, An American Slave* (1845).

11. See Henry Louis Gates, Jr., *Figures in Black: Words, Signs, and the "Racial" Self* (New York: Oxford University Press, 1989), pp. 107–8.

12. Robert Steptoe, "Sharing the Thunder: The Literary Exchanges of Harriet Beecher Stowe, Henry Bibb, and Frederick Douglass," in *New Essays on*

"Uncle Tom's Cabin," ed. Eric J. Sundquist (Cambridge: Cambridge University Press, 1986), pp. 135–54.

13. For an analysis that claims, on the contrary, that Douglass remained skeptical about his white readers, see Robert B. Steptoe, "Distrust of the Reader in Afro-American Narratives," in *Reconstructing American Literary History*, pp. 300–322, especially pp. 301–4.

14. See William L. Andrews's discussion of Douglass's tale in *To Tell a Free Story: The First Century of Afro-American Autobiography, 1760–1865* (Urbana: University of Illinois Press, 1986), pp. 185–88.

15. Ezra Pound, "The Serious Artist" (1913), in *Literary Essays of Ezra Pound,* ed. T. S. Eliot (New York: New Directions, 1968), pp. 43–44.

16. Hans Robert Jauss, *Toward an Aesthetics of Reception*, trans. Timothy Bahti (Minneapolis: University of Minnesota Press, 1982), pp. 21–25.

17. Douglas, *Feminization of American Culture*, p. 357.

18. Ibid., pp. 357–58.

INDEX